State of Halakha
Israel's History in Jewish Law

Yeshivat Har Etzion ישיבת הר עציון

מגיד
MAGGID

Aviad Tabory

STATE OF HALAKHA

ISRAEL'S HISTORY IN JEWISH LAW

Yeshivat Har Etzion
Maggid Books

State of Halakha
Israel's History in Jewish Law
First Edition, 2023

Maggid Books
An imprint of Koren Publishers Jerusalem Ltd.

POB 8531, New Milford, CT 06776-8531, USA
& POB 4044, Jerusalem 9104001, Israel
www.korenpub.com

Cover photo: *Raising the Ink Flag at Umm Rashrash,*
March 10, 1949 (photograph by Micha Perry, IDF Spokesperson's Unit).
A handmade ink-drawn Israeli flag is raised at
Umm Rashrash on the shores of the Red Sea (now Eilat).

The publication of this book was made possible
through the generous support of *The Jewish Book Trust.*

ISBN 978-1-59264-553-4, *hardcover*

Printed and bound in the United States

Dedicated by Tabby and John Corré
in loving memory of their parents

Sally and Maurice Silas

and

Rose and Eric Corré

Dedicated to my 8th grade Rebbe
at Yavneh Hebrew Academy (1969)
and Rebbe to our sons Zev (2000–2002) and
Joshua (2010–2012) who attended Har Etzion

Rav Binyamin Tabory z"l

עשה לך רב וקנה לך חבר

May his wife, Rabbanit Naomi Tabory,
have a long life with much naches from
her children and grandchildren.

With much gratitude for over fifty years
of friendship and study of Torah

Ronnie and Cheryl Nagel
Los Angeles, California

מוקדש באהבה לזכר

הרב בנימין תבורי זצ״ל

ר״מ בישיבת הר עציון,
אשר חינך את בנינו בדרכי אהבת התורה,
לימוד התורה ומסירות לעם ישראל בארץ ובעולם.

משפחת שור

In memory of our dear friend and esteemed teacher

Rabbi Binyamin Tabory ז״ל

And in honor of our dear and honored friend

Mrs. Naomi Tabory תלח״א

Who graced our community and our lives
as living exemplars of Torah values.

Phil and Faygie Schwartz

Dedicated by

Deena and Gilad Ottensoser (YHE '88)
and family

in appreciation for Yeshivat Har Etzion

Contents

Introduction

Throughout Jewish history, the religious community has constantly been confronted by new developments and circumstances. From historic and revolutionary events to medical and technological innovations, rabbis have always been able to respond to new halakhic situations. By finding precedents in Jewish sources and applying them to their times, the religious leadership succeeded in answering new challenges. For example, when electricity was harnessed, the rabbis had to decide how to react; they argued about which already known models of *melakha* (forbidden work) on Shabbat mentioned in the Talmud would apply in the specific case.

However, the establishment of the State of Israel in 1948 created a very different challenge. Laws dealing with government and sovereignty, questions regarding economic models for a country, and wartime moral and ethical dilemmas had not been discussed in a practical sense for over two thousand years. The halakhic models of the past hundreds of years responded to individuals and to communities. This new model of a Jewish state had been unknown to our rabbis for centuries. Does the well-known concept of *pikuaḥ nefesh* (preserving life) change when applied on a national level? Should the modern state coerce its citizens to keep the Torah? What is the halakhic status of a secular government? Who is obligated to join the Jewish army? Should the laws of conversion remain the same or should the waves of immigration to Israel influence them? These are just a few of the questions that were raised.

The great rabbis of the twentieth century, who believed that the events that followed the establishment of the Jewish state were miraculous and recognized the biblical prophecies that were coming true, had to add new sections, as it were, to the *Shulḥan Arukh* in order to deal with the new reality. This book pays tribute to the great rabbis who redefined and created new halakhic concepts with their broad knowledge and deep insight. Their names appear throughout; they are true heroes, and we are indebted to them.

Beginning with Israel's establishment in 1948, this book follows over seventy years of the state's history. The same flag that was made from a rag and ink and raised on the shores of the Gulf of Eilat in 1949, symbolizing the end of the War of Independence (chapter 2), returns at the end of the book, when we examine the questions that relate to the state sending an Israeli flag to the moon (chapter 33). These two very different flags symbolize the astonishing achievements of the Jewish people that occurred in such a short time. During decades of war and terrorism, our people have worked relentlessly to create a modern Jewish country which serves as a model to the entire world. In the current book, we journey through the young state's history and examine the halakhic questions that it faced.

There are many family members, friends, colleagues, and mentors whom I must thank. I have had the privilege over the past twenty-five years to teach Torah in several *batei midrash*. The topics presented in this book have always been favorites of mine, and I must thank all the wonderful institutions that have given me the opportunity to develop each and every lesson. However, there are two main *batei midrash* in which the bulk of these themes were developed. Over the past two decades I have taught in two leading educational institutions, Yeshivat Eretz Hatzvi in Jerusalem and Camp Stone in Sugar Grove, Pennsylvania, both dedicated to the principles and beliefs of Modern Orthodoxy and Religious Zionism. I am grateful to the wonderful rabbis and educators who lead these educational centers for their friendship and support and particularly for giving me the opportunity to develop and teach these ideas. From Camp Stone, I am indebted to Adina and Yehuda Rothner as well as Estee and Yaakov Fleischmann; from Yeshiva Eretz Hatzvi, Rabbis David Ebner, Yehudah Susman, and Benni Pflanzer.

A discussion with my good friend Rabbi Alex Israel was crucial in turning these lessons into a series that followed the history of the State of Israel. My friends and neighbors, Rabbi Yitzchak Blau and Jeremy Brody, have read the manuscript, and each has offered critical insights.

The Israel Koschitzky Virtual Beit Midrash of Yeshivat Har Etzion published the *shiurim* which ultimately led to this book. My thanks go to Rabbi Reuven Ziegler and Debra Berkowitz. I would also like to thank Matthew Miller of Koren Publishers/Maggid Books, as well as Aryeh Grossman, Deena Glickman, Ita Olesker, Nechama Unterman, and Tomi Mager for the skill and professionalism they brought to the editing and production of this book.

The realization of this book was made possible through the generosity of my dear friends Tabby and John Corré, as well as my parents' close friends Phil and Faygie Schwartz and Ronnie and Cheryl Nagel. I am also most appreciative of the support given by Julie and Jacob Schorr.

My parents-in-law, Syma and Henry Weinberg, have always been helpful with their advice and support. Many of my preliminary drafts were read by them and I am grateful for their insightful comments. My dear mother, Naomi, reviewed many of the articles in this book and I found her suggestions to be most valuable.

My wife Debra, together with our children Shira and Yoni, Yair, Talya, and Yishai are the center of my life and have supported my journey of teaching Torah, for which I shall be eternally grateful.

This book is dedicated to my beloved father and teacher, Rabbi Binyamin Tabory of blessed memory, who bravely fought ALS, a grave illness, for many years. His wisdom and vast Torah knowledge, together with his loving personality, charm, and wonderful sense of humor, influenced me throughout the years and continue to do so even after his death in September 2019. My Abba, a devoted student of Rabbi Soloveitchik, was a master teacher. He passionately believed in the importance of imparting Torah and ensuring that knowledge would be passed on to the next generation. A great advocate of Zionism, he, together with my mother and sister Adina, made aliya in 1971. I was raised in a home that believed in and practiced *Torah va'avoda* and thus the main theme of this book – the integration of Torah with the State of Israel – derives from the inspirational education I received from him. Finally, I want to express my thanks to *HaKadosh Barukh Hu,* who has granted me the opportunity to learn and teach Torah in *Medinat Yisrael.* I pray and hope that this book will spread the love of *Torat Eretz Yisrael,* and may we see the rest of our prophets' prophecies come true *bimheira beyamenu.*

Aviad Tabory
Alon Shevut
Av 5782/August 2022

1

The Declaration of Independence, 1948

Can Yom HaAtzma'ut Be Celebrated Earlier Than the Original Date?

On Friday, May 14, 1948, David Ben-Gurion declared Israel's independence. The Hebrew date was 5 Iyar 5708. The declaration, which took place in Tel Aviv, was scheduled about eight hours before the end of the British mandate at midnight on Shabbat. The leaders of the Jewish community in Palestine at the time were aware that the result of such a move would be an immediate invasion by the surrounding Arab nations.

The decision was not an easy one. The opposition, both external and internal, was strong and fierce. Many of Ben-Gurion's advisers urged him to postpone the declaration. For many years, it was rumored that the final vote for the declaration had passed by a slight majority – six to four.[1]

1. Historian Mordechai Naor published a letter of Ben-Gurion, who argues that no vote took place. See "Yom Revi'i HaGadol," *Haaretz*, May 1, 2006, https://www.haaretz.co.il/misc/1.1102622.

Even though the White House supported the move, the State Department was vehemently opposed. The following description of events by Clark Clifford, a close adviser of President Truman, contains valuable insight into the opposition faced by Israel:

> The President regarded his Secretary of State, General of the Army George C. Marshall, as "the greatest living American." Yet the two men were on a collision course over Mideast policy, which, if not resolved, threatened to split and wreck the Administration. British control of Palestine would run out in two days, and when it did, the Jewish Agency intended to announce the creation of a new state, still unnamed, in part of Palestine.
>
> Marshall firmly opposed American recognition of the new Jewish state.... Marshall's opposition was shared by almost every member of the brilliant and now-legendary group of men, later referred to as "the Wise Men," who were then in the process of creating a postwar foreign policy that would endure for more than forty years...
>
> Some months earlier, during one of our weekly breakfasts at his elegant Georgetown home, Forrestal [James Vincent Forrestal, the secretary of defense] had spoken emotionally and frankly to me concerning his opposition to helping the Zionists, as advocates of the creation of a Jewish state were called. "You fellows over at the White House are just not facing up to the realities in the Middle East. There are thirty million Arabs on one side and about six hundred thousand Jews on the other. It is clear that in any contest, the Arabs are going to overwhelm the Jews. Why don't you face up to the realities? Just look at the numbers!"[2]

As noted, within Ben-Gurion's own cabinet there was fierce opposition to declaring the state. On the day the cabinet had to vote on the proposal, discouraging news arrived both from the king of Jordan, who

2. Clark M. Clifford and Richard C. Holbrooke, *Counsel to the President: A Memoir* (New York: Random House, 1991); excerpt taken from http://jcpa.org/article/president-truman%E2%80%99s-decision-to-recognize-israel/.

replied negatively to Israel's request for a truce, and from Moshe Sharett (appointed foreign minister that very week), who informed Ben-Gurion that not only would America not recognize the new Jewish state, but in the inevitable war which would follow any kind of declaration, the United States would not come to Israel's aid.

Nobel Prize laureate S. Y. Agnon describes the courage it took for Ben-Gurion to make the decision:

> We all wanted a Jewish state. Of course we did. But we were afraid of saying so out loud. And when the test came, we thought perhaps we should not risk it, perhaps we should postpone it for a generation, but Ben-Gurion had the courage to proclaim the end of Jewish statelessness in our time.[3]

YOM HAATZMA'UT AND ITS HALAKHIC IMPLICATIONS

Rabbi Tzvi Yehuda Kook (Jerusalem, 1891–1982) explored the unique *kedushat hayom* (sanctity of the day) of Yom HaAtzma'ut in a passionate address.[4] He explains that the greatest miracle of the establishment of the State of Israel was not the military victory of a fledgling state over the armies of enemy countries, but the remarkable courage to make that fateful decision and announce the establishment of an independent state. He defends this idea by quoting the Gemara (Bava Metzia 106a), which states that a shepherd's rescue of his flock from a lion or a bear may be considered a miracle. Where exactly is the miracle in this act? The Tosafists explain that the miracle is to be found in the shepherd's "spirit of courage and willingness to fight."[5] This spirit of valor is a miracle from above, an inspired inner greatness spurring one to rise to the needs of the hour.

Similarly, Sephardi Chief Rabbi Ben-Zion Uziel writes about the ramifications of the declaration itself:

3. S. Y. Agnon, *MeAtzmi El Atzmi* (Tel Aviv: Shocken, 2000), 330.
4. The article appears in the introduction to Nachum Rakover's *Hilkhot Yom HaAtzma'ut VeYom Yerushalayim* (Jerusalem: unknown publisher, 1985), 5–6.
5. Bava Metzia 106a, s.v. *Mativ*.

> "This day you have become the people of the Lord your God" (Deut. 27:9), because on this day we were released from the enslavement of a foreign kingdom in the Land of Israel, which wanted to choke us to death.
>
> This daring declaration has made the Jewish people into an independent nation. It has given courage to the soldiers of Israel and it has opened up the gates of the Land of Israel to all Jews scattered around the world. This declaration has enabled the Jewish people to take their rightful place as a nation among the nations of the world. "This is the day the Lord has made; let us rejoice and be glad in it" (Ps. 118:24).[6]

Both rabbis emphasize, each in his own way, the significance that the declaration itself plays within the miraculous events of 1948. Do these opinions have halakhic ramifications?

Since 1949, the observant world has celebrated Yom HaAtzma'ut both as a religious day and as a national holiday. Questions have been asked about reciting Hallel, the *Sheheḥeyanu* blessing ("Who has kept us alive"; the blessing for special occasions), and the *SheAsa Nissim* blessing ("Who has performed miracles"). Many articles and books deal with these subjects.

The *Sheheḥeyanu* Blessing on Yom HaAtzma'ut

In one of the many discussions about reciting *Sheheḥeyanu*, Rabbi Yehoshua Menachem Ehrenberg (Hungary/Israel, 1904–1976) argues against reciting the blessing.[7] He explains the difference between Yom HaAtzma'ut and Ḥanukka in the following way: While the miraculous events of Ḥanukka actually took place beginning on 25 Kislev, the miracles which we celebrate on our Independence Day occurred either on the last day of the 1948 war, when the ceasefire was signed, or on November

6. Quoted in Rabbi Shimon Federbush, *Torah UMelukha* (Jerusalem: Mosad HaRav Kook, 1961), 169.
7. Rakover, *Hilkhot Yom HaAtzma'ut*, 240. Rabbi Ehrenberg was a hasidic scholar who served as the rabbi of the British detention camps in Cyprus and later as an *av beit din* (chief of the religious court) in Tel Aviv.

29, 1947, the day the UN voted for the Partition Plan. Thus, no miracle actually occurred on the fifth of Iyar. Therefore, he concludes, the blessing should not be recited. Obviously, based on the views of Rabbis Kook and Uziel, one could argue the opposite.

Hallel on the Fifth of Iyar

The fifth of Iyar was designated by the Israeli government as the official day to celebrate Israel's independence, and a law was passed to that effect. Israel's Remembrance Day for fallen soldiers, Yom HaZikaron, was set on the previous day, the fourth of Iyar. However, concerns about the desecration of Shabbat over the years have necessitated moving these days. Thus, if the fifth of Iyar falls on Friday or Shabbat, Yom HaAtzma'ut is moved to Thursday and Yom HaZikaron to Wednesday; if the fourth of Iyar falls on Sunday, Yom HaZikaron is pushed off until Monday and Yom HaAtzma'ut to Tuesday. (This was codified by the Knesset in 1950 as an amendment to the Yom HaAtzma'ut law.) The result is that in most cases Yom HaAtzma'ut is not celebrated on its original date of the fifth of Iyar. The rabbis discuss the proper halakhic response to this situation.

Chief Rabbi Shlomo Goren (Poland/Israel, 1917–1994) argues that even if the national day has been changed to a different date, Hallel must be recited on the original date, the fifth of Iyar.[8] His reasoning is that the sources that require us to recite Hallel on miraculous days seem to indicate that the prayer can only be recited on the actual day of the historical miraculous event. He quotes Rabbi Menachem Meiri (on Pesaḥim 117a), who argues that any person who has been saved miraculously from danger may celebrate that date every year with the recital of Hallel. He then cites the *Ḥatam Sofer* (Rabbi Moshe Sofer; Pressburg, 1762–1839; *Yoreh De'ah* 133), who believes that celebrating a holiday and reciting Hallel for miracles may be based on a biblical source. Both sources, argues Rabbi Goren, limit the celebrations to the actual date itself. Rabbi Goren maintains, as a matter of fact, that all salvation and victories in the 1948 war are connected to the fifth of Iyar, the day the nation of Israel declared its independence.

8. *Torat HaShabbat VeHaMoed* (Jerusalem: World Zionist Organization, 1982), 432.

A further reason for his ruling has to do with the original decision to celebrate Yom HaAtzma'ut on the fifth of Iyar each year. Rabbi Goren argues that the original decision did not take into account the possibilities of changing the date; the changes, therefore, cannot be made today.

Today's custom, however, is to celebrate Yom HaAtzma'ut with the recital of Hallel on the day chosen by the state. Rabbi Yaakov Ariel, in an article on this topic, explains that there is a precedent for this in Jewish law.[9] When Purim falls on Shabbat (in our calendar, this would be when Shushan Purim is observed on Shabbat in Jerusalem and other walled cities), the reading of the Megilla is pushed back to Friday while the other commandments of the day are celebrated either on Sunday or on Shabbat. The reading of the Megilla, claims R. Naḥman in the Gemara (Megilla 14a), is parallel to Hallel, proving that Hallel can be recited on an alternative date.

Nevertheless, some might argue that we divide the days' commandments differently. On the alternative date, we should celebrate the national side of Yom HaAtzma'ut together as an entire state, but we should maintain the religious side of Yom HaAtzma'ut on Shabbat (as Rabbi Goren suggests). Rabbi Ariel strongly disagrees. In this case, he argues, we would be committing the terrible "sin" of creating a separation between religion and state. The message would be that the national side of Yom HaAtzma'ut is separate from the religious dimension.

Rabbi Yaakov Medan addresses this question and concurs with Rabbi Ariel.[10] He brings to our attention that, as noted earlier, Ben-Gurion himself declared independence on Friday, May 14, even though the official date for the expiration of the mandate was May 15. This was due to his consideration of not desecrating the Shabbat. Even from the very beginning, the date of Yom HaAtzma'ut was based upon the consideration of not violating Shabbat.

---

9. "Yom HaAtzmaut SheḤal BeShabbat O BeErev Shabbat," *Teḥumin* 8 (1986/1987): 59.
10. In the *Be'er Miriam* series, *Yom HaAtzma'ut VeYom Shiḥrur Yerushalayim* (Alon Shevut: Har Etzion, 2017), 268.

The Jewish nation's declaration of sovereignty in its land posed halakhic questions that the religious leadership had to answer. Ultimately, after the rabbis debated this matter, their ruling became the custom practiced by Israelis and Jews worldwide.

2

Operation Uvda, 1949

Are One or Two Days of Yom Tov Celebrated in Eilat?

The War of Independence (*Milḥemet HaShiḥrur*) officially began on May 14, 1948, with David Ben-Gurion's Declaration of Independence, and ended over a year later, on July 20, 1949. During this period, Israeli forces fought successfully against armies from several Arab countries, including Syria, Jordan, and Egypt. Over six thousand Israelis, 1 percent of Israel's population at the time, were killed.

The Israel government signed separate armistice agreements with each neighboring country – with Egypt on February 24, Lebanon on March 23, Jordan on April 3, and Syria on July 20. The armistice lines saw Israel holding close to 80 percent of British-Mandate Palestine, which was around 20 percent more than the original UN Partition Plan had allotted.

However, during the armistice negotiations, the Jordanians, contrary to the UN's plan, claimed control over the Negev. As a result, the Israeli army was ordered to "create facts" on the ground and conquer the Negev. The target was to reach the shores of the Red Sea as quickly as possible. The young Israeli army assigned two separate units to meet the challenge: the Golani Brigade and the Negev Brigade. Each unit was given a different route but they shared a target – to reach the Jordanian police station which sits on the shores of the Red Sea, Umm Rashrash.

On March 10 at three in the afternoon, the Negev Brigade completed the mission. The Golani Brigade arrived two hours later. But when the soldiers reached the abandoned police station, they realized that they had forgotten to bring an Israeli flag; they created their own, drawing a Magen David on a cloth using ink from a pen. Thus, the famous "ink flag" was hoisted on a pole and Eilat was declared the southern border of the State of Israel.

Operation Uvda ("fact"), as it was known, was the last military operation of the 1948 war. The commanders of both units sent a telegram at the conclusion of the operation: "On Hagana Day, the 11th of Adar, the Palmach Negev Brigade and the Golani Brigade present the Gulf of Eilat to the State of Israel."

THE BORDERS OF THE STATE: HALAKHIC RAMIFICATIONS

Many halakhic rules and laws relate to the Land of Israel. Determining the exact borders has halakhic ramifications – for example, *Shemitta* (the Sabbatical year) and other *mitzvot hatluyot baAretz* (commandments related to the land); the commandment to live in Israel; the prohibition against leaving Israel; and keeping one or two days of Yom Tov (holiday, when work is not allowed).

Is Eilat considered part of Israel? Do the unique laws that apply only to Israel apply to this southern city? Eilat's status has a number of important halakhic ramifications.

Yom Tov Sheni

Originally, Jewish custom was to declare Rosh Ḥodesh (the beginning of each month) based on the testimony of two witnesses and the official declaration of the Jewish courts. Once the day was decided upon, messengers would be sent out to Jewish communities, letting them know when the holidays of that specific month would be celebrated.

The Gemara explains that in the Diaspora, two days of Yom Tov must be kept. The original reason for this custom was that the messengers did not reach Jewish communities which were distanced from Jerusalem; as the communities were unsure which was the exact day of Rosh Ḥodesh, they celebrated two. Although nowadays we have a fixed calendar, the Gemara rules that these communities must continue the custom (Beitza 4b).

According to this logic, two days of Yom Tov should be celebrated in all areas to which messengers did not arrive. But this would also include large areas of present-day Israel. In fact, this is the view of the Rambam (Rabbi Moshe ben Maimon or Maimonides; Spain/Egypt, 1138–1204):

> Whenever the distance between Jerusalem and a particular place exceeds a ten-day journey, the inhabitants should observe [the holidays] for two days, as was their previous custom.
>
> [The following rules apply when, by contrast,] places are a ten-day journey or less from Jerusalem, and thus it is possible that the messengers could have reached them: We see whether that place is [located in the portions of] the Land of Israel that were inhabited by Jews during the time the calendar was established on the basis of the sighting [of the moon] during the second conquest [of the land] – e.g., Usha, Shefaram, Luz, Yavneh, Nov, Tiberias, and the like, [the inhabitants of these places] should celebrate only one day.
>
> If the place is part of Syria – e.g., Tyre, Damascus, Ashkelon, and the like – they should follow the custom of their ancestors. If [the custom was to celebrate] one day, [they should celebrate] one day. [If the custom was] two days, [they should celebrate] two days.[1]

1. *Mishneh Torah, Hilkhot Kiddush HaḤodesh* 5:11–12. All translations of *Mishneh Torah* are based on Eliyahu Touger's volumes (New York: Moznaim, 1986–). Small changes have been made to translations for uniformity and clarity.

Regarding places without a specific tradition, the Rambam rules that:

> When a place is located within a journey of ten days or less from Jerusalem, and it is part of Syria or the Diaspora, and [its inhabitants] have no [established] custom conveyed [from previous generations], they should celebrate two days, as is customary in the world at large. [The same rules apply to] a city that was created in the desert of the Land of Israel, or a city first populated by Jews in the present era.

Based on this logic there are those who hold that even in new neighborhoods of Jerusalem, two days should be kept.[2]

However, today most follow the opinion of the Ritva (Yom Tov Asevilli; Seville, ca. 1260–1320), who argues that the custom is based on the rule of majority. In the past, most of the Jews living in Israel kept one day while most Jews in the Diaspora kept two; thus, the same practice remains today. Accordingly, all cities and towns in Israel keep only one day. However, for this issue (*Yom Tov Sheni*), we must define what is considered Israel. Is it based on geographical borders? And if so, what are these borders?

Kedushat Eretz Yisrael

Aside from the question of *Yom Tov Sheni*, the issue of the land's status as sacred has ramifications for any number of commandments. *Kedushat Eretz Yisrael*, the sanctity of the Land of Israel, is a concept that must be taken into consideration.

The Land of Israel is both unique and sacred. The Torah states that at all times the "eyes of God" are on it (Deut. 11:12). Certain commandments apply only in Israel and certain rituals, like ordaining rabbis, *Kiddush HaḤodesh* (sanctifying the new moon), *Egla Arufa* (the ceremony conducted upon discovering a corpse outside of town), and even prophecy can only be practiced in Israel.

---

2. Rabbi Moshe Sternbuch points out that both the *Ḥazon Ish* in Bnei Brak and the Brisker Rabbi, Rabbi Yitzchok Zev Soloveitchik, celebrated two days of Yom Tov. See Sternbuch, *Mo'adim UZmanim* (Jerusalem: self-pub., 1996), 8:55.

Besides the specific border markings mentioned in the Torah, we must note that there are two other "models" of Israeli borders. One is *gevul olei Mitzrayim* (the border of the immigrants from Egypt), referring to the areas which were captured in the days of Yehoshua; the other is the border defined by the settlements of returnees from the Babylonian exiles (*olei Bavel*), in the days of Ezra and Neḥemya.

Our discussion must take note of the different forms the Land of Israel has taken over the years.

According to the rabbis, the *kedusha* – sanctity – of the land can be annulled. Although the details of this matter are greatly disputed, we will follow the Rambam's ruling that the first *kedusha* which was established in the days of Yehoshua was annulled with the destruction of the First Temple. The sanctity was restored to the land with the return of the Jewish immigrants from Babylonia in the days of Ezra and Neḥemya.

This second *kedusha* remains forever and was not affected by the destruction of the Second Temple.[3] Accordingly, there are areas in Israel today that do not have *kedusha* – for example, the Jordan valley and the Negev, where no Jews lived during the Second Temple period.

What is the status of these territories today? Are they part of the Land of Israel? Does the lack of *kedushat Eretz Yisrael* in Eilat affect our question regarding one or two days of Yom Tov?

Distinction Between *Shem* and *Kedusha*

An idea mentioned and explained by many commentators can shed light on our discussion.[4] When referring to the uniqueness of Israel, these commentators relate,[5] one must distinguish between two principles:

---

3. *Mishneh Torah, Hilkhot Beit HaBeḥira* 6:16. According to the Rambam, the reason for the difference between the first and second *kedusha* is that the first *kedusha* was created by conquering the land while the second was by settling the land. For the explanation of this difference see Rabbi Joseph B. Soloveitchik, *On Repentance* (Jerusalem: Oroth, 1980), 332–34, as well as *The Rav Speaks* (New York: Judaica Press, 2002), 66–67.
4. See Rabbi Avraham Yitzchak Kook, *Shabbat HaAretz* (Jerusalem: Mosad HaRav Kook, 1993), 115; Rabbi Shlomo Yosef Zevin, *LeOr HaHalakha* (Jerusalem: Kol Mevaser, 2004), 91; Rabbi Yechiel Michel Tukachinsky, *Sefer Eretz Yisrael* (Jerusalem: Levin-Epstein, 1954/1955), 90–91.
5. See Rabbi Joseph B. Soloveitchik, *Iggerot HaGrid* (Riverdale, NY: Morasha Foundation, 2001), 265; Rabbi Ahron Soloveichik, "Kedushat Eretz Yisrael VeShem Eretz

- ***Shem Eretz Yisrael*** (the name of the Land of Israel): This principle refers to the land itself regardless of the people living there. Its uniqueness lies in its being the land of God. This sanctity is not dependent on anyone and cannot change. The land that possesses this status is based on the biblical borders; it is a mystical uniqueness.
- ***Kedushat Eretz Yisrael***: This sanctity is dependent upon the nation of Israel, which creates the *kedusha*. It can be made and can be annulled. Its borders are dependent upon the historical presence of the people of Israel. This is a technical, halakhic definition.

For each and every commandment, one must investigate whether it is connected to the uniqueness of Israel or is a direct result of the sanctity of the land. Rabbinical ordination, prophecy, the sanctification of the new moon, and the commandment to live in Israel depend on *shem Eretz Yisrael* and thus apply at all times. However, most *mitzvot hatluyot baAretz* depend upon the *kedusha* of the land. Thus, fascinatingly, the Jordan valley may be exempt from *Shemitta* but prophecy could be achieved there.

Rabbi Yechiel Michel Tukachinsky (1871–1955, Belarus/Land of Israel) explains that the question of whether to keep one or two days of Yom Tov has nothing to do with the *kedusha* of Israel. Rather it depends on the definition of the Land of Israel. However, what are these borders? Is Eilat included in biblical Israel?

Biblical Borders

The Torah contains two descriptions of borders – one in Genesis and the other in Numbers. In the main covenant, known as *Brit bein HaBetarim* (the Covenant between the Pieces), God promises the Land of Israel to Avraham. The borders described in the covenant include an enormous territory "from the Nile to the Euphrates": "On that day God made a covenant with Avram, saying: To your descendants I will give this land, from the river of Egypt [the Nile] to the great river Euphrates, the land of the Kenites, Kenizzites [the ten nations]..." (Gen. 15:18–19). Accordingly, the borders of Israel extend in the northeast from the Euphrates

---

Yisrael," *Beit Yitzḥak* 13 (Nisan 1967): 82; Shlomo Pick, *Mo'adei HaRav* (Ramat Gan: HaMakhon HaGavoha, Bar-Ilan University, 2003), 226.

River that flows from northern Syria to the Persian Gulf, and in the southwest from the sources of the Nile River in Ethiopia down to the port city of Alexandria.

However, the book of Numbers, using the well-known borders of the land of Canaan, minimizes the land to a much smaller area: "And the Lord spoke to Moshe saying: Command the Israelites, and say to them: As you enter the land of Canaan – this is the land that will become your possession, the land of Canaan with its borders" (Num. 34:1–2). Regarding the exact southern border, the Torah describes it in great detail:

> Your southern sector shall extend from the desert of Zin along Edom, and your southern border to the east begins at the end of the Dead Sea. The border shall then turn south of Maaleh Akrabim and cross toward Zin; its outer limit shall be south of Kadesh Barnea, extending to Hazar Addar and continuing toward Azmon.
>
> The border shall then turn from Azmon to the ravine of Egypt, and its ends shall be to the sea. (Num. 34:3–5)

Many commentators have attempted to identify the exact locations of these geographical sites. When it comes to the western (Mediterranean Sea) and eastern (Jordan River) natural borders, things are straightforward. However, the northern and southern borders are in dispute.

Southern Border

What is the river of Egypt (Num. 34:5)? Many commentators, like Rabbi Saadia Gaon (Egypt/Babylonia, ca. 882/892–942), maintain that this is the river of El Arish.[6] This means that the southern border begins at the southern tip of the Dead Sea and extends to El Arish, i.e, slightly south of the Beer Sheva-Gaza line in the northern part of the Negev. Accordingly, Eilat would not be included in the Land of Israel. However, Rabbi Saadia Gaon also identifies Maaleh Akrabim as Aqabah, which is basically the Eilat of today.[7]

6. See *Shut HaRadbaz*, 6:206.
7. As quoted by Rabbi Yosef Schwarz in his book *Tevuat HaAretz* (Jerusalem, 1899), 24–25.

The Opinions of Israeli Rabbis

Rabbi Tukachinsky was asked by the minister of religions, Rabbi Maimon, to compose a book on the laws and customs of Israel. In his book, *Sefer Eretz Yisrael*, he recalls how together with Chief Rabbi Herzog he sent out a letter to eighteen rabbis with the question: How many days of Yom Tov should be observed in Eilat?[8]

Before he quotes these rabbis' rulings, he voices his own opinion. First, he explains that the Rambam and the Ritva debated this. Regarding the borders which define one or two days of Yom Tov, the Rambam refers to the borders of the returnees from the Babylonian exile,[9] while the Ritva notes that even people who live distances of fifteen to twenty days from Jerusalem keep one day of Yom Tov, suggesting that he follows the biblical borders of the book of Numbers.

As we saw above, the accepted custom is to follow the Ritva's opinion when it comes to celebrating one day of Yom Tov in all of Israel. Therefore, it makes sense that we should follow his opinion here as well.

And indeed, all of the rabbis, in their responses, agreed that one day should be observed in Eilat. Among them were both chief rabbis, Rabbi Herzog and Rabbi Uziel, as well as the *Ḥazon Ish* (Avraham Yeshaya Karelitz; Belarus/Israel, 1878–1953). Chief rabbi of Jerusalem, Rabbi Tzvi Pesach Frank (Kovno/Jerusalem, 1873–1960), ruled in his book that Eilat is definitely part of Israel and one day should be observed there.[10]

Rabbi Shlomo Zalman Auerbach (1910–1995) also responded to the letter and he ruled similarly. However, he adds a very interesting and original angle to our discussion. He suggests that perhaps the fact that Eilat is part of the State of Israel and "shares" its sovereignty is a halakhic reason to observe one day there.[11]

MITZVOT HATLUYOT BAARETZ

Do the commandments which are dependent on *kedushat haAretz* like *Shemitta* and offerings and tithes (*terumot* and *maasrot*) apply to Eilat?

8. See ibid., 35–43.
9. *Mishneh Torah, Hilkhot Kiddush HaḤodesh* 5:11.
10. *Mikra'ei Kodesh* (Jerusalem: Mekhon Ha-Rav Frank, 1974), 2:196.
11. *Minḥat Shlomo* (Jerusalem: Otzrot Shlomo, 2011), vol. 2–3, tanina, 46.

According to our above discussion, these commandments only apply to the areas of Israel which were settled in the days of the Second Temple (Ezra and Neḥemya). As there were no Jews living in Eilat during that period, it seems that fruit and vegetables that grow there do not have *kedusha*; thus, these commandments do not apply there.

During the war of 1948, Rabbi Shmuel Yosef Zevin (Minsk/Israel, 1888–1978) wondered whether the IDF's occupation of the Negev had the power to retrieve or recreate the *kedusha* of the Land of Israel. If so, the special mitzvot of *Shemitta* and offerings and tithes would apply today. Much like the original *kedusha* of the Land of Israel, could there be a sanctity that was achieved by conquering the land?

Rabbi Tukachinsky also refers to this question and elaborates. He explains that Israeli sovereignty over the Negev might not be considered a new type of *kedusha*, but perhaps it has the ability to bring back the original one. He quotes the Radbaz (David ben Solomon ibn Zimra; Spain/Safed, 1479–1573), who claims that the second type of *kedusha* was attained by an oral declaration (*kedusha bapeh*) which would require an ordained *beit din* (rabbinical court) and therefore cannot be accomplished today. Unlike the second *kedusha*, the first type of *kedusha* was attained solely by conquering the land. Thus, he suggests the conquering of the Negev in 1948 may even have created a third *kedusha*.[12]

Rabbi Yaakov Ariel argues that even according to the Radbaz, *kedusha* created by the power of conquest does not require an oral declaration; an intention to create *kedusha* is still necessary. He questions if such an intention was thought of by the Israeli government. Therefore, he questions the validity of the *kedusha* of the Negev in 1948.[13]

Rabbi Zev Weitman, chief rabbi of Alon Shevut, wrote an important book about fulfilling the laws of *Shemitta* nowadays. He refers to our question and quotes opinions that state that even areas occupied by Israeli forces that are outside of the biblical borders have some level of *kedushat haAretz*. In his conclusion, he suggests that due to the possibility

12. This possibility is also suggested by Rabbi Waldenberg. See *Tzitz Eliezer* (n.p.: Waldenberg, 1985), 10:1.

13. "HaNegev VeHaArava – HaIm Nitkadshu BiKedushat HaAretz," *Teḥumin* 29 (2008/2009): 305.

of the renewal today of *kedushat haAretz*, one should avoid planting harvests in the southern parts of Israel during the *Shemitta* year.[14]

Israel's conquest of Eilat, an area that was likely not part of the biblical Land of Israel, raises numerous questions about the commandments that must be observed there, most prominently how many days of Yom Tov must be celebrated there and whether *mitzvot hatluyot baAretz* must be observed. This was a practical halakhic question, and in order to answer it, the decisors had to delve into the meaning of the land's *kedusha*.

14. *Likrat Shemitta Mamlakhtit BiMedinat Yisrael* (Alon Shevut: Tzomet, 1993), 143–49.

3

Herzl's Burial in Jerusalem, 1949

What Is Halakha's Approach to Secular Zionism?

Theodor (Binyamin Ze'ev) Herzl was only forty-four when he died in 1904 (20 Tamuz 5664). During his short life, he became the most important leader of the Zionist movement, paving the way for the establishment of the State of Israel in 1948.

Born in Budapest, Herzl came from an assimilated family with no connection to Jewish tradition, but he was intrigued by the future of the Jewish people. Early on, he considered assimilation as a solution to the antisemitism which he encountered; however, he soon came to the conclusion that the only real strategy for the survival of the Jewish people was the establishment of a homeland. Working as a journalist, Herzl wrote articles, plays, and a book discussing his Zionist vision of a Jewish state in the Land of Israel. One of his greatest achievements was contacting heads of state, including the Sultan of the Ottoman Empire and Kaiser Wilhelm II. In 1897, he inaugurated the First Zionist Congress in Basel, Switzerland.

In his writings, Herzl asked to be buried in the Jewish state of which he dreamt. His wish came true in August 1949, when an official ceremony was conducted by the Israeli government on a desolate mountaintop in Jerusalem, capital of the new state. Mount Herzl became the official cemetery for the leaders of the State of Israel as well as the IDF's main military cemetery.

ORTHODOX ATTITUDES TOWARD SECULAR JEWRY AND THE ZIONIST MOVEMENT

The religious world was ambivalent in its attitude toward the Zionist movement and particularly its secular leaders. As Herzl was the face of modern Zionism, much of the criticism targeted him. Below, we examine the Orthodox community's different approaches toward secular Jews, specifically those who were part of the Zionist community. In this study, the responses and eulogies delivered after Herzl's death can provide significant insight.[1]

Orthodoxy and Secular Jews: An Evolution

The question of how the Torah relates to secular Jews has been around for a very long time.[2] The original fundamental halakhic attitude toward secular Jews is very harsh and strict, without much room for understanding

---

1. In 2018 a collection of eulogies for Herzl in Hebrew, delivered by rabbis throughout the Jewish world, was published. This book, *Lev HaUmma* (Jerusalem, 2017), was edited by Moshe Nahmani. It serves as proof that Herzl was greatly admired and adored by religious communities.
2. In Hebrew see Rabbi Ohad Fixler, "Maamado Shel Mi SheEino Shomer Torah UMitzvot," The Israel Koschitzky Torat Har Etzion VBM, December 30, 2015, https://www.etzion.org.il/he/talmud/seder-nezikin/massekhet-avoda-zara/עז-דף-כו-מעמדו-של-מי-שאינו-שומר-תורה-ומצוות; in English, see Rabbi Chaim Navon, "The Status of 'Chilonim' in Halakha (1)," The Israel Koschitzky Torat Har Etzion VBM, December 25, 2016, https://www.etzion.org.il/en/status-chilonim-halakha-part-1, and Rabbi Chaim Navon, "The Status of 'Chilonim' in Halakha (2)," The Israel Koschitzky Torat Har Etzion VBM, December 25, 2016, https://www.etzion.org.il/en/status-chilonim-halakha-part-2.

or tolerance; some even recommend violence against those Jews who deny the Torah.[3]

Rabbi Yehuda Amital (Romania/Israel, 1924–2010) explains that there is a gap between the Written and the Oral Torah.[4] While the Written Torah talks in the language of *middat hadin,* the attribute of justice, the Oral Torah speaks the language of *middat haraḥamim,* the attribute of mercy. This might explain why the way we relate to secular Jews in practice is very different from the written law.

Since the nineteenth century, some rabbis – for example, Rabbi Yaakov Ettlinger (Germany, 1798–1871) – have suggested that the Orthodox approach to secular Jews should change due to the changing circumstances of the time. His main argument was that in the past, Jews who did not practice their religion were leaving the Jewish nation. In current times, he argued, secular Jews were still connected to tradition and Judaism in other ways.[5] Some, like the *Ḥazon Ish,* have argued that in our times a more sensitive and tolerant attitude toward secular Jews should be taken. The *Ḥazon Ish* may have modeled his approach on the well-known halakhic concept of *tinok shenishba,* which literally translates as "a child taken captive." This idea is mentioned by the Rambam:[6]

> The children of these errant people and their grandchildren whose parents led them away and they were born among these Karaites and raised according to their conception, they are considered as children captured and raised by them. Such a child may not be eager to follow the path of commandments, for it is as if he was compelled not to. Even if later he hears that he is Jewish and sees Jews and their faith, he is still considered as one who was compelled against observance, for he was raised according to their mistaken path.

---

3. See Rambam, *Mishneh Torah, Hilkhot Eidut* 11:10 and *Hilkhot Rotze'aḥ* 4:10.
4. See Rabbi Amital's article, "A Torah Perspective on the Status of Secular Jews Today," *Tradition* 23, no. 4 (Summer 1988): 1–13, found online at: https://traditiononline.org/a-torah-perspective-on-the-status-of-secular-jews-today/.
5. *Binyan Tziyon* (Vilna: Y. L. Mets, 1878), *se'if* 23.
6. *Mishneh Torah, Hilkhot Mamrim* 3:3.

> This applies to those whom we mentioned who follow the erroneous Karaite path of their ancestors. Therefore, it is appropriate to motivate them to repent and draw them to the power of the Torah with words of peace.

Accordingly, the *Ḥazon Ish* instructs his students:

> And it seems that this law (a harsh rule against secular Jews) applies only in times when God's supervision is clear, like in the time when there were miracles and a heavenly voice and the righteous of the generation were under clear personal supervision. Heretics were then especially perverse in swaying the impulses toward lust and lawlessness, and at that time clearing out the evildoers was protection of the world, for all knew that pushing the generation away [from the ways of the Torah] brings punishment to the world and causes pestilence, war, and hunger to come upon the world.
>
> But when divine supervision is hidden, and faith has been uprooted from the doorways of the nation, such acts do not build a fence against lawlessness but add to the lawlessness, for they will see it as an act of destruction and violence, God forbid. Since we are supposed to fix things, we should not apply this law when it does not lead to correction. Rather, we must bring them back through ties of love and put them in the rays of light as much as we can.[7]

Secular Jews in the Zionist Age

What is the religious attitude toward the Zionist movement? The Zionist ideology creates a dilemma for many of the Orthodox, and much confusion. On one hand, the ideology is rooted in the Torah and Jewish tradition. On the other hand, many of its leaders distance themselves from the Torah and its values.

---

7. *Ḥazon Ish, Yoreh De'ah, Hilkhot Sheḥita* 2:16.

The different approaches of Orthodox Judaism toward Herzl and the Zionist movement are reflected in the current attitudes toward the State of Israel and more specifically toward secular Jews in Israel.

Rabbi Elchanan Wasserman (Lithuania, 1874–1941), considered to be one of the greatest Torah leaders of the twentieth century, was radically opposed to the Zionist movement. A martyr who was killed by the Nazis, Rabbi Wasserman opposed those who chose to emigrate to Israel or even the US because of the spiritual dangers he believed existed in both countries.

In a booklet dedicated to his reading into the difficult times of the Holocaust, he claims that his time is that of *ikveta diMeshiḥa,* the footsteps of the Messiah. He rejects all modern ideologies like socialism and Zionism, then sweeping through the Jewish communities of Europe. It is his opinion that God-fearing Jews must immerse themselves completely in Torah studies; all other philosophies and ideologies are modern forms of idolatry. He appears to be referring directly to Theodor Herzl when he writes: "The father of the modern national idea in Israel ... who lived sixty years ago and fought all his life with great bitterness against the Torah." He goes on to explain that Zionism sees itself as an alternative to the Torah: "Apparently, he thought that the Torah had lost its significance and that he was to succeed it; for this reason, he created an alternative to Torah in the shape of the national idea."

Rabbi Wasserman points out that the source of Herzl's inspiration was not the Torah but rather the historical events of the times, specifically the Balkan revolutions:

> In fact, this was not the absolute origin of the national idea. At that time, the era of the Balkan revolutions, all the small Balkan people[s] thought in terms of nationalism, seeking to throw the yoke of the Turks from their necks. The opportunity presented itself for him to take the finished article and replant it on Jewish soil. The main feature of this idea is that to be a Jew means to subscribe to the national idea and nothing more. His successors bring "their rabbi's Torah" to perfection by their pronouncement that even an apostate is to be reckoned equal to any Jewish nationalist.

He then questions:

> What is the opinion of the Torah regarding such an idea? There are clear laws for such a concept. In thirty-six places the Torah warns that the convert is to be pampered as a father pampers his only son. What must be the convert's origin? Even if he is a descendant of Haman, the law of the convert applies to him. On the other hand, an Israelite who proves disloyal to his faith, even if he is the son of the greatest, comes under the ruling "We lower them into the pit and do not raise them out of it." He is worse than the dog to which the law of "We lower" does not apply.

He then concludes:

> We see, therefore, that one's origin alone without Torah is valueless, so that the nationalist idea is nothing but a modern idol, not recognized by the Torah. It is fundamentally idolatry.[8]

This extreme opposition to Zionism was also expressed by other great rabbis of the twentieth century and laid the foundation to the claim that secular Zionism holds nothing new or beneficial for the traditional Jewish community. Thus, the classic rejection of secular Jews, in Rabbi Wasserman's view, should be applied in our days as well.

Religious Zionism Confronts Secular Zionism

The Religious Zionist philosophy toward the secular community has two main approaches which reflect the different interpretations it holds of Zionism.[9] One is pragmatic, while the other is filled with messianic leanings.

---

8. The entire article, "Ikvasa DeMeshiḥa," was printed in a collection of Rabbi Wasserman's articles, *Kovetz Maamarim* (Tel Aviv: E. S. Wasserman, 1983–1984). It can be found online in Hebrew at: http://www.daat.ac.il/daat/ezrachut/tsiyonut/ikveta.pdf, and in English as "Epoch of the Messiah," https://www.truetorahjews.org/images/Epoch_of_the_Messiah.pdf.
9. See Michael Tzvi Nehorai, "HaRav Reines VeHaRav Kook: Shtei Gishot LeTziyonut," in *Yovel Orot*, ed. Benjamin Ish-Shalom and Shalom Rosenberg (Jerusalem: World Zionist Organization, 1985), 209–20.

A common attitude in the early twentieth century was a pragmatic and practical approach which believed that Zionism was the best way to save the Jewish people from assimilation and antisemitism. Rabbi Yitzchak Ya'akov Reines (Lithuania, 1839–1915), founder of the Mizrachi Religious Zionist movement, was a believer in this approach.

We will quote from a eulogy written by Rabbi Avraham Eliyahu (Elya) Kaplan (Lithuania, 1890–1924) for Theodor Herzl. Rabbi Kaplan, who died tragically at a very young age, was the *rosh yeshiva* of the Hildesheimer Rabbinical Seminary in Berlin. In 1919 he delivered the following tribute in Telz (Telšiai), Lithuania:

> He did not teach us Torah; he did not teach us halakha or Aggada. He did not teach us any Jewish studies nor *musar* (Jewish ethics), as he was never taught these subjects. He was raised in surroundings where this knowledge did not exist.
>
> However, he taught us two words, words that we never dared to pronounce (Jonah 1:9): "*Ivri anokhi*," "I am a Hebrew man!" In our *beit midrash* we could make this claim, we could even write it in our newspapers; but there was one place in which we could not, in the international arena...
>
> Herzl taught us what we know today: to stand tall and proud before the world and demand our right to return to our homeland.[10]

Similar thoughts and ideas focusing on the great impact Herzl's life had on the Jewish nation were raised by other Religious Zionist rabbis and leaders. These approaches and understandings allowed the religious world to distinguish between the negative secular side of the Zionist leaders and the positive side of the Zionist movement which they believed would bring safety, peace, and prosperity to the Jewish people.

Rabbi Avraham Yitzchak Kook's "Lamentation in Jerusalem"

The eulogy of Rabbi Avraham Yitzchak Kook (Russia/Land of Israel, 1865–1935) for Herzl, the "Lamentation in Jerusalem," was as original as

10. *BeIkvot HaYira* (Jerusalem: Mosad HaRav Kook, 1988), 85–91.

it was daring, and it received much attention in the Jewish world, not necessarily positive.[11] In it, Rav Kook discusses the struggle between the tribe of Yehuda and the tribe of Yosef. He explains that each of the tribes symbolizes separate characteristics of leadership that are needed to guide the nation:

> So, it came about that throughout the Exile there is a see-saw effect of these two opposing forces. At times, there is exhibited a drive toward material, worldly success that flows primarily from the foundation of Joseph and Ephraim; other times there is a stirring of the spiritual drive for observance of Torah and spiritual development, for awe and love of God. Since it is impossible for our nation to attain its lofty destiny other than by actualizing these two components – the universal symbolized by Joseph, and the distinctive symbolized by Judah – there arise in the nation proponents of each aspect. Those who would enhance spirituality prepare the way for Messiah son of David, whose focus is the final destiny. Truly the focus of life is spiritual attainment, except that the spiritual can only develop properly if it is accompanied by all the material acquisitions of which a full-bodied nation is in need. Those who redress the material, general aspects of life prepare the way for Messiah son of Joseph.
>
> When these two forces work at cross purposes as a result of the calamity of exile, shortsightedness, and disarray, these are the "birth pangs of Messiah," or to be more exact, the "birth pangs of Messiahs" (plural).

He indirectly refers to Herzl as the Messiah from the tribe of Yosef, whose responsibility is to maintain the physical existence of the nation:

11. The entire eulogy is printed in a collection of Rav Kook's articles, *Maamarei HaRaaya* (Jerusalem: HaKeren Al Shem Golda Katz, 1984), 94–99. The translation to English appears in Bezalel Naor, *When God Becomes History: Historical Essays of Rabbi Abraham Isaac Hakohen Kook* (New York: Orot, 2003). It can be found online in Hebrew at: https://he.wikisource.org/wiki/מאמרי_הראיה/המספד_בירושלים, and in English at: https://www.machonso.org/uploads/images/13-D-10-lamentation.pdf.

> The Zionist vision manifest in our generation might best be symbolized as the "footstep of Messiah son of Joseph" (*'ikva de-Mashiah ben Yosef*). Zionism tends to universalism (as opposed to Jewish particularism). It is unequipped to realize that the development of Israel's general aspect is but the foundation for Israel's singularity. The leadership of the Zionist movement must be greatly influenced by the gifted few of the generation, the righteous and the sages of Israel. On the other hand, the ideal of Israel's national renaissance, including all the material accouterment – which is a proper thing when joined to the spiritual goal – to date has not succeeded, and the lack of success has brought on infighting, until finally, *the leader of the movement has fallen,* a victim of frustration. (Emphasis mine.)

This radical approach led to a unique attitude toward the secular side of the Zionist movement. Rav Kook's understanding explained why he valued the pioneering Jews of his time although they did not keep Torah and commandments. He believed that their intentions were good and that they were part of the redemption plan to bring the Jewish people back to their homeland.

In fact, Rav Kook writes that many of the actions and the ideals of these secular Jews do not contradict Judaism; rather, in certain respects, these "rebels" are more "religious" than many religious practicing Jews:

> The soul of Israel's transgressors, who, in the footsteps of the Messiah, are lovingly connected to the affairs of all of Israel, to the Land of Israel and to the renewal of the nation, is more amenable than the soul of those who have no faith in Israel.[12]

12. *Orot HaTeḥiya* (Jerusalem: Machon Har Bracha, 2017), chap. 43.

4

Receiving Reparations from Germany, 1952

Should the Jewish State Accept Charity from Other Nations?

On September 10, 1952, an agreement was signed between West Germany and Israel in Luxembourg. According to the agreement, West Germany was to pay the State of Israel for the costs of "resettling so great a number of uprooted and destitute Jewish refugees,"[1] and, as the Claims Conference (the Conference on Jewish Material Claims Against Germany, charged with arranging restitution for victims of the Nazis) states in its mission statement, to compensate Holocaust survivors for the "suffering and losses resulting from Nazi persecution."[2]

The idea of accepting reparations from Germany began immediately after the end of World War II, but it was only in the early 1950s

1. The full agreement can be found online at: https://treaties.un.org/doc/Publication/UNTS/Volume%20162/volume-162-I-2137-English.pdf.
2. Available at: http://www.claimscon.org/forms/CC_AR_2007.pdf.

that the Israeli government put forward a claim of a billion and a half dollars. This calculation was based on three thousand dollars for each of the half a million European refugees that Israel resettled.

Following the War of Independence, the new Israeli state was struggling. Jewish refugees were pouring into the country, which had yet to recover from a war that had killed 1 percent of the population. The economy was failing, and David Ben-Gurion, the prime minister at the time, realized the potential these payments had to boost the country's economy. Ben-Gurion made strong arguments in order to convince his colleagues in the Knesset to vote for the agreement. Quoting the famous verse from I Kings 21:19, "*Haratzaḥta vegam yarashta?*" ("Have you murdered and also taken possession?"), he posited that Israel should not allow the German murderers to benefit from the death of their victims. He also asserted that the greatest revenge against the atrocities of the Nazis would be to use their money to build a Jewish homeland.

The fierce and violent opposition to the agreement, led by Menachem Begin, resulted in demonstrations against the government. In public rallies, Begin called the agreement an act of treason and betrayal. In a dramatic speech to the Knesset, Begin appealed to his colleagues, begging them to vote against the payments, and even suggesting holding a referendum.[3] Turning to the religious members of the Knesset, he argued:

> You went to your constituents during the election not with this issue in mind. You went to the people for the sake of the Jewish religion, for the dignity of the Torah of the nation of Israel. But what does the Torah of the nation of Israel have to do with the negotiations with Amalek? By doing so you might as well erase a holy and sacred verse from the Torah that states that God carries His war against Amalek "from generation to generation" (Ex. 17:16). How would God fight Amalek if you, the protectors

3. The minister of transportation at the time sent an official request to Rabbi Eliezer Waldenberg, asking about the Torah's opinion regarding holding a referendum. Rabbi Waldenberg responded that he was against it. See *Sefer Hilkhot Medina* (Jerusalem, Waldenberg, 1951), 3:89–97.

> of religion, vote for making peace with Amalek, merely for the sake of accepting money from him?[4]

The debate over the reparations issue was probably the fiercest and most heated in Israel's history. On January 7, 1952, the day of the debate, the Knesset was stormed by demonstrators and objects were thrown at members of Knesset.

HALAKHIC QUESTIONS ABOUT REPARATIONS

In Jewish communities around the world, as well as in Israel, rabbis expressed deep emotions when arguing against the agreement. Some of the rabbis, echoing Begin, referred to the Germans as Amalek, thereby stirring up profound emotional and religious feelings. There are reports that in America, Rabbi Yaakov Kamenetsky (Lithuania/US, 1891–1986) announced at a rabbinical conference that "the majority opinion sides with the opinion of Rabbi Aharon Kotler, who opposed all negotiations with Germany even if large sums of reparations can be obtained."[5]

Rabbi Hershel Schachter[6] records that Rabbi Joseph B. Soloveitchik (Pruzhany/US, 1903–1993) opposed the agreement for two reasons: one, accepting the money might indicate that the Jewish people had forgiven the Germans for the atrocities they had committed; two, he believed that the Germans maintained the status of Amalek and therefore Jews were not allowed to enjoy any benefit from them. Rabbi Soloveitchik understood that Amalek was not a specific race of people but rather any entity that wishes to destroy the Jewish people.[7] My friend and colleague, Rabbi Dr. Nechemia Kleinman, told me that he, as a Holocaust survivor, was entitled to accept money from Germany. He asked Rabbi Soloveitchik for his opinion. Rabbi Soloveitchik responded that even though he opposed accepting any money, once the money was being

---

4. For the entire speech (in Hebrew) see "Menachem Begin – Mivḥar Ne'umim BaKnesset: HaShilumim BeGermania," Daat: Mikhlelet Herzog, accessed June 23, 2021, ḥttp://www.daat.ac.il/daat/ezraḥut/begin/neum4-2.ḥtm.
5. Rabbi Tzvi Weinman, *MiKatowice Ad Heh BeIyar* (Jerusalem: Vatikin, 1995), 213.
6. *Nefesh HaRav* (Jerusalem: Reishit Yerushalayim, 1994), 87.
7. See *Kol Dodi Dofek* (New York: Yeshiva University, 2006), 111, n. 23, in the name of his father, Rabbi Moshe Soloveitchik.

distributed, one was allowed to accept it. In later years, Rabbi Schachter added, he heard that Rabbi Soloveitchik admitted that he may have been mistaken in opposing the payments; in retrospect the reparations saved the Jewish state.[8]

In Israel, the chief rabbi of Petach Tikva, Rabbi Reuven Katz,[9] argued passionately against the agreement. An article on the question was published in his book of essays on contemporary halakhic matters. He makes three points: First, like Rabbi Soloveitchik, he argues that the German nation has the status of Amalek. Second, he is concerned that the State of Israel would be accepting not only money but also products, machinery, and technology from the Germans, built and made by Jewish blood: "How can a Jewish hand touch machinery and products that are soaked in Jewish blood?" Finally, he mentions one last reason: building the Jewish state with blood money would be a disgrace and a *ḥillul Hashem* (desecration of the name of God). It would appear to the world that Jewish blood can be bought and sold.

Is this strong opposition to reparations based on purely emotional reactions to the horrors of the Holocaust, or is it predicated on halakhic principles?

Biblical Precedents

In several places the Torah mentions that the nation of Israel left Egypt with great wealth.[10] Some commentators were concerned by this; it suggests that the nation of Israel gained this wealth by means of deceit. The Torah mentions that *Am Yisrael* "borrowed" the wealth without the intention of returning it.[11]

---

8. See Rabbi Howard Jachter in *Mentor of Generations: Reflections on Rabbi Joseph B. Soloveitchik*, ed. Zev Eleff (Jersey City, NJ: Ktav Publishing House, 2008), 331.
9. *Shaar Reuven* (Jerusalem: Hotzaat HaSefarim HaEretz-Yisraelit BeSiyua Mosad HaRav Kook, 1952), 301–4.
10. At the Burning Bush: Ex. 3:22; before the plague of the firstborn: 11:2–3; and when the Israelites left: 12:35–36.
11. See Gerald Blidstein, *Iyunim BeMaḥshevet HaHalakha VeHaAggada* (Beer Sheva: Ben-Gurion University, 2004), 11–23. Both Nehama Leibowitz in *Iyunim Ḥadashim BeSefer Shemot* (Jerusalem: World Zionist Organization, 1984), 129–34, and Rabbi Elchanan Samet in his second series of *Iyunim BeParashat HaShavua* (Maale Adumim: Maaliyot, 2002), 263–85 discuss this matter at length.

The Gemara recalls how this issue was discussed centuries later:

> The people of Egypt came to judgment with the Jewish people before Alexander of Macedon. The Egyptian people said to Alexander: It says in the Torah: "And the Lord gave the people favor in the eyes of Egypt, and they lent them" (Ex. 12:36). Give us the silver and gold that you took from us; you claimed that you were borrowing it and you never returned it. (Sanhedrin 91a)

A Jew named Geviha ben Pesisa was chosen to respond, and he began his opening response with the question:

> From where are you citing proof that you are entitled to the silver and gold? They said to him: From the Torah.

He responded:

> I too will cite proof to you only from the Torah, as it is stated: "And the sojourning of the children of Israel, who dwelt in Egypt, was four hundred and thirty years" (Ex. 12:40), during which they were enslaved to Egypt, engaged in hard manual labor. Give us the wages for the work performed by the 600,000 men above the age of twenty whom you enslaved in Egypt for four hundred and thirty years!

The gemara here is responding to those who feel "uncomfortable" with the source of the Jews' wealth. The Jewish nation earned this wealth (and more) through hard work over a long period of time.

Perhaps this biblical story can serve as a precedent, a source to justify receiving the money from Germany – money that is a drop in the bucket when compared to the wealth stolen by the Germans.

Rabbinic Views on Reparations

In 1976, Rabbi Yosef Shalom Elyashiv (1910–2012) was asked if it would be permissible to accept money from the German government for the purpose of printing manuscripts of *Rishonim*, the rabbis of the eleventh to fifteenth centuries. In his article,[12] he mentions the different talmudic sources that prohibit accepting charity from non-Jews. He then quotes a ruling from Rabbi Yosef Karo (Toledo, 1488–1575)[13] that while it is forbidden to accept charity from a non-Jew in public, it is permitted to do so in a private, subtle manner. This ruling is based on the gemara in Sanhedrin 26b, which explains that a Jew who accepts charity from non-Jews cannot act as a witness. The gemara limits this rule to a person who accepts money in public and adds that if the Jew has no other option but to accept donations in public, he is permitted to do so for his livelihood. Meiri (ad loc.) explains that in the latter case the gemara permits accepting funds because of *pikuaḥ nefesh,* which overrides most halakhic considerations.

Some explain[14] that the reason for the prohibition has to do with the *ḥillul Hashem* which would ensue if a Jew were to take the money, as this suggests that the Jewish community is turning its back on its own people. Rabbi Shabbetai Kohen (the *Shakh*; Lithuania/Moravia, 1622–1663) explains that the *ḥillul Hashem* is created when a Jew supplicates in public.[15]

The matter is also discussed in Bava Batra 10b. Here the gemara argues that Jews may not accept charity for a different reason: the concern is that by accepting the donations the Jewish people would be crediting the non-Jews with merit (*zekhut*), which in return would grant them the heavenly legitimacy to continue their rule over the Jewish people. The gemara does allow accepting the money in certain cases, e.g., in a situation in which rejecting the money would disrupt the good relations between the government and the Jewish community (*shelom malkhut*). Even so, the gemara requires that the money be divided only among the poor of the non-Jewish community.

Is there a halakhic difference between the two arguments? In other words, why does Rabbi Yosef Karo not seem to take Bava Batra

12. "Teshuva BeInyan Netilat Tzedaka Min HaGoyim," *Moriya* 15, no. 5–6 (Adar 1987): 33–35.
13. *Yoreh De'ah* 254:1.
14. *Ḥokhmat Adam, Hilkhot Tzedaka* 146b.
15. *Shakh, Yoreh De'ah* 254:1.

10b into account? If a poor person accepts donations privately, is it not still a problem to give merit to non-Jews?

Rabbi David HaLevi Segal (also known as the *Turei Zahav* or *Taz*; Poland, 1586–1667) argues that the gemara in Bava Batra is only concerned with cases in which the non-Jew specifically directs his charity toward Jews. In situations in which the non-Jew is donating charity out of the goodness of his heart and does not designate his charity to Jews, we are not concerned about the fact that he is receiving merit for the commandment of giving charity.

Rabbi Eliezer Waldenberg (Jerusalem, 1915–2006)[16] and Rav Kook[17] explain that each source is discussing a different situation. While the gemara in Bava Batra is referring to aid from a public body like a government, the gemara in Sanhedrin is referring to charity given from one individual to another. *Ḥillul Hashem* only applies in the latter case, in which a Jew is living off the generosity of a non-Jew, as this involves shame and disgrace. However, the concern of giving the non-Jew merit by accepting his donations refers to foreign governments. Because of this understanding, Rabbi Waldenberg permits accepting donations from private funds if no *ḥillul Hashem* occurs.

Based on these sources, it seems that it would be improper to accept the German payments. Even if one were to argue that that there is no issue of *ḥillul Hashem* when a country accepts money from another country, the argument of the gemara in Bava Batra would surely apply.

Rabbi Elyashiv permits accepting donations (specifically for publishing manuscripts for Torah study) for a few reasons. First, he quotes *Rishonim*[18] who argue that presents, unlike charity, are acceptable. The difference between a present and charity is that the giver of a present sometimes does so out of self-interest. Case in point, argues Rabbi Elyashiv: the Germans are paying for the manuscripts because they are honored that these esteemed authors were born in Germany. Second, he quotes the commentators mentioned before, who in difficult times allow payments to be accepted. Last, he mentions the law which

16. *Tzitz Eliezer,* 15:33.

17. *Daat Kohen* (Jerusalem: Mosad HaRav Kook, 1984), *se'if* 132.

18. *Yad Rama,* Bava Batra 10b.

states that a non-Jew who donates money to a synagogue is permitted to do so, as this is similar to donating a sacrifice to the Temple, which is allowed. The money in this case is going for a religious cause, and it would therefore be permitted.

In an article addressing America's foreign aid to Israel, Rabbi Mordechai Fromm, a former rebbe in Yeshivat Mercaz HaRav, discusses the halakhic questions regarding accepting charity from non-Jewish governments.[19] Even though there are vast differences between Germany's reparations and America's foreign aid, there are some halakhic arguments that are similar. Rabbi Fromm questions if money given by governments is considered charity. Quoting the *Taz* mentioned above, he argues that America distributes funds to other countries as well as Israel. The American government is not acting out of kindness but rather in its own national self-interest.

Rabbi Fromm recognizes that both gemaras refer to Jewish communities as well as to Jewish individuals. The gemara in Bava Batra is concerned that accepting funds from non-Jewish governments might give the donors merits which might empower them to rule over the Jewish people. However, explains Rabbi Fromm, the question before us is an entirely different one. Everything changes once we have an independent Jewish state. Permitting the Jewish state to accept foreign aid would lead to the opposite result, as this money would in fact strengthen the Israeli state; building a strong Jewish country would weaken other nations' rule over us. Finally, he mentions that in times of great need, especially in situations involving *pikuaḥ nefesh*, one is permitted to accept donations. The State of Israel desperately needs these funds in order to sustain its security and economy; therefore, the country is allowed to accept the aid.

It seems to me that the last argument mentioned could be used to argue in favor of the German agreement. The money accepted from the Germans changed Israel's financial status. Putting emotional reactions aside, the understanding that we are not dealing with individuals, but rather with international agreements between independent nations, creates a new reality. This reality – of a Jewish state that may or may not accept money from other governments – was a new one for the halakhic world.

19. *Zekhor Zot LeYa'akov* (Jerusalem: Mosad HaRav Kook, 1971), 81.

5

Ben-Gurion's Call for Opinions on Jewish Identity, 1958

Who Is a Jew?

In the early days of the State of Israel, the definition of "Who is a Jew" had not yet been decided; it was only a matter of time until the question arose. Dr. Zerach Warhaftig (1906–2002), a signatory of the Declaration of Independence and a minister in Ben-Gurion's cabinet, later wrote that, in the beginning, it was assumed the status quo would remain: Jewish identity was primarily religious and hence should be based upon Jewish law.[1]

In March 1958, Israel's minister of internal affairs, Israel Bar-Yehuda, decided that parents could declare their children Jewish even in cases in which the mother was not Jewish. The decision created an uproar in the country and led to a coalition crisis. As a result, Prime Minister Ben-Gurion elected to establish a committee consisting of himself and two other ministers.[2] The group was tasked with examining the rules

1. In his book *Ḥukka LeYisrael Dat UMedina* (Jerusalem: Mesilot, 1988), 153–78.
2. Ben-Gurion's son had married a non-Jewish woman, and it therefore seems that he may have taken a personal interest in this matter. See Anita Shapira, *Ben-Gurion:*

for the registration of children of mixed marriages. It was also encouraged to solicit the opinions of Jewish scholars both in Israel and abroad on this subject before making its decision. The government decided to focus on children and not on adults. In the latter case, it was decided that to be registered as a Jew, it was sufficient for an adult to "feel" Jewish.

On October 27, 1958, a letter was sent out to over fifty leading poets, scholars, and rabbis, asking them to share their views on the following question: "How should the State of Israel register a child in a case where both the non-Jewish mother and Jewish father wish the child to be registered as Jewish?"[3] In total, the committee received forty-six written responses.[4] As might be expected, all Orthodox rabbis and scholars were adamant that this was a religious question and should therefore be decided based on Jewish law.[5] The response of the Lubavitcher Rebbe, Rabbi Menachem Mendel Schneerson (1902–1994), was typical:

> My opinion is absolutely clear, following the Torah and the tradition accepted for generations, that in these matters there can be no validity whatsoever to a verbal declaration expressing the desire to register as a Jew. Such a declaration has no power to change the reality.
>
> According to the Torah and the tradition throughout the ages, a Jew is a person born to a Jewish mother, or a convert who had been converted following the procedure laid down in the authoritative codes of Judaism from ancient times down to the Shulchan Arukh.[6]

Demuto Shel Manhig (Tel Aviv: Am Oved, 2015), 127–29.

3. The entire letter can be found online at Toldot, Atar Historia, accessed June 24, 2021, https://toldotofakim.cet.ac.il/ShowItem.aspx?ItemID=a7e56358-9249-4e6a-84e8-9047e8fdab14&lang=HEB.
4. All the responses were collected and published by the government in a collection called *Kovetz Mihu Yehudi* (Jerusalem, 1959). A summary of all the answers can be found in Avraham Korman's book *Yehudi: Mihu UMahu* (Tel Aviv: Avraham Korman, 1976).
5. The majority of responses agreed that the definition of who is a Jew is a religious one. Ironically, the responses were never addressed properly by the government.
6. The original letter was published in the journal *HaPardes* 34, no. 1 (1959): 34. It can also be found in English at: "David Ben-Gurion Asks 'Who is a Jew?'" TheRebbe.org,

Rabbi Joseph Soloveitchik responded in a letter written jointly with his friend and colleague Rabbi Hayyim Heller, stating the obvious but adding their concern:[7]

> We are indeed perplexed that the State of Israel now seeks to hew down our traditional branches and thereby smear the ancient glory of Israel, which has long been sanctified through spilt blood and sufferings of preceding generations.... Will the State of Israel be built up by the destruction of the sanctity of the Jewish people?

HALAKHIC SOURCES ON RELIGIOUS IDENTITY

What is the source for following the mother rather than the father (matrilineal descent) regarding the question of how to determine a child's religion?

The gemara in Kiddushin (68b) asks: "From where do we derive that her [the Jewish woman who marries a non-Jew] offspring is like her?" R. Yoḥanan in the name of R. Shimon b. Yoḥai answers the question by quoting a text from Deuteronomy (7:3–4) which prohibits intermarriage: "You shall not give your daughter to his son... for he will turn away your son from following Me." He then argues the following:

> [Since the verse is concerned that after one's daughter marries a non-Jew, the father will lead his children away from the service of God this indicates that] your son [i.e., your grandson] from a Jewish woman is called "your son" [by the Torah], but your son from a non-Jewish woman is not called your son, but her son.

Rabbi Baruch Epstein (1860–1942) in his biblical commentary[8] explains the gemara's proof. After the Torah prohibits intermarriage for both men

accessed June 24, 2021, https://www.chabad.org/therebbe/letters/default_cdo/aid/2064625/jewish/David-Ben-Gurion-Asks-Who-is-a-Jew.htm.

7. A complete translation of the letter can be found in Rabbi Soloveitchik's *Community, Covenant and Commitment*, ed. Nathaniel Helfgot (Jersey City, NJ: Ktav, 2005), 168–69.

8. *Torah Temima*, Deut. 7:3–4: "Do not intermarry with them: your daughter you shall not give to his son, nor take his daughter for your son. For he will turn away your

and women, it explains the danger and the result of such a marriage: "He will turn your son away…" Surely, the Torah should have used plural language: **they** will turn your **sons** away, thus referring to both your son and daughter marrying non-Jews. Therefore, the understanding is that the Torah accepts that the son of a non-Jewish woman is not considered "your son" anymore.

The gemara in Yevamot (45a) rules that the offspring of a non-Jew or a slave who engages in intercourse with a Jewish woman is Jewish, and he or she may marry into the congregation of Israel. However, according to other sources, it is unclear if this practice was respected in early times. In Leviticus (24:10–11) we read:

> The son of an Israelite woman – and he was the son of an Egyptian man – went out among the Israelites, and they quarreled in the camp: this son of the Israelite woman and an Israelite man. And the son of the Israelite woman pronounced the [Divine] Name and cursed.

According to a *midrash halakha,*[9] the "son of the Israelite woman" and the "Egyptian man" cursed God after Moshe's court ruled that he was not entitled to inherit land in Israel as an Israelite. The midrash understands that having an Israelite mother does not make one Jewish if the father is Egyptian. The midrash even adds that the "son of the Israelite woman" converted to Judaism.

The Ramban (Nahmanides; Girona, 1194–1270; ad loc.) questions the midrash's interpretation, as it contradicts the normative halakha that Jewish identity follows the mother. He quotes an opinion in the name of French sages (*Tzarfatim*) who argue that before the Torah was given at Mount Sinai, the custom was to define Jewish identity by the father, as is implied by the midrash. Ramban disagrees and argues that the Torah's rule of following the mother was always in effect. He understands the midrash as referring to several halakhot in which we follow

son from following Me to serve other gods, and the Lord's anger will burn against you and will quickly destroy you."

9. *Sifra, Emor* 4.

the father's lineage – for example, inheritance laws and priesthood. As for the midrash's reference to conversion, Ramban explains that this was not real conversion; rather he chose to follow his mother's family rather than his non-Jewish father's family.

The most direct source from biblical times that the practice was to follow the mother's side can be found in the book of Ezra (10:1–4).

> As Ezra prayed and confessed, weeping as he knelt down on his knees before the House of God, a very large crowd of Israelites gathered around him: men, women, and children, weeping a great deal. Then Shekhanya son of Yeḥiel, of the sons of Eilam, spoke up, saying to Ezra: "We have indeed been unfaithful to our God by marrying foreign women of the peoples of the land; even so, there is still hope for Israel in this matter. Now, let us make a covenant with our God *to send away all these women and their offspring*, according to the counsel of the Lord and of those who fear our God's commandments; everyone shall abide by the law. Rise up, for it is your duty to take care of this matter; we will be with you. Be strong and take action." (Emphasis mine.)

The covenant made by Ezra mentions sending away the non-Jewish women and their children. The children of non-Jewish men are not mentioned; presumably they remained within the Jewish community.

Rabbi Yechiel Yaakov Weinberg, a prominent leading *posek* (decisor) of the twentieth century (Poland/Switzerland, 1884–1966), also responded to Ben-Gurion's letter. In his response, he suggests reasons for the Torah's ruling that we follow the mother's religion to decide who is a Jew.

> According to the laws of the Torah, Jewish identity follows the mother. We do not claim to know the reasons of the Torah's laws, yet suggestions have been made as to the reason for this law. Some say that it is a biological reason, as the child develops in its mother's womb. Some say that it has a moral reason, since the mother and her constant influence determine the education of the child...and others see the reason as the unquestionable certainty

> that the child is born to his mother. However, whatever the reason may be, it is not the rational element but rather the religious element that was the deciding factor in shaping the character of the nation and shaping the Hebrew family.[10]

At least twice more in later years[11] the question of defining "Who is a Jew" created major crises, both in the State in Israel and abroad. Rabbi Immanuel Jakobovits, chief rabbi of the British Commonwealth from the late sixties until the early nineties, describes the uniqueness of our question: "No single issue has epitomized the challenge to traditional Jewish norms created by the restoration of Jewish statehood more than this ongoing debate on the definition of Jewish personal status."[12]

Why is this true? What makes this issue so compelling and unique? Why does the "restoration of Jewish statehood" have such an impact on the "Who is a Jew" question? I believe that there are two main reasons.

First, the question of who is a Jew is not just an internal problem of the State of Israel; rather, it affects Jews around the world. The decisions made by Israel's government and courts threatened to split the Jewish world. The Lubavitcher Rebbe writes in his letter:

> The question of registration, or however it may be described, is not a matter confined to Israel alone. It goes without saying – as explained in your letter – that no one may raise a barrier between the Jews of Israel and those of the Diaspora. On the contrary, all our brethren, wherever they may be, have constituted one people from the moment of their emergence, in spite of their dispersion in all the corners of the world. Consequently, the solution of the

10. The entire letter was published in his book *LiFrakim* (Jerusalem: HaVaad LeHotzaat Kitvei HaGaon HaRav Yechiel Yaakov Weinberg, 2004), 301–11.
11. In 1968, the Shalit affair arose. Benjamin Shalit, an Israeli officer, married a non-Jewish woman. In 1970, the Supreme Court ruled that his children could be registered as Jews. Throughout the seventies, a major crisis erupted within the government regarding the question of recognizing Reform and Conservative conversions.
12. Immanuel Jakobovits, *If Only My People: Zionism in My Life* (London: Weidenfeld and Nicolson, 1984), 193.

> problem must be one that is acceptable to all members of the Jewish people everywhere...

Secondly, there was deep concern within the Jewish world that the State of Israel was creating a new Judaism. The fear was that secular Zionism was attempting to redefine Jewish nationality. Judaism had always been defined as both religion and nationality. Throughout the long years of exile, it was the religious dimension that preserved our Jewish identity. Would the new State of Israel change that? Were new criteria developing to define the Jewish people that would reject the central place of religion?

Rabbi Aharon Lichtenstein (US/Israel, 1933–2015) appears to address this same issue in his important article about Brother Daniel.[13] Brother Daniel (Shmuel Oswald Rufeisen, 1922–1998) was born to a Jewish family in Poland. While hiding from the Nazis, he converted to Christianity. In the 1950s, Rufeisen applied for Israeli citizenship. He maintained that although he was not an observant Jew, according to Jewish law, he was still considered Jewish.

The Israeli government denied Brother Daniel's request on the grounds that he had converted to Christianity. The case reached the Supreme Court, and in 1962 the court upheld the government's decision: any Jew converting to another religion would lose their ancestral right to immigrate to Israel.

In the introduction to his article, Rabbi Lichtenstein points out the changes that the State of Israel brought to the ongoing discussion about who is a Jew:

> The existence of the State has radically changed the character of the problem itself. Its establishment opened up the possibility that political and geographic elements might supplement or supplant racial and religious criteria in determining membership in the community of Israel. The possibility was of course two-edged. On the one hand, it might be contended that Jews living in Israel were

13. "Brother Daniel and the Jewish Fraternity," *Judaism: A Quarterly Journal of Jewish Life and Thought* 12, no. 3 (Summer 1963): 260–80; reprinted in *Leaves of Faith: The World of Jewish Living* (Jersey City, NJ: Ktav, 2003), 57–83.

> somehow "more Jewish" than their co-religionists elsewhere.... On the other hand, arguing for inclusion rather than exclusion, one might hold that non-Jewish residents of the state are also, in a sense, within the "community of Israel."

While opinions have been expressed across the spectrum, the halakhic question and the national definitions continue to concern Jews worldwide. Even today, in the twenty-first century, "Who is a Jew" is a major question for Jews both within the State of Israel and in the Diaspora.

6

The Capture of Adolf Eichmann, 1961

Are There Halakhic Issues Regarding Bringing Murderers to Justice?

On May 23, 1960, David Ben-Gurion, prime minister of Israel, announced before the Knesset:

> I must inform the Knesset that not long ago the security services found one of the great Nazi war criminals: Adolf Eichmann, who was responsible, along with other Nazi leaders, for what they called the Final Solution to the Jewish problem – that is, the extermination of six million Jews in Europe. Adolf Eichmann is already under arrest in Israel and will soon face trial in Israel, in keeping with the laws governing justice for the Nazis and their helpers.[1]

1. For the original in Hebrew, see "Pirsum Meyuḥad: MeAḥorei HaKla'im Shel Mishpat Eichmann," Arkhiyon HaMedina, accessed December 21, 2021, https://catalog.archives.gov.il/chapter/the-eichmann-trial-behind-the-scenes/.

A few days earlier, Israeli Mossad agents had kidnapped Adolf Eichmann, who was hiding in Argentina under the alias Ricardo Klement. In a daring mission, the Israeli agents were able to smuggle Eichmann out of the country and bring him to Israel to stand trial. The response both in Israel and abroad was sensational. Argentina complained that Israel had committed a crime in their country and demanded reparations.

Eichmann's trial began on April 11, 1961, and ended on December 15, 1961. Gideon Hausner, Israel's attorney general, served as the prosecutor. His famous, passionate speech began with the words:

> When I stand before you here, judges of Israel, to lead the prosecution of Adolf Eichmann, I am not standing alone; with me are six million accusers. However, they cannot rise to their feet and point an accusing finger toward him who sits in the dock and cry: "I accuse." For their ashes are piled up on the hills of Auschwitz and the fields of Treblinka, and are strewn in the forests of Poland; their graves are scattered throughout the length and breadth of Europe; their blood cries out, but their voice is not heard. Therefore, I will be their spokesman, and in their name I will unfold the awesome indictment.[2]

In his testimony, Eichmann insisted he had no choice but to follow orders, as he was bound by an oath of loyalty to Hitler. This defense was similarly used by some defendants in the 1945–1946 Nuremberg trials. On December 15, 1961, Eichmann was sentenced to death by hanging. In his appeal, Eichmann claimed: "There is a need to draw a line between the leaders responsible and the people like me forced to serve as mere instruments in the hands of the leaders. I was not a responsible leader, and as such do not feel myself guilty." On June 1, 1962, after his final appeal was rejected, Eichmann was hanged, his body cremated, and his ashes scattered over the sea.

The trial was followed closely around the world and raised awareness of the atrocities that had taken place during the Holocaust. In Israel,

2. *Reshumot Mishpato Shel Adolf Eichmann* (Jerusalem: Misrad HaMishpatim, 1982), 1:55.

it was the first time that the people were exposed to the personal stories of the many survivors living in the country.

At the same time, certain questions and dilemmas were raised regarding the trial and its verdict. Isaiah Berlin, the Jewish philosopher, questioned the purpose of conducting a trial. Requests from all over the world were sent to Yitzhak Ben-Zvi, Israel's president, asking him to consider commuting the sentence to life in prison. A petition, signed by famous figures such as Martin Buber, Hugo Bergman, and poet Leah Goldberg, argued that executing Eichmann would belittle the magnitude of the Holocaust. In the letter attached, they said that if this Nazi criminal could make the Jews employ an executioner, that would be a victory for the Nazis. Jew-haters worldwide, they warned, would claim that Eichmann's death had atoned for the Nazis' crimes against the Jews.[3] Newly published protocols[4] from Ben-Gurion's cabinet meetings show that ministers Yosef Burg, Abba Eban, and Levi Eshkol hesitated when making the final decision not to grant clemency. Eichmann's wife, too, sent a telegram, pleading to spare his life.

The president's response to all these requests was negative. In a handwritten note which he attached to the telegram, he quoted the words of the prophet Shmuel as he killed the king of Amalek: "As your sword has made women childless, so your mother shall be childless among women" (I Sam. 15:33).

THE RABBINIC VIEW OF JUSTICE FOR MURDERERS

In articles published by rabbis at the time, it seems that other questions and concerns were raised: How much money and effort should be invested in the hunting of Nazi criminals? Should the state assassinate Nazis or bring them to justice? Does Jewish law recommend the death penalty? The halakhic discussion revolved around precedents from the Torah and rabbinic literature.

3. The complete letter, dated May 30, 1962, with list of signatories, can be found on the Israel State Archives website: http://www.archives.gov.il/archives/#/Archive/0b0717068001c167/File/0b07170684d1cd84/Item/0907170684d1ce34.

4. See the protocol, dated May 29, 1962, on the Israel State Archives website: http://www.archives.gov.il/archives/#/Archive/0b0717068031be30/File/0b07170680348 35a/Item/0907170680348915.

Goel HaDam: The Blood Redeemer

In normal situations, court authorities are responsible for punishing trespassers and criminals. However, the Torah recognizes that in certain circumstances a person is permitted to avenge the death of his relative. If a *goel hadam* (blood avenger) finds that the murderer of his relative has escaped from an *ir miklat* (city of refuge for people who have killed unintentionally), R. Yosei the Galilean rules, avenging the blood of one's relative is considered a commandment (Makkot 11b).

The Rambam rules that the *goel hadam* has responsibilities within the trial process:

> It is a commandment for the blood redeemer to kill the murderer, as the Torah states: "The blood redeemer shall put the murderer to death" (Num. 35:19). Whoever is fit to inherit the victim's estate becomes the redeemer of his blood. If the blood redeemer does not desire or is unable to kill the murderer, or if the victim does not have a relative to redeem his blood, the court executes the murderer by decapitation.[5]

Unlike the Rambam, the Ramban considers the acts of the *goel hadam* a commandment in and of itself, and he counts it as one of the 613 commandments.[6] He explains that the blood relative is responsible for chasing the murderer and bringing him to justice. He further notes that if there is no blood relative, the court must appoint a representative to avenge the blood of the murdered person.

In the seventeenth century, Rabbi Menachem Mendel Krochmal (1600–1661), rabbi of Nikolsburg, was asked about a case in which a man is murdered and the murderer's identity is known. Can one force the blood relative to chase the murderer? Is he expected by Jewish law to pay for the expenses involved in bringing the man to justice? Here, it must be noted, the context of this responsum is key; it was around the terrible time of the Khmelnitsky massacres (1648–1657).

---

5. *Mishneh Torah, Hilkhot Rotze'aḥ* 1:2.
6. Ramban's Glosses on Rambam's *Sefer HaMitzvot,* positive commandment 13.

In his response, Rabbi Krochmal argues that this commandment is similar to all others: one is obligated to pay the normal expenses to perform the commandment. He adds that the law is the same if the murderer is a non-Jew. At the end of his responsum, he states that one cannot expect the relative to pay large amounts of money (for example, exorbitant bribes); rather, the community is expected to pay these expenses. He testifies that he applied these laws in his community: "Our custom is to raise the money required to chase murderers even if we realize that we cannot always succeed in avenging the death of our murdered brethren, because Jewish blood is not to be considered *hefker* (ownerless, i.e., cheap)."[7]

Rabbi Shimon Federbush (1892–1969), chief rabbi of Finland, wrote an article about the Eichmann trial.[8] After mentioning Rabbi Krochmal's responsum, he quotes Rabbi Menachem of Riesbürg (Germany, early fifteenth century), who argues that one may violate Shabbat in order to pursue murderers.[9] This comes from an understanding that punishing murderers is an essential deterrent to prevent future attacks on the Jewish community.[10]

Regarding Gideon Hausner's opening remarks, that with him stand six million prosecutors, Rabbi Federbush adds an interesting comment. As mentioned before, the Torah sees the *goel hadam* as solely responsible for bringing the murderer to justice. Accordingly, he should also act as the prosecutor in the trial. He quotes Rabbeinu Nissim of Girona (or Ran; 1320–1376), who writes: "It is a commandment for the *goel hadam* to prosecute the murderer of his relative before the courts. If there is no *goel hadam*, then the courts must appoint an alternate prosecutor to speak on behalf of the victim."[11] Therefore, concludes Rabbi Federbush, appointing the country's head prosecutor to speak on behalf of the millions who perished in the Holocaust was correct.

---

7. *Teshuvot Tzemaḥ Tzedek* #111.
8. "Mishpat Eichmann LeOr HaHalakha," in *Ḥikrei Yahadut* (Jerusalem: Mosad HaRav Kook, 1966), 236–42.
9. It is unclear if he permits violating rabbinical laws or even biblical ones.
10. *Nimmukei Maharam MiRiesbürg,* printed at the end of *Shut Mahari Weil.*
11. *Ḥiddushei HaRan,* Sanhedrin 45a.

Ein Shaliaḥ LiDvar Aveira

As mentioned before, Eichmann claimed that he was following the orders of his superiors and therefore should not be culpable. Rabbi Moshe-Zvi Neria, the founding *rosh yeshiva* of Yeshivat Kfar HaRo'eh, a Member of Knesset, and founder of Bnei Akiva (1913–1995), argues that there is no halakhic basis for this argument.[12] In Joshua (1:18) we are taught that the punishment for disobeying the king is death. However, the gemara in Sanhedrin 49a teaches us that this is not the case if the king's order contradicts a law of the Torah.

Rabbi Neria quotes other sources that indicate that if a Noahide, or non-Jew, is commanded or even forced to kill, he must object even if he is killed for disobeying the order. The source for this law is based on common sense (or *sevara*): "What makes you think your blood is redder than his?" This line appears in Sanhedrin 74a (in Rashi's version of the text). Obviously, this logical statement applies equally to Jew and non-Jew.

Some might argue that Eichmann did not actually kill anyone directly; rather, he gave orders to others. Rabbi Natan Tzvi Friedman (1914–1993), a neighborhood rabbi in Bnei Brak, comments that this argument has no basis in Jewish law.[13] He quotes the Rambam, *Hilkhot Melakhim* 9:4:

> A non-Jew who slays any soul, even a fetus in its mother's womb, must be executed in retribution for its death. Similarly, if he slays a person who would have otherwise died in the near future, places a person bound before a lion, or starves a person to death, since ultimately, he has caused a death, he must be executed. Similarly, he must be executed if he used deadly force against an assailant who could have been neutralized by wounding. This is not the case when it comes to a Jew.

This law proves that a non-Jew is responsible for murder even if it is committed indirectly. Furthermore, Jewish law does not exempt those who send others to perform murder.

---

12. "Mishpat Tzorer HaYehudim BaHalakha," in *Shana BeShana* (1961): 105–19.
13. "Mishpat Eichmann LeOr HaHalakha," *Gevilin* 14–15 (Tammuz 1961): 25–27.

This issue is discussed by Rabbi Neria and relates to the concept of *sheliḥut* in Jewish law. Normally, Jewish law recognizes that a *shaliaḥ* (appointed emissary) can perform legal acts on behalf of the *meshale'aḥ* (dispatcher). The gemara in Kiddushin (42b) limits this by introducing the concept of "*Ein shaliaḥ lidvar aveira*," "There is no agency for transgression." One is held accountable for a transgression one commits even if commissioned to do so by another. The *meshale'aḥ*, or dispatcher, is not punished for the transgression despite having sent the violator to commit the act.

The gemara cites textual sources from the Torah for this halakha but also suggests a logical argument: "*Divrei harav vedivrei hatalmid, divrei mi shomin*?" This literally translates as: "The words of the teacher and the words of the student – whose words does one obey?" Essentially, the *meshale'aḥ* cannot be held responsible for commissioning the act, because he could not have expected the *shaliaḥ* to carry out the mission. The *meshale'aḥ* did not actually anticipate the *shaliaḥ*'s compliance with his request, as it involved violating the Torah. If so, argues Rabbi Neria, this logic should apply in our case. So can Eichmann use this for his defense?

The answer is found in the works of Rabbi Shimon ben Tzemach Duran (the Rashbatz; Spain, 1361–1444), who limits this logic to circumstances in which the *meshale'aḥ* could actually claim that he did not anticipate that the *shaliaḥ* would listen to him.[14] If it clear to the *meshale'aḥ* that the *shaliaḥ* would follow his orders, the *meshale'aḥ* is liable. Accordingly, if an officer gives an order to soldiers to commit murder and knows without a doubt that the soldiers will carry out the task, the *meshale'aḥ* is guilty of murder.

Furthermore, Rabbi Neria quotes many opinions that *ein shaliaḥ lidvar aveira* does not apply in the case of a non-Jew.

The Death Penalty

Many *posekim* have discussed the Torah's opinion regarding the application of the death penalty today.[15] In 1954, the Knesset voted to abolish the

---

14. *Tashbetz*, vol. 1, 156.
15. For a detailed summary of the many opinions, see Yaron Unger, "Onesh HaMavet," http://main.knesset.gov.il/Activity/Info/LegalDepartmentSurveys/Survey251113.pdf.

death penalty for the crime of murder. The death penalty was retained for war crimes, crimes against humanity, crimes against the Jewish people, treason, and certain crimes under military law during wartime. Nonetheless, this question arises every few years; it is a complex matter both for the Israeli public and in the halakhic literature.

On one hand, those who oppose the death penalty quote this famous passage:

> A Sanhedrin that executes once in seven years is characterized as a destructive tribunal. R. Elazar b. Azarya says: Once in seventy years. R. Akiva and R. Tarfon say: If we had been on the Sanhedrin, no one would have ever been executed. (Mishna Makkot 1:10)

On the other hand, those who are in favor quote opinions of the Gemara and *posekim* emphasizing that the government is permitted and even obligated to use extreme measures in order to sustain law and order and to ensure that justice prevails.

The Rambam is very clear, as he writes:

> When a Jewish king desires to slay any of these murderers and the like – who are not liable for execution by the court – by virtue of his regal authority, in order to perfect society, he has the license.
>
> Similarly, if the court sees a need for a temporary measure to execute them, because this is required at the time, they have the license to do as they see fit.[16]

In their conclusions, Rabbi Neria, Rabbi Federbush, and Rabbi Friedman all believe that, based on Jewish law, the Israeli government has the right and obligation to bring murderers of the Jewish people to justice and, if need be, to put them to death.

I wish to end with the powerful words of Rabbi Friedman:

16. *Mishneh Torah, Hilkhot Rotze'aḥ UShemirat Nefesh* 2:4.

> Now that the *tzorer* (enemy) has been caught and put on trial, there are those who are merciful to him. Let us listen to the words of our prophets. Yeshayahu (5:16) declares: "The Lord of Hosts is exalted through justice and the Holy God is sanctified through righteousness."

In the midrash, R. Shimon b. Yoḥai claims that God appears in His greatness when the wicked are punished. Yeḥezkel says (38:23): "I will be magnified, I will be sanctified, and I will make Myself known in the eyes of many nations – and they will know that I am the Lord."

7

Our Man in Damascus: Eli Cohen, 1965

How Far May One Go to Protect the State of Israel?

Eli Cohen was born in 1924 in Alexandria, Egypt. He was involved in the Zionist movement there and made aliya in 1957. In Israel, the Mossad recognized his great potential and recruited him. The Mossad created a new false identity for him as a Syrian businessman returning home after living in Argentina; he was given the name Kamel Amin Thaabet. Part of his training process included learning Muslim prayers and religious customs.[1] After living for some time in Buenos Aires, he arrived in Damascus in February 1962.

Eli became a well-known figure in Damascus high society. He made contact with the elite of the Syrian community, including ministers, businessmen, and highly placed officials. "Thaabet" was a wealthy nationalist who hosted parties rich in alcohol and women and was generous

1. Yeshayahu Ben Porat and Uri Dan, *HaMeragel SheBa MiYisrael: Parashat Eli Cohen* (Tel Aviv: Masada, 1968), 48.

with both loans and advice.[2] At these parties, Eli, feigning intoxication, was able to gather important information.

Eli Cohen provided an extensive range of intelligence to the Israeli army over a period of four years (1961–1965). He sent information to Israel by radio, secret letters, and occasionally in person. The intelligence he provided played a major role in Israel's victory in the Six-Day War. While visiting the Golan Heights, he collected information on the Syrian fortifications. Under the pretense of protecting the soldiers, who were exposed to the sun, he had trees planted at every position. The trees were later used as markers by the Israeli military, enabling the young state to capture the Golan Heights with relative ease.

On January 24, 1965, the Syrian security services broke into Cohen's apartment and arrested him. Until today, it is unclear who revealed his true identity and how.

After a trial before a military tribunal, Cohen was found guilty of espionage and sentenced to death. He was said to have been repeatedly tortured. Israel staged an international campaign for clemency, hoping to persuade the Syrians not to execute him. Despite international appeals to commute the death sentence, the sentence was upheld.

On May 18, 1965, Cohen was hanged in Al Marjeh Square in Damascus. On the day of his execution, Eli Cohen's last wish, to see a rabbi, was granted by the prison authorities. To this very day, the Syrian authorities refuse to release his body.

What is perhaps most amazing about Eli Cohen is that he was genuinely liked, even loved, by so many of the top Syrian leaders. He was never suspected of being a spy until the very end.

CAN A JEW APPEAR AS A NON-JEW?

Taking on the fictitious identity of a non-Jew involves halakhic questions. Rabbi Yosef Karo brings the following law: "It is prohibited for a Jew to claim that he is an idolater even if this is for saving one's life. However, it is permitted to dress as an idolater to escape persecution."[3] The Rema (Rav Moshe Isserles, 1530–1572) comments on the law, adding

2. Ben Porat and Dan, *HaMeragel*, 119.
3. *Shulḥan Arukh, Yoreh De'ah* 157:2.

that "even though it is prohibited for a Jew to claim that he is an idolater, it is permitted to trick the non-Jew into thinking that he is one. This is only permitted at times when one is in grave danger."

Accordingly, Rabbi Shlomo Goren[4] wonders: Under what halakhic premises can the Israeli secret services send spies who take on the identity of non-Jews? In Muslim countries, Israeli spies are required to be faithful religious Muslims. They must pray and act in accordance with all Muslim laws. They must be able to convince their acquaintances that they are who they claim to be: genuine Muslims. They must take upon themselves the Muslim faith.

Normally one could argue that all Jewish laws are suspended in the case of *pikuaḥ nefesh* (lives in danger). However, it is a well-known law that even in order to save one's life, one may not worship idols. The source for this law is in the Gemara:

> [It was] concluded in the upper story of the house of Nitza in Lod: All transgressions in the Torah, if a person is told, "Transgress and you will not be killed," he may transgress except for idol worship (*avoda zara*), forbidden sexual relations (*gilui arayot*), and bloodshed. (Sanhedrin 74a)

Is Islam Considered Idol Worship?

Rabbi Goren explains that the *heter* (dispensation) is based on the halakhic ruling of the Rambam that Muslims are not considered idolaters. He refers to the Rambam's letter to Ovadya HaGer (Ovadya the convert):

> These Ishmaelites [i.e., Muslims] are not idolaters at all. [Idolatry] has been eradicated from their mouths and hearts. They unify God without question.... Likewise all contemporary Muslims, including women and children, have eradicated idolatrous beliefs; their errors and foolishness are manifest in other matters.... In respect of the unity of God, they are in no error at all.[5]

---

4. *Mishnat HaMedina* (Jerusalem: HaIdra Rabba, 1999), 140–44.
5. *Teshuvot HaRambam*, #448.

This ruling appears again in a discussion regarding the *heter* to derive benefit from wine of a Muslim. The law of *yayin nesekh* (wine used for idol worship) prohibits Jews from drinking wine of idolaters as well as deriving benefit from it. If the non-Jew is not halakhically categorized as an idolater, then one may derive benefit.

> Similarly, concerning any non-Jew who does not serve idols, such as the Ishmaelites (Muslims), though their wine may not be drunk, it is permitted to benefit from it. So have all the *Geonim* ruled. We may derive no benefit, however, from the wine of idolaters.[6]

Rabbi Ovadia Yosef, basing himself on the Rambam's opinion, permits Jews to walk into a mosque.

> Regarding Jewish soldiers who requested from the prince to give them a place to pray, and he gave them a mosque, are they permitted to pray there?... He [Rabbi Isaac Elchanan, *Ein Yitzḥak, Oraḥ Ḥayim* 11] answered that since it is clear in the *Tur* ([*Yoreh De'ah*] 124) in the name of *Geonim*, Rambam, and Rashba, that the Ishmaelites are not idolatrous, and so wrote the Rema ([*Yoreh De'ah*] 146:5), one may easily permit praying there.[7]

It is therefore understandable that the Rambam believes that people do not have to give up their lives in a situation in which they are faced with the choice to convert to Islam or die:

> One who preferred to suffer martyrdom in order not to pronounce the Mohammedan confession has done nobly and well, and his reward is great before the Lord. He may be regarded as supremely virtuous, as he was willing to surrender his life for the sanctification of the name of God, blessed be He. Should

6. *Mishneh Torah, Hilkhot Maakhalot Asurot* 11:7.
7. *Yabia Omer, Yoreh De'ah* 7:12. Translation taken from the Sefaria website: https://www.sefaria.org.il/sheets/66223.10?lang=bi&with=all&lang2=he.

> one, however, inquire of me, "Shall I be slain or pronounce the Mohammedan confession?" my answer would be: "Utter the formula and live."[8]

However, even though most *posekim* agree with the Rambam that the Muslim faith is not idolatry,[9] not all agree with his conclusion that conversion to Islam overrides a life-threatening situation.[10] The Radbaz disagrees with Rambam's position and argues that Jews must give up their lives rather than convert to Islam. His rationale is based on the argument that giving agreement to Muhammad's prophetic mission is the equivalent of denying the validity of Torah.[11]

Marrying a Non-Jew

Rabbi Goren notes that another significant halakhic issue must be addressed in this context. In order to maintain their false identity, spies might be required to make unexpected sacrifices. An older bachelor, for example, in the Muslim world might arouse suspicion; therefore, it might be necessary to arrange a fictitious marriage. Here the issue that arises is forbidden relations, *gilui arayot,* another commandment which must be kept at all costs, even if the alternative is death. How far can a spy carry on with his or her deception? May he marry a non-Jewish woman to convince his acquaintances that he is one of them?[12]

Rabbi Goren debates this question and quotes Rabbeinu Tam (Troyes, 1100–1171), who holds that the famous principle of *gilui arayot* overriding *pikuaḥ nefesh* is only true when both the people involved are

8. Rambam, *Iggeret HaShmad.*
9. See Marc Shapiro, "Islam and the Halakha," *Judaism* 42, no. 3 (Summer 1993): 332–43.
10. Haym Soloveitchik argues that the opinion of the Rambam on this topic as it is potrayed in this letter is very different from his true halakhic opinion. See his article: "Maimonides' 'Iggeret ha-Shemad': Law or Rhetoric," in *Rabbi Joseph H. Lookstein Memorial Volume,* ed. Leo Landman (New York: Ktav, 1980), 281–320.
11. *Shut HaRadbaz,* 4:92; 5:40.
12. For a lengthy article regarding this question, see Rabbi Ari Shvat, "Gilui Arayot Lemaan Bitḥon HaMedina," *Teḥumin* 30 (2009/2010): 68–81.

Jewish. However, if one is a non-Jew, the Jew is permitted to have relations to save a life.[13]

However, maintains Rabbi Goren, there is an additional issue to address. The Torah prohibits marrying non-Jewish women: "Do not intermarry with them; do not give your daughters to their sons in marriage or take their daughters for your sons" (Deut. 7:3). This law theoretically must be suspended in our case. Although this is a *lo taaseh* (a prohibition), the rule is simple. *Pikuaḥ nefesh* takes precedence over all commandments, except the three mentioned above. However, explains the Rambam, this prohibition is different and unique:

> Although this transgression is not punishable by execution by the court, it should not be regarded lightly, for it leads to a detriment that has no parallel among all the other forbidden sexual relations. For a child conceived from any other forbidden sexual union is [the father's] son with regard to all matters and is considered a member of the Jewish people, even if he is a *mamzer* (a person born of a forbidden relationship). A son conceived by a non-Jewish woman, by contrast, is not considered his son.
>
> This matter causes one to cling to the non-Jewish nations from whom the Holy One, blessed be He, has separated us, and to turn away from following God and to betray Him.[14]

Rabbi Goren suggests that this idea, mentioned in the Rambam, may be a reason for the prohibition of intermarriage even in life-threatening situations. Rabbi Goren therefore suggests an alternative reason for permitting *gilui arayot* in specific situations.

Pikuaḥ Nefesh of the Jewish People

The Gemara discusses the actions of Yael, who killed the Canaanite general Sisera and helped win the war between Hazor and the Israelites (Judges 4). The Gemara's understanding is that Yael seduced Sisera in

13. *Tosafot*, Ketubbot 3b, s.v. *Velidrosh*.

14. *Mishneh Torah, Hilkhot Issurei Bia* 11:5–7.

order to kill him. Even though Yael committed a transgression, the Talmud justifies her actions:

> [A transgression for the sake of Heaven] is equivalent to a mitzva not for its own sake, as it is written, "Blessed above women shall Yael be, the wife of Ḥever the Kenite; above women in the tent shall she be blessed" (Judges 5:24). Who are the "women in the tent"? Sara, Rivka, Raḥel, and Leah.
>
> R. Yoḥanan said: That wicked one [Sisera] engaged in seven acts of sexual intercourse [with Yael] at that time, as it is stated, "Between her legs, he sunk, he fell, he lay" (Judges 5:27). (Nazir 23b)

The Gemara justifies Yael's actions even though she commits the transgression of *gilui arayot*. The explanation, claims Rabbi Goren, is that Yael saves the Jewish people rather than just herself. When the Gemara argues that one must give up one's life when faced with *gilui arayot,* it is referring to saving the lives of individuals. When the entire body of the Jewish people is in danger, one is permitted to violate all of the Torah's prohibitions.[15]

Installing a spy in enemy countries, argues Rabbi Goren, is considered an act of *pikuaḥ nefesh* for the entire Jewish people. Therefore, it is permissible for a Jew to violate halakha even if *gilui arayot* is involved.

Eli Cohen's story illustrates for us only some of the issues that a spy might confront. In the decades since Israel's founding, halakhic authorities have relied on earlier halakhic rulings to examine what a spy may and may not do in the service of the Jewish state.

15. This idea is mentioned by Rabbi Menachem Meiri. See his commentary on Sanhedrin 74b.

8

The Six-Day War, 1967

Are People – and Soldiers in Particular – Permitted to Enter the Temple Mount?

The great miracles of the Six-Day War can only be fully understood and appreciated if one internalizes the events that took place in the weeks leading up to June 1967. Egyptian President Gamal Abdel Nasser created a united front with Syria and Jordan, putting Israel in a chokehold. The purpose and goal of this united front was clear: to destroy the Jewish state. There was real fear and even some panic in the Jewish world, as well as in the State of Israel. Memories of the Holocaust resurfaced, reminding the people of how real the threat of annihilation could be.

The young state pleaded with King Hussein of Jordan to refrain from entering the war; he was promised by Prime Minister Levi Eshkol that Israel would not attack first. The king, convinced by rumors he had heard on the radio that Egyptian forces were victorious, ignored the appeal.

As news of the successful daring attack of the Israeli Air Force on the morning of June 5 spread around the world, fear and anxiety turned to relief and joy. However, nothing prepared Israel and the Jewish people for the dramatic events that took place two days later, when the Israeli army entered the Old City of Jerusalem and liberated *Har HaBayit,* the Temple Mount. Motta Gur, commander of the Paratroopers' Brigade, made a historic announcement on the radio: "*Har HaBayit beyadeinu!,*" "The Temple Mount is in our hands!" With Gur's permission, an Israeli flag was fastened to a pole topped with an Islamic crescent.

However, total sovereignty over the holy site was not to last for long. Moshe Dayan, the defense minister at the time, standing on Mount Scopus, watched the events through binoculars. As the flag was raised, he radioed Gur demanding that he remove the flag immediately. After the war, Dayan met with the Muslim *waqf,* who governed the site, and formally returned the Temple Mount to its control.

Dayan and the Muslim leaders came to an arrangement: While Israel would be responsible for security, the *waqf* (property endowment) would determine who would pray at the holy site. In other words, although Jews would be allowed on the mount, they would be denied the right to pray. This status quo has remained in place ever since.

The irony is that Moshe Dayan received support from the rabbis, who agreed with him that Jews should refrain from entering the Temple Mount. In the summer of 1967, a poster prohibiting entrance to the Temple Mount was published. The declaration was signed by many rabbis, among them the chief rabbis of Israel, Rabbi Nissim and Rabbi Unterman. Besides forbidding Jews from entering, the poster also noted that this had been the common custom for generations. But what were the reasons behind the rabbis' strong opposition? Why was it felt that Jews must not ascend the Temple Mount?

JEWS ON THE TEMPLE MOUNT: THE HALAKHIC PERSPECTIVE

Kedushat Har HaBayit

The Rambam explains the halakhic ramifications of the *kedusha* (sanctity) of the Temple Mount:

> The Temple Mount is holier than [the city of Jerusalem]. Neither men who have the flux nor women who have the flux, are menstruating, or have recently given birth may enter there. [However,] a corpse itself may be brought onto the Temple Mount, so obviously one who has contracted ritual impurity from a corpse may enter there.
>
> The *Ḥeil* is holier than *Har HaBayit*. Non-Jews and those who have contracted impurity through contact with a corpse… may not enter there.[1]

The *Ḥeil* was the enclosed section on the mountain, containing the courtyards and the Temple itself. The punishment for trespassing on certain parts of the Temple grounds is *karet* (death by God's hands).[2]

Regarding whether or not this *kedusha* applies at all times is a *maḥloket*, or disagreement, between the Rambam and his famous critic, the Raavad (Rabbi Avraham ben David; Provence, ca. 1125–1198). While the Rambam contends that the Temple Mount retains its sanctity at all times,[3] the Raavad argues that the *kedusha* was abolished at the time of destruction:[4]

> According to the opinion in the Talmud which states that it was not originally consecrated for eternity, no differentiation was made between the Temple, Jerusalem, and the remainder of the Land of Israel.... Therefore, entering [the Temple grounds] in our days is not punishable by *karet* (excision).

There are some who are of the opinion that the Raavad's understanding would be the basis for permission to walk in the Temple area itself.[5] Others, like Rav Kook,[6] explain that the Raavad is arguing with the Rambam

1. *Mishneh Torah, Hilkhot Beit HaBeḥira* 7:15.
2. Ibid., 7:18.
3. Ibid., 6:16–17.
4. In his footnotes on the Rambam above.
5. See Meiri, *Beit HaBeḥira*, Shevuot 16a.
6. *Mishpat Kohen: Teshuvot BeMitzvot HaTluyot BaAretz* (Jerusalem: Mosad HaRav Kook, 1966), *siman* 96.

about the level of transgression of entering the Temple Mount; these people are confident that the Raavad would nevertheless agree that it is forbidden to walk in the area where the Temple stood.

The Rambam's opinion is commonly accepted, and no halakhic authority today permits entering the area on which the Temple stood.[7] Theoretically, if people claimed to know the location of the original Temple, they would be permitted to enter the Temple Mount on the conditions that they purified themselves by immersing in a *mikve* (ritual bath) and were careful not to walk on the original borders of the Temple. A *mikve* would purify a person only from *tuma hayotzeit migufo* (an impurity that emanates from his body) and not the impurity that is the result of coming in contact with a corpse. For that, they would require the ashes of a red heifer, which we do not currently have.

The reason that so many rabbis oppose entering the Temple Mount today is the concern that we do not know exactly the location of the original Temple. Some rabbis are concerned that even if we claim to know the original borders, permission to ascend would bring many people who do not follow the strict laws of *tuma vetahara* (ritual impurity and purity) to violate the *kedusha* of the Temple site.

Immediately following the Six-Day War, Rabbi Shlomo Goren, chief rabbi of the Israeli army, began measuring the Temple Mount in order to establish the original borders of the Temple. His findings led him to the conclusion that in certain areas of the mountain, it is permissible for Jews to walk.[8] Moreover, the Mishna (Middot 2:1) states that the Temple Mount measured five hundred by five hundred *amot* (cubits), an area of approximately 62,500 square meters. Today the area referred to as the Temple Mount is a rectangle that is twice as long, covering about 145,500 square meters. Rabbis who permit entry to parts of the mountain suggest there are areas in the south and north that were clearly added by King Herod and thus do not have *kedusha*.

7. See Rabbi Eliezer Waldenberg, *Tzitz Eliezer* (n.p.: Waldenberg, 1985), 10:1, par. 5.
8. For a detailed summary of the different opinions, see Rabbi Shmuel Weingarten, "Har HaBayit VeKedushato," *Torah SheBe'al Peh* 11 (1969): 146–81.

Mora Beit HaMikdash

Besides the prohibition of entering the Temple and the Temple Mount in a state of impurity, the Torah commands us to fear the Temple and to treat it with proper awe and reverence (*mora*; Lev. 19:3). This includes not entering the Temple Mount while wearing leather shoes or with a walking stick or purse. One may not spit, have dust on one's feet, use the Temple Mount as a shortcut, or engage in idle chatter while there (Berakhot 54a). The Rambam also adds that this law permits entrance to the Temple only for *dvar mitzva* (a religious purpose).[9]

The Rambam, while explaining the meaning of this law, argues that it applies at all times, even when the Temple is destroyed:

> Even though the Temple is now in ruins because of our sins, a person must hold its [site] in awe, as one would regard it when it was standing. [Therefore,] one should only enter a region which he is permitted to enter. He should not sit in [the area of] the Temple Courtyard, nor should he act frivolously when standing before [the place of] the Eastern Gate...[10]

Rabbi Aharon Lichtenstein argues that it is possible that the Raavad, whose opinion was mentioned above, disagrees with the Rambam only about impure people entering the Temple but would still agree that the commandment of fearing the Temple applies at all times.[11]

Both opinions, for and against ascending to the Temple Mount, use the commandment of *Mora HaMikdash* for their argument. Some *posekim* note that this commandment includes precautions one must take not to come close to the holy mountain. Others argue that by following the strict halakhot of *Mora HaMikdash* together with immersion

9. *Mishneh Torah, Hilkhot Beit HaBeḥira* 7:2.
10. Ibid., 7:7.
11. "Visiting the Temple Mount in Our Time," trans. David Strauss, The Israel Koschitzky Torat Har Etzion VBM, September 21, 2014, https://etzion.org.il/en/visiting-Temple-mount-our-time.

in a *mikve*,[12] a person should be able to fulfill this commandment in the correct fashion and even fulfill other commandments, such as *Shemirat HaMikdash* (guarding the Temple), as well as showing a great yearning and desire for building the Temple.

MAY ONE ASCEND THE TEMPLE MOUNT TODAY?

Can today's observant Jews, with access to the mount that once housed the Temple, visit the holy site? What are the parameters of a walk on the mount today?

Ascending the Mount: Precedents

Rabbi Shlomo Goren finds evidence of a Jewish presence on the Temple Mount from the Second Temple period up until three hundred years ago.[13] He mentions the Rambam, who on his visit to Jerusalem on 6 Marḥeshvan, 4925 (1164), prayed on the Temple Mount.[14] In his letter, the Rambam writes: "I entered the great and holy house and prayed there."

Rabbi Ovadia Yosef forbids visiting the Temple Mount for some of the reasons discussed above.[15] In fact, he tells a story about the great Jewish philanthropist, Sir Moses Montefiore, who entered the Temple Mount on his visit to Israel in the year 1856. As a result, certain rabbis declared a *ḥerem* (excommunication) on him. Even though it was later lifted as result of Montefiore's admission of his mistake, we can see how delicate and sensitive this matter was at all times.

---

12. For a detailed list of halakhot of preparations for ascending to the Temple Mount, see Rav Yosef Tzvi Rimon's article, "Hilkhot Aliya LeHar HaBayit," The Israel Koschitzky Torat Har Etzion VBM, accessed August 1, 2021, http://www.etzion.gush.net/vbm/archive/10-halak/16alia.php.
13. Rabbi Shlomo Goren, *Har HaBayit* (Jerusalem: Yedioth Ahronoth, 1992), chap. 26, 340–58.
14. This letter is recorded in the *Sefer Ḥaredim, Shaar Teshuva,* chap. 4. There are those who doubt the letter and its meaning. For further discussion, see Gedalia Meyer and Henoch Messner, "Entering the Temple Mount in Halacha and Jewish History," *Hakirah* 10 (2010): 63.
15. *Yabia Omer, Yoreh De'ah* 5:26; "BeInyan Kedushat Har HaBayit VeHaMikdash," *Torah SheBe'al Peh* 47 (2008): 14–22.

Guarding the Temple Mount

One final practical question related to our discussion is about the soldiers guarding the Temple Mount. At first, the religious soldiers stationed on the mount refused to enter due to the halakhic restrictions mentioned before. In fact, the soldiers argued, let the secular soldiers who are not concerned with the halakhic issues guard the mountain; we will remain outside the entrance.

In the early seventies, the commander of the soldiers stationed on the Temple Mount asked Rabbi Avraham Sherman, a rabbinical judge who served in the Israeli rabbinical court, for a halakhic ruling. Rabbi Sherman forwarded the question to one of the prominent *posekim* of the generation, Rabbi Yosef Shalom Elyashiv.[16] Due to an understanding that keeping guard on the Temple Mount is an action of *pikuaḥ nefesh* (saving lives), Rabbi Elyashiv permitted soldiers to walk on all areas of the mount. At the same time, he argued, the soldiers and police should only ascend the mount after immersion in a *mikve*. They should not wander around for no reason, they should wear shoes without leather, and they should observe the commandment of *Mora HaMikdash* to the best of their ability.

Interestingly enough, Rabbi Elyashiv argued that it is preferable for the observant soldiers to guard the Temple Mount itself, as they would take precautions to keep the laws of *Mora HaMikdash*.

Jewish Presence on the Temple Mount

The rabbis who permit ascending the Temple Mount argue that under today's political circumstances, abandoning the mountain to the *waqf* and the Muslim world would be a terrible mistake. It would convey to the world that the Jews and Israel are not interested in this holy site and constitute a tacit agreement that it is a Muslim site.

Ironically, as Rabbi Goren argues, praying by the Western Wall is a relatively new custom which began three hundred years ago, while the Temple Mount is the space that Jews have known to be sacred for centuries. In a letter written to Prime Minister Yitzhak Rabin he says:

---

16. Rabbi Avraham Sherman "BeGidrei Issur Knisa LeMitḥam Har HaBayit BeYamenu," *Torah SheBe'al Peh* (2008): 116–18.

> The prayers taking place by the Western Wall symbolize the exile of the Jewish people and our expulsion from the Temple Mount. However, prayers on the Temple Mount symbolize the return of our people to their land and the site of the Temple.[17]

Rabbi Goren's understanding that until a few centuries ago Jews ascended the Temple Mount with no qualms gives us an important perspective on the subject. The question of Jewish presence on the Temple Mount is one that will continue to be debated by halakhic authorities.

17. The entire letter appears in Rabbi Eliezer Melamed's *Peninei Halakha: Likutim BiInyanei HaAm VeHaAretz* (Har Bracha: Machon Har Bracha, 2005), 288–93.

9

The Loss of Israeli Dakar Submarine, 1968

Is Burial at Sea Considered *Kever Yisrael*?

On January 9, 1968, Israel's newly purchased submarine, the *INS Dakar*, set sail from Portsmouth, England. It was expected to arrive in Haifa on February 2. On board were sixty-nine sailors from the Israeli Navy. On January 25, after the submarine failed to deliver its scheduled broadcast, the navy declared that it had lost contact with the vessel. As a result, an international search-and-rescue operation began.

On March 6, Defense Minister Moshe Dayan officially declared that the *Dakar* and its entire crew had been lost. A day of national mourning was announced.[1] The IDF Rabbinate declared the missing sailors dead and instructed the families to sit *shiva* (mark a week of mourning). This decision led Rabbi Shlomo Goren, chief rabbi of the IDF, to declare

1. Admiral Shlomo Erell, commander of the Israeli Navy, wrote a summary of the events. See his book *Lefanekha HaYam: Sipuro Shel Yamai* (Tel Aviv: Defense Ministry, 1998), 298–305.

that all the wives of the missing sailors were permitted to remarry.[2] The official *yom hapetira* (day of death) was set on 29 Tevet.

On February 9, 1969, a buoy washed up on the shores of Israel. It was examined and found to be the *Dakar*'s emergency buoy. While it was hoped that this would help solve the mystery of the *Dakar*'s disappearance, it was not to be. For the next thirty years, Israel continued searching for the lost vessel.

Many speculations and wild theories circulated about what might have happened. A rumor about the sailors being taken prisoner was just one of many. There was talk of Russian involvement, as the Russians strengthened their hold in the Middle East after the Six-Day War. Others speculated that Egypt might have been involved, as it had recently sunk an Israeli warship, killing forty-seven sailors. The Israeli government's official explanation was that a malfunction was most probably the reason for the submarine's disappearance; no evidence proved otherwise.

On May 24, 1999, a joint US-Israeli search team detected a wreck on the seabed between Crete and Cyprus, at a depth of some three thousand meters. On May 28, the first images were taken; it became clear that the *Dakar* had been found. A great hole was discovered in the submarine's hull. Some artifacts were recovered, including the bridge and many small items.

At the time, top Israeli officials discussed the possibility of raising the submarine. Some argued that although such a complicated task would cost a fortune, no price should prevent the government from doing all it could to bring the bodies of Israeli servicemen to Jewish burial.

THE COMMANDMENT OF *KEVER YISRAEL*

Jewish law is very particular about where and how Jews must be buried, but does halakha recognize burial at sea as a legitimate religious burial? And if the answer is negative, should the commandment of Jewish burial be kept at all cost?

---

2. Rabbi Goren's responsum appears in *Meshiv Milḥama* (Jerusalem: HaIdra Rabba, 1985–86), 3:99–213; see the ruling on pp. 212–13.

There appear to be two main sources for the commandment of burial (*kevura*). First, the Torah teaches us that *harugei beit din* (Jews condemned to death and executed by a religious court) must be buried on the same day: "You shall not let his corpse remain all night upon the post. You must bury him that [same] day" (Deut. 21:23). Although the verse is referring to *harugei beit din*, Jews executed by the *beit din*, the Rambam believes that the law applies to all Jews.[3] He writes: "There is a positive commandment to bury all *harugei beit din* on the day of execution … and not only *harugei beit din*, but whoever leaves his deceased [relative] overnight violates a prohibition as well."[4] It seems that the Rambam understands that this verse is not only a source for the prohibition of leaving the dead unburied overnight, but also a source for a positive commandment to bury the dead. The following law mentioned by the Rambam regarding a man who requested that he not be buried in the ground at the time of his death is significant: "If, however, he directed that he should not be buried, we do not listen to his request, for *burial is a commandment*, as the Torah states: 'For you shall certainly bury him.'"[5]

The other source has to do with the commandment of *gemilut ḥasadim* (performing acts of kindness). The Gemara discusses the origin of the obligation:

> R. Ḥama b. R. Ḥanina says: What is [the meaning of that] which is written: "After the Lord your God shall you walk" (Deut. 13:5)? But is it possible for a person to follow the Divine Presence? But hasn't it already been stated: "For the Lord your God is a devouring fire" (Deut. 4:24)? Rather, [the meaning is] that one should follow the attributes of the Holy One, blessed be He …
>
> The Holy one, blessed be He, buried the dead, as it is written, "And He was buried in the valley" (Deut. 34:6), so, too, [should] you bury the dead. (Sota 14a)

3. For a detailed discussion regarding this source see Rabbi Aharon Lichtenstein, "The Mitzva of Burial," The Israel Koschitzky Torat Har Etzion VBM, September 21, 2014, https://etzion.org.il/en/talmud/seder-nezikin/massekhet-sanhedrin/mitzva-burial.
4. *Mishneh Torah, Hilkhot Sanhedrin* 15:8.
5. Ibid., *Hilkhot Avel* 12:1.

Burial at Sea

The Jewish custom is to bury the dead directly in the ground. The *Shulḥan Arukh* explains: "If one buries the dead in a coffin and not in the ground, he transgresses the law of burial. If the coffin is buried in the ground, he is not transgressing. However, it is preferable to bury the dead directly in the earth."[6]

Accordingly, questions Rabbi Shabbetai Kohen (the *Shakh*), how does one explain our custom today of burying the dead in coffins?[7] He gives two answers: First, the custom today is to scatter earth on the body which is put in a coffin. This practice is considered burial in the ground. Second, all coffins have holes in them, which connect the bodies to the earth. Rabbi Benayahu Bruner, a rabbinical judge and *rosh yeshiva* in Safed, argues that based on both reasons, the bodies of the *Dakar*'s sailors are halakhically considered to be buried in the ground.[8]

Furthermore, under the circumstances, it is not clear that the sailors' bodies must be buried in the ground. By the time the submarine was found, it was possible that all that was left of the bodies was bones. The law of burial in the ground does not apply to bones. In the past, the Jewish custom was to wait until the body had decomposed and only then to collect the bones to be put in a coffin.[9] In fact, the Mishna (Moed Katan 1:5) reports that deceased family members were traditionally placed inside a family burial cave. After some months, when the organs had decomposed, the family performed *likut atzamot* (gathering of the bones) and placed them into a pit within the cave that contained the bones of all their ancestors.

Based on this logic, Rabbi Yigal Ariel of Nov, in the Golan Heights, argues that the halakha does not require burying the bones in the ground. Additionally, there is no concern of *bizui hameit* (dishonoring the dead), as the bodies are resting peacefully on the bottom of the sea.[10]

---

6. *Yoreh De'ah* 362:1.
7. Ad loc.
8. "Kevurat Ḥalalei HaTzolelet *Dakar*," *Teḥumin* 20 (1999/2000): 181–87.
9. See *Beit Yosef, Yoreh De'ah* 363.
10. "Kevod HaḤayim O Kevod HaMeitim," *Teḥumin* 20 (1999/2000): 171–80.

Is It Permissible to Move Bodies?

If the sailors of the *Dakar* are considered, according to halakha, buried, moving them to another burial site might be problematic. The Gemara lists ten *takkanot* (decrees) that Yehoshua made as the Jewish people entered the Land of Israel (Bava Kama 81a). One of them has to do with a *meit mitzva* (a body that one finds abandoned). The *takkana* states that the body should be buried at the site at which it has been found. The reason for this is the concern that moving the body may take time and create *bizui hameit*. The Gemara understands that a soldier killed in action is always considered a *meit mitzva*, even if there are those who can bury him (Eiruvin 17a).

The Radbaz explains that there is a concern that in war, soldiers are preoccupied with their battle responsibilities, which would again result in *bizui hameit*, with bodies remaining outside or in transit for hours or days. As a result, he argues that soldiers killed by accident are also considered *meit mitzva*[11] and should be buried at the site at which they died.

Although there seems to be a *maḥloket* among *Rishonim* if burying a *meit mitzva* on site is a *ḥova* (obligation) or *reshut* (option), Chief Rabbi Ben-Zion Meir Uziel understands that it is an obligatory law[12] and a *meit mitzva* must be buried on site.

The custom today, explain the *posekim*, is to bury a *meit mitzva* in a proper cemetery. Burying them on site, they assert, would not protect the bodies from robbers who might dig up the bodies, leading to *bizui hameit*.[13] In the case of the *INS Dakar*, this logic does not seem to apply; there is no fear that the bodies will be disturbed. Furthermore, removing the bones might entail more *bizui hameit*.

At What Cost Should Bodies Be Moved?

If it were possible to raise the vessel, it would involve a huge expense. Even then, there is no assurance that body parts would be found. Does

11. Radbaz's commentary on Rambam, *Mishneh Torah, Hilkhot Melakhim* 6:13.
12. *Piskei Uziel BeShe'elot HaZman* (Jerusalem: Mosad HaRav Kook, 1977), 190.
13. *Shakh* in the name of Maharshal, *Shulḥan Arukh, Yoreh De'ah* 364:3, 10.

the commandment of burial justify spending such vast amounts of money?

Rav Avraham Yitzchak Kook, when asked about renovations to the military cemetery on Mount Scopus, addressed a similar dilemma in his responsum. Although he encouraged the renovations, he raises the concern that the budget should be limited to the minimum because of the principle "The Torah spared the money of the Jewish people" (Yoma 39a). He also concluded that the custom of the Jewish people is not to spend vast sums on the dead but rather to use the money on the living.[14]

Some might argue that we are not merely dealing with the commandment of burial but rather with a highly sensitive issue that has major ramifications for the morale of Israeli soldiers. We shall, God willing, discuss this topic in a subsequent chapter (see chapter 11). Perhaps the soldiers' morale should be taken into account within the halakhic discussion.

Teḥiyat HaMeitim

One final concern on the subject is that bodies which have not been buried properly in a Jewish cemetery will not experience *teḥiyat hameitim,* the resurrection of the dead which will take place upon the Messiah's arrival. I believe it is only appropriate to end this highly sensitive discussion with the powerful words of Rav Kook:

> It is obvious that the commandment of burial strengthens our faith in *teḥiyat hameitim,* which is one of the thirteen principles of our faith.
>
> However, it is clear that in situations in which people have not been properly buried, the Almighty will collect all scattered body parts.... [Therefore] all the martyrs of Israel will one day arise from the dead...[15]

14. *Daat Kohen: Teshuvot BeHalakhot Shulḥan Arukh Yoreh De'ah* (Jerusalem: Mosad HaRav Kook, 1969), *siman* 212.
15. Ibid., 197.

10

The Yom Kippur War, 1973

What Is the Religious Meaning of the War?

On Saturday, October 6, 1973, just after two in the afternoon, the Egyptian and Syrian armies launched a two-front offensive on Israel. The date of the surprise attack was no accident, for that fateful day was Yom Kippur – a day when the country completely shuts down, a day when hundreds of thousands of Israelis, including soldiers, are in synagogue fasting and praying.

The attack caught the Israeli army off-guard and unprepared. Even though there had been numerous signs and indications that war was inevitable, Israeli intelligence ignored them all. Over the first three days, both Arab armies advanced quickly, capturing the Hermon outpost in the north and territories in the Sinai Peninsula to the south.[1] When the shocking news of the Arab successes reached the Israeli public, there was deep concern and fear that the State of Israel faced an existential threat.

1. For a detailed description of the entire war see Chaim Herzog, *Milḥemet Yom HaDin: Arba'im Shana LeMilḥemet Yom Kippur* (Tel Aviv: Yedioth Ahronoth, 2013).

Defense Minister Moshe Dayan was rumored to refer to the situation as a potential "destruction of the Third Temple."

The prayers and religious services on that first, holy day were interrupted as thousands of reserve soldiers were called up and sent straight to the bloody battlefields. The feeling of many was that they were fighting for their home. In those first days, many soldiers were killed, injured, or taken captive. Due to the heavy losses, the IDF Chief Rabbinate created temporary cemeteries. The fallen soldiers were buried in these temporary graves, and only after the war were the bodies exhumed and reinterred in military cemeteries. In some cases, family members were only informed weeks later that a soldier had been killed. Many soldiers' bodies were never found. Confusion and chaos were everywhere – and yet, within a few days, after heroic battles, the IDF was able to hold the line and stop the enemy's advances.

The dramatic change in the course of the war took place over Sukkot. In the north, on the first day of Sukkot (five days after Yom Kippur), Israeli forces ended their defense, transitioning to offense. Over the next few days, the IDF fought bravely in the Golan Heights against Iraqi and Jordanian forces that had come to the aid of the Syrian forces.

Down south, the campaign took somewhat longer. On October 15, the fourth day of Ḥol HaMoed Sukkot, the army began a counterattack that continued until the end of the war, with the IDF crossing over the Suez Canal and laying siege to the Egyptian army. The ceasefire, which was forced on Israel by Russian pressure, found Israeli tanks a mere one hundred kilometers from Cairo and thirty-five kilometers from Damascus. As a result of the radical transformation in such a short time, from the abyss of disaster to a stunning victory against overwhelming forces of multiple armies, many recognized the battles of this war to be no less than miraculous.

After the war, a committee was appointed by the government to investigate the IDF's unpreparedness and its failure to properly analyze military intelligence. The committee was headed by Shimon Agranat, chief justice of Israel's Supreme Court, and thus it was named the Agranat Commission.

In its report, the committee was critical of what it referred to as the military intelligence's "concept." The prevailing conception had been based on the assumption that Egypt would only attack if it had the ability to take on the Israeli Air Force. Military intelligence also believed that Syria would only attack if Egypt did. In the absence of any upgrade to Egypt's air force, IDF intelligence had concluded there was no threat of imminent war.

THE RELIGIOUS MEANING OF THE WAR

The difficult questions, shock, and bewilderment were also felt in the religious world. The Air Force's chief chaplain, Rabbi A. H. Rabinowitz, describes the prevailing atmosphere at that time:

> "Rabbi, why did it happen on *Yom Kippur*?" The question was voiced by a young female trainee during one of my sessions at the officer's training school. She did not ask why it happened; she knew that only too well. Every youngster in Israel grows up with the feeling that he may well have to fight to live. His brothers, sisters, parents, uncles and aunts have all done and are doing just that. Why should his lot be different in a hostile world? "But, Rabbi, what was the significance of it happening on *Yom Kippur*?" The question rang across the hall then and it has been resounding in my ears ever since. For the first time in my life, I was almost at a loss for words. This youngster sensed the deeper significance of it having occurred on *Yom Kippur*. She sensed it; I could not explain it. My lame response hardly bears repeating. I failed her dismally. Perhaps I failed myself even more so. Why did it have to be *Yom Kippur*? What Jewish historical logic lies beneath the surface? Where in the maze of the bewildering labyrinth of Messianic times lies the key? The Jewish soul and consciousness were stirred in an unfathomable manner that relate to the essence of Jewish being. Why *Yom Kippur*?[2]

Rabbi Rabinowitz understands the war as a wakeup call to the entire Jewish state. The horrors of the war require the people of Israel to ask themselves the "big" questions about the relationship between being

---

2. A. H. Rabinowitz, "Why Yom Kippur?" *Tradition* 15, no. 3 (Fall 1975): 13–32.

Israeli and being Jewish. He attributes great significance to the fact that the war began on our holiest day of the year:

> It had to be *Yom Kippur*. It could only have happened on *Yom Kippur*. Because *Yom Kippur* is that moment in Jewish life when a man faces himself. When a people comes face to face with its being, with its past and with its future.

Rabbi Norman Lamm (1927–2020), addressing the lessons to be learned from the Six-Day War, reflects on his thoughts in the aftermath of the Yom Kippur War. In his opinion, the great euphoria created by the success of Six-Day War led to arrogance and forgetting God:

> That both conflicting emotions – the Messianic euphoria and the military self-assurance – were unrealistic, was proven by the Arab surprise attack on Yom Kippur 1973, which punctured the balloon of Israel's imaginary invincibility. Israel was unprepared, the troops untrained for war, supplies were largely unavailable when and where needed, and so on. The successful counterattack by the Israelis, no matter how brilliant, did not make up for the sudden feeling that we had all been "taken"...
>
> My mind, during this period, inevitably turned to the powerful passage (in Devarim [Deut.] 8:11–18): "Beware lest you forget the Lord your God...lest when you have eaten and are full and you say in your heart, 'My power and the might of my hand have gotten me this wealth.' But you should remember the Lord your God: for it is He who gives you the power to get wealth, that He may establish His covenant which He swore to your fathers, as it is this day."
>
> What happened to cause such a reversal of fortune? What happened was that self-confidence morphed into arrogance, and arrogance into unforgivable carelessness.
>
> We forgot the God of Israel and learned nothing from the triumph of the Six-Day War...[3]

3. Norman Lamm, "Remembering the Six-Day War: Then and Now," *Tradition* 40, no. 2 (Summer 2007): 7–13.

Yeshivat Har Etzion lost eight students during the war. Rabbi Amital, the founding *rosh yeshiva,* was torn between personal anguish and the need to strengthen and give hope to his students, as well as the desire to understand the meaning of this seeming reversal in the process of redemption. He questioned the meaning of the war, whether or not this was a retreat from God's plan of redemption. Were we still living in the times of *atḥalta dige'ula* (the beginning of the redemption)?[4]

His redemptive reading of events was darkened, but unshaken. In his theological response to the traumatic events, he writes, "It is clear that we are in the process of redemption."[5] He argues that there are three compelling reasons to see this war as part of a larger messianic plan:[6]

1. The battles were directly connected to the rebuilding of *Malkhut Yisrael,* Jewish sovereignty.
2. Many Arab states participated in the war, which almost resulted in a US-Soviet nuclear confrontation.
3. The final victory was great, miraculous, and of biblical proportions.

Regarding the last point, Rabbi Amital mentions that with all the pain and sadness that came with war, we still have an obligation to thank God for the great miracles which occurred during the battles.[7]

As a matter of fact, following the great debate among the *posekim* regarding the recital of Hallel on Yom HaAtzma'ut, Rabbi Shlomo Goren declared after the Yom Kippur War that now more than ever Hallel must be recited with a blessing.[8] This stemmed from his understanding that the victories of this war may have been the most miraculous of all wars.[9]

---

4. All the following quotes and sources of Rabbi Amital are taken from "LeMashma'utah Shel Milḥemet Yom HaKippurim," in Rabbi Amital's book, *HaMaalot MiMaamakim: Devarim BeSugiyat HaDor Al Teshuot Ve'al Milḥamot* (Alon Shevut: Agudat Yeshivat Har Etzion, 1974).
5. Ibid., 31–32.
6. Ibid., 22–24.
7. Ibid., 17.
8. A. Doron, "BeYom HaAtzma'ut HaShana Yesh Lomar 'Hallel' BiVrakha," *HaTzofeh,* April 17, 1974.
9. See Herzog, *Milḥemet Yom HaDin,* 250, who calls this war the greatest achievement of the Israeli army in all of its history.

Rabbi Chaim David HaLevi, chief rabbi of Tel Aviv from 1973 to 1998 (1924–1998), addressed the meaning of the war at the annual gathering of rabbis at Mosad HaRav Kook in Jerusalem.[10] On one hand, he questioned Rabbi Menachem Kasher's opinion that this war should be considered *milḥemet Gog uMagog* (a climactic battle that will precipitate the Messianic redemption). On the other hand, he assured his audience that the process of redemption that began with the establishment of State of Israel was still intact.

When looking for the meaning of the terrible blow the country received, he mentioned that the lack of commitment to the Land of Israel and especially to the newly liberated territories of Yehuda, Shomron, and Gaza might have been a reason. It is interesting to note that in fact the war quickened the messianic energies of the settler movement, which crystallized into Gush Emunim (the movement that began settling Yehuda and Shomron).

These attempts to explain the meaning of historical events and to interpret God's hand in history has deep roots in the classical philosophers of religious Zionism.[11] Rabbi Amital himself explains in the beginning of his article why the search for meaning is so important:

> A Jew who believes that events touching on the life of the nation of Israel are guided by divine providence will naturally inquire as to their meaning and significance. The Torah and the prophets command us unceasingly to pay attention. It is also a natural intellectual inquiry for one based in faith. If events pass one by without one attempting to penetrate the depth of their true meaning, the Sages consider such a person dead.[12]

10. "Mekomah Shel Milḥemet Yom HaKippurim BeMaarkhot Ge'ulat Yisrael," *Torah SheBe'al Peh* (1975): 63–68.
11. For more about this idea, especially in the works of Rabbi Amital, see Reuven Ziegler and Yehudah Mirsky, "'We Have Fled from You to You': Rav Amital and the Shoah," The Israel Koschitzky Torat Har Etzion VBM, https://www.etzion.org.il/en/holidays/asara-betevet/"we-have-fled-you-you"-rav-amital-and-shoah.
12. Amital, *HaMaalot MiMaamakim,* 11.

Yet I believe that in the following words, one can sense that Rabbi Amital is adamant that there are limitations to man's attempt to completely understand the meanings of history.

> Clearly, we do not have the tools to know the secrets of God and to know the considerations, motives, and intentions of divine providence, "for My thoughts are not your thoughts" (Is. 55:8). However, this does not exempt us from our obligation to observe and to delve. It is Torah, and we must study it.[13]

13. Ibid., 11.

11

The Yom Kippur War, 1973

Are Warfare and Burial Permitted on Shabbat and Yom Tov?

The war in 1973 caught the IDF and the Israeli people completely unprepared, and the chaos was felt on every level, both on the battlefield and in the combat support units. The IDF's Military Rabbinate, for its part, was suddenly challenged with the tragic and gruesome task of dealing with the deaths of thousands of soldiers. This job was comprised of different components, including gathering the bodies, identifying them, and burying them – as well as delivering the terrible news to families.

As a result of the complexity involved, many halakhic questions arose.

SHABBAT AND YOM TOV IN MILITARY HALAKHA

War and death raise a number of halakhic questions; some of the most fascinating ones relate to what may and may not be done on Shabbat and Yom Tov.

Dealing with Bodies on Shabbat and Yom Tov

A dead body may not be moved on Shabbat or Yom Tov, as it is *muktzeh* (an item that the rabbis prohibited from moving on Shabbat). The Gemara proclaims: "[For the] deceased David, king of Israel, one does not desecrate Shabbat" (Shabbat 151b). Rabbi Yosef Karo permits asking non-Jews to take care of dead bodies on Yom Tov but prohibits it on Shabbat and Yom Kippur.[1] The prohibition to deal with the burial of the dead on Shabbat and Yom Kippur (which are more halakhically restrictive than Yom Tov), Rabbi Karo believes, is because it is considered disrespectful to the dead to have Shabbat desecrated because of them.[2]

The book of Maccabees mentions that even during war, this law was strictly enforced:

> After the battle, Judas led his men to the town of Adullam. It was the day before the Sabbath, so they purified themselves according to Jewish custom and then observed the holy day. By the following day (after Shabbat) it was urgent that they gather up the bodies of the men who had been killed in battle and bury them in their family tombs. (II Macc. 12:38–40)

Even caring for a *meit mitzva* (a body that is found for which there is no infrastructure for proper burial) may not involved violating Shabbat (*ḥillul Shabbat*).[3]

There are circumstances, though, where exceptions exist to this rule. A body may be removed to a safe area if leaving it where it is conflicts with *kevod haberiyot* (human dignity). If, for example, the body is in danger of being destroyed by fire or if it smells very bad, one is permitted to move it on Shabbat. This *heter* is limited to violating an *issur derabbanan* (rabbinical prohibition) only.[4]

Obviously, in cases of great need, when *pikuaḥ nefesh* conflicts with the prohibition of not dealing with bodies, Shabbat must be

1. *Shulḥan Arukh, Oraḥ Ḥayim* 426:3.
2. *Mishna Berura* 17 to *Shulḥan Arukh, Oraḥ Ḥayim* 426:3.
3. See Sanhedrin 35b.
4. See *Shulḥan Arukh, Oraḥ Ḥayim* 311:1–2.

violated. A good example of this is mentioned by Rabbi Avraham Avidan, deputy chief rabbi of the IDF, who argues that on Shabbat during wartime, bodies may be removed from vehicles that are needed for fighting.[5]

During the War of Attrition (1969–1970), many Israeli soldiers were killed in bunkers scattered along the banks of the Suez Canal. Rabbi Shlomo Goren, chief rabbi of the IDF, was asked if the bodies could be moved on Shabbat. In a letter sent to Rabbi Mordechai Halpern, an IDF chaplain then and today a renowned expert in the field of medical ethics, he wrote:

> Although the halakha is clear that bodies cannot be moved on Shabbat, in circumstances in which keeping the dead in the army post will hurt the morale of the other soldiers and thus have an ill effect on the motivation to fight the enemy, we permit [soldiers] to move the dead to the closest area. In cases where it is dangerous, the task may be done using vehicles.[6]

Rabbi Avidan explains that this ruling of Rabbi Goren is part of the unique *heter* given by the Torah for fighting on Shabbat.[7]

Fighting a War on Shabbat and Yom Kippur

It is a well-known law that when a life is in danger, it is a commandment and obligation to violate Shabbat. This profound law is based on the verse in Leviticus (18:5) "*Vaḥai bahem,*" "And live by them." The Gemara (Yoma 85b) learns from these words that the obligation to preserve human life overrides the obligation to observe other commandments. If the only way to preserve life is to transgress a religious prohibition, the preservation of life takes precedence.

---

5. Based on his experiences, Rabbi Avidan wrote a detailed book on the laws of burial named *Darkhei Ḥesed* (Jerusalem, 1978). See there 10:2 (p. 125).
6. See Rabbi Shlomo Goren, *Meshiv Milḥama* (Jerusalem: HaIdra Rabba, 1983–84), 2:217–20.
7. *Shabbat UMoed BeTzahal* (Jerusalem: Yeshivat Shaalvim, 1990), 17. A similar idea is expressed by Rabbi Gad Navon, chief rabbi of the IDF, in "Pinui Ḥalalim BeShabbat," *Teḥumin* 5 (1983/1984): 55–57.

From where do we learn that it is permissible to fight on Shabbat? Some argue that this is based on "*Vaḥai bahem.*" Other *posekim* explain that there is a separate source in the Torah for fighting on Shabbat.[8] The Torah states: "When you lay siege to a town and wage war against it for many days to capture it...until the town that has made war against you falls (*ad ridtah*)" (Deut. 20:19–20). The Gemara (Shabbat 19a) understands that this verse teaches us that it is permissible to extend fighting even to Shabbat, until the enemy submits. But why does the Gemara need a separate verse to prove what we already know, that Shabbat can be violated in life-threatening situations?

Rabbi Goren answers that this verse does not limit the *heter* to fighting only in life-threatening situations; rather it enlarges the *heter* of fighting to include all military goals. This means that it is permissible to violate Shabbat in wartime in any situations necessary to reach total victory and accomplish the goals of the war. Accordingly, ensuring a high level of morale among the fighters must be taken as a profound consideration that may overcome other halakhot.

A similar law, which unfortunately came up in the Yom Kippur War as well as in other wars, is whether soldiers' lives may be endangered while searching for their fallen friends. At first glance, it seems simple that it would be prohibited due the laws of *pikuaḥ nefesh*, yet the custom of the IDF is to permit it in certain situations.[9] Here again the logic is that in wartime, soldiers are affected by the way the army treats their comrades in arms. Assuring soldiers that their country will do everything possible to bring their bodies to burial is essential to the morale of the soldiers, and their level of motivation can affect the outcome in combat.

The question, of course, is the following: How can one assess the damaging effect to the soldiers' morale when they view corpses in their vicinity? At what point may this justify violating Shabbat? Rabbi Shlomo Zalman Auerbach explains that the criteria for permitting *ḥillul*

8. See Goren, *Meshiv Milḥama*, and Rabbi Moshe-Zvi Neria, *Milḥamot Shabbat* (Jerusalem: HaIdra Rabba, 1982–83), 1:88–91.
9. See Rabbi Yitzchak Kaufman, *HaTzava KaHalakha* (Jerusalem: Kol Mevaser, 1994), 194–95; and Rabbi Yehuda Zoldan, *Shevut Yehuda VeYisrael* (Jerusalem: Jerusalem College of Technology, 2007), 345–58.

Shabbat should be based on parallel cases, which, if they were to occur on regular weekdays, would require immediate evacuation.[10]

In an article on this subject, Rabbi Goren adds another reason to permit the removal of bodies on Shabbat. Since Arab armies use our soldiers' bodies as a way of pressuring us in negotiations and even making demands to exchange their live soldiers for our fallen, retrieving our dead and preventing the enemy from taking them is considered halakhically part of the war effort and therefore justifies *ḥillul Shabbat.*

Rabbi Mordechai Halpern was an IDF chaplain in the Sinai Peninsula during the Yom Kippur War. In an article he published about his experiences, he describes his dilemmas regarding this question.[11] On Simḥat Torah, he was told that there were dead bodies at an army post which had been recaptured by Israeli forces and asked whether they could be removed. He gave his permission for two reasons: first, because on Yom Tov the level of prohibitions involved are only rabbinical, or *derabbanan*; and second, he relies on Rabbi Goren's ruling that the negative impact on the morale of the living soldiers would be dangerous. Although the report about the dead soldiers proved to be false, Rabbi Halpern was convinced that the ruling was justified.

On the following Shabbat, *Shabbat Bereshit,* while stationed down south, the chaplaincy received reports about dozens of dead Israeli soldiers lying by the side of the road while their comrades were fighting the enemy. At first, the rabbis were skeptical due the prior false report received on Simḥat Torah; however, as soon as they independently verified the report, the same ruling was given and the chaplaincy sent soldiers on Shabbat to evacuate the bodies during the battle.[12]

Rabbi Halpern mentions that after the war, he discussed the case with Rabbi Shlomo Zalman Auerbach and Rabbi Yisrael Gustman, two prominent *posekim,* both of whom agreed with his ruling.

10. Rabbi Avidan in his name; see *Darkhei Ḥesed* 10:2.
11. "Pinui Ḥalalim BeShabbat," *Teḥumin* 22 (2001/2002): 104–15.
12. In his article, Rabbi Halpern mentions as an afterthought that on that Shabbat he met Rabbi Goren, who at the time was already Ashkenazi chief rabbi of Israel. The fact that the chief rabbi of Israel traveled down to the front during wartime to join the soldiers is a testimony to his spectacular dedication.

Rabbi Yehoshua Ben-Meir, founding *rosh yeshiva* of Yeshivat Hesder Shevut Yisrael, was an army chaplain in the Golan Heights during the war. In a letter to his colleague, Rabbi Halperin, he describes his experiences.[13] He was also asked to evacuate bodies that were scattered around the battlefield on the first day of Sukkot. He expresses his dilemma, as the standing orders of the IDF Rabbinate were not to remove bodies on Shabbat or Yom Tov. His *heter,* he explains, was based both on the fact that some of the bodies were lying in tanks, preventing the vehicles from being used, and on the impact that the bodies had on the soldiers' spirits. When his team questioned his authority, he replied that as of now he believed that this was the correct ruling but assured them that after the war he would consult with his own rabbi, Rabbi Shlomo Zalman Auerbach.

After the ceasefire came into effect, Rabbi Ben-Meir met with Rabbi Auerbach. He presented all his dilemmas. Regarding his ruling to allow driving on Yom Tov to evacuate bodies, the rabbi responded: "You are asking the question of an *am haaretz* (a simpleton). You put yourself and your soldiers into danger by entering a battlefield for the evacuation of bodies. If you saw fit to endanger your lives, surely it is permitted to break Shabbat and Yom Tov."

At this point, Rabbi Ben-Meir asked: "Was I allowed to endanger their lives under the circumstance?" The rabbi replied that he believed it was allowed. He then quoted Rabbi Goren who had allowed soldiers to be sent to the front in order to make IDF kitchens kosher for Pesaḥ during the War of Attrition. Rabbi Auerbach justified this ruling by arguing that *ḥillul Shabbat* is permissible even to boost IDF morale, as crucial a part of military effort as any.

Finally, Rabbi Ben-Meir asked the rabbi if, for identification purposes, it is permitted to write on Shabbat, taking into account *hatarat agunot,* the need to release women whose husbands had been lost. Rabbi Auerbach realized that this issue would become a raw nerve for the Israeli public and claimed that he saw logic in allowing the violation

13. See Yehoshua Ben-Meir, "Pinui Ḥalalim BeShabbat VeḤag BeMilḥemet Yom HaKippurim," Daat: Atar Limudei Yahadut VeRuaḥ, 23 Tishrei 5762, http://www.daat.ac.il/daat/tsava/maamar/benmeir-1.htm.

of Shabbat for this purpose, again explaining the effect of such a ruling on soldiers' morale.

Rabbi Ben-Meir pressed on. "Does the rabbi permit writing *beshinui* with the left hand (an act that would be violating Shabbat on a rabbinical level)?" The great *posek* replied: "Who am I to give such a ruling? After the war, we must gather all the rabbis and decide together." Rabbi Ben-Meir was troubled, "But until then, Rebbe, what do we do?" "Until then," he explained, "we go by the rule: *kol hashoel, harei zeh shofekh damim* (all those who ask are murderers)," implying that it is permitted until decided otherwise.

Let us end with the words of the prophet Yeshayahu (25:8): "He will swallow up death forever, and the Lord God will wipe every tear from every face; He will sweep His people's shame away from all the earth, for the Lord has spoken."

12

Operation Yonatan: The Raid on Entebbe, 1976

What Is the Halakhic Response to a Miraculous Rescue?

On July 4, 1976, the Israeli army stunned the world with one of the most daring and courageous hostage-rescue missions of all time. Just a few days earlier, on June 27, an Air France flight from Israel to France had been hijacked by pro-Palestinian terrorists. Four terrorists boarded the plane at a stopover in Athens before seizing the plane. After refueling the plane in Libya, they forced the pilot to fly the plane with its 250 passengers to Entebbe, Uganda, where they were joined by three additional terrorists.

The kidnappers began their negotiations with the authorities by releasing the non-Jewish passengers. At the time, the leader of Uganda was President Idi Amin, previously a friend of Israel, but at this point a sympathizer of the pro-Palestinian movement. The guerrillas threatened to kill all hostages unless fifty-three terrorists were freed from Israeli prisons and a $5 million ransom was paid.

Yitzhak Rabin, the prime minister of Israel, ordered the army to plan a rescue mission. Ultimately, it was decided that four planes filled with elite soldiers would be sent, and they would attack the terminal, kill the terrorists, and free the hostages. To confuse the terrorists, the soldiers got hold of a replica of Idi Amin's car; a soldier dressed as him to make the terrorists think he was approaching. During the assault, the soldiers killed all seven terrorists as well as over forty Ugandan soldiers, who were backing the terrorists. The commander of *Sayeret Matkal* (Israel's most elite commando unit), Yoni Netanyahu, and three hostages were killed in the attempt.

This was not the first hijacking of an Israeli plane or of its citizens. In December 1968, an El Al plane was hijacked on its way from Rome to Israel and was forced to land in Algeria. While the Israeli army prepared for a surprise attack, Israel ended up negotiating with the terrorist organization and freed over twenty Palestinian prisoners. In May 1972, a Belgian Sabena plane was hijacked by the Black September terrorist group and forced to land in Lod. A successful attack on the plane killed the terrorists and freed the hostages.

However, it was Operation Yonatan, as it was later named for Yoni Netanyahu, which shocked the world and contributed to the growing myth of the Israeli army in the world. It was then that the world began to view Israel's military as a model for fighting terrorism.

HALAKHIC TOPICS IN OPERATION YONATAN

Operation Yonatan, and others like it, raised a number of interesting halakhic questions that must be answered.

Salvation at the Hands of the Secular

Operation Yonatan, also called Operation Entebbe, shook the religious world as well. While the Religious Zionist community praised the operation and recognized in it a miracle, the *ḥaredi* – or ultra-Orthodox – world was confused and split in its response. The Chief Rabbinate of Israel, as recorded in its archives and later published by Rabbi Shmuel Katz, put out a letter praising the Israeli government for the success of the attack, as well as declaring that special prayers should be recited that Shabbat thanking God for the miracles that had taken place.

Rabbi Ovadia Yosef, the Sephardi chief rabbi at the time, wrote a responsum about the operation. The article itself addresses halakhic questions; between the lines, however, Rav Ovadia makes it obvious what he thinks about the attack. In a footnote added when the responsum was printed in his book *Yabia Omer* (10:17), he praises the attack and gives thanks to God for performing miracles:

> Praise be to God, who has increased His grace and His wonders with His people. All the nations of the world have seen the salvation of our God, and have been astonished and amazed by the heroism of [the soldiers of] Israel, who with the help of God saved the lives of the captives and brought them to [the Land of] Israel…

Outside of Israel, however, things were slightly different. From the responses that we have, it is obvious that some religious Jews were stunned by the success of the operation and troubled by it from a theological perspective. How can the salvation of God occur through secular Jews? How should we respond to the event itself? Was the operation a miracle?

Although many of these theological questions had already been raised by religious thinkers in 1948 and 1967, due to the astounding success of Entebbe, these questions resurfaced.

Rabbi Moshe Feinstein (Minsk/US, 1895–1986) writes the following:

> Concerning the matter of the Jews who were hijacked to Uganda and then were saved by [Israeli] soldiers who went to Uganda, it is reasonable that this should be considered an open miracle. This is because in the normal course of events, it would not be possible for such a thing to be successful. Whatever is done in the world is only by the hand of God – whether it is for the good or whether it is, God forbid, the opposite…

> He caused that these Jews be captured, but He also caused that they were rescued by means of giving these soldiers special courage and motivation so that they were able to save the captives. He also arranged circumstances so the soldiers in fact were successful. Nevertheless, the reason that God did a miracle through sinners is hidden from us. Furthermore, it is prohibited for any man to be "wise" and raise questions against God's actions. Rather, it is necessary for us to be wholehearted and accepting of whatever God does, as it explicitly says in the Torah (Deut. 18:13).[1]

During the 1960s, Chabad and Satmar were engaged in a dramatic conflict. Following the Six-Day War, the Lubavitcher Rebbe voiced his opinion about the results of the war and expressed his feelings that great miracles had occurred and that the war was considered a *milḥemet mitzva* (an obligatory or commanded war). Over the course of the following years, the Rebbe continued to express support for the State of Israel, ultimately changing his movement's opinion about Zionism. In both letters and addresses he gave following the operation in Entebbe, he described the event as "miraculous."[2]

In a personal letter, the Rebbe wrote:

> Here my thoughts turn to the recent miraculous rescue of the hostages from Uganda. One cannot fail to note the extraordinary aspects at both ends of the hijacking: on the one hand, the ease with which the four terrorists hijacked the Airbus in Athens; and on the other hand, the extraordinary success of the rescue operation. In other words, both the initial tragedy and eventual deliverance clearly point to the Hand of God.[3]

---

1. *Iggerot Moshe, Yoreh De'ah* 4:8.
2. See *Iggerot HaKodesh* (Israel: Kehot, 2015), 31:11.
3. "The Miracle of Entebbe," TheRebbe.org, accessed June 28, 2021, https://www.chabad.org/therebbe/letters/default_cdo/aid/397865/jewish/The-Miracle-of-Entebbe.htm.

Apparently, articles in the Yiddish papers associated with Satmar condemned the attack, arguing that Israel should not have put the hostages' lives in danger, but rather should have negotiated with the terrorists.

Rabbi J. David Bleich, in his article about the operation, states:

> Some persons influenced by Neturei Karta ideology denied that soldiers of a secularist Jewish state could possibly be agents of divine providence. The Central Rabbinical Congress, known as the *Hitaḥdut ha-Rabbanim,* issued a formal declaration dated 15 Av 5736 expressing criticism of the operation and of the acclaim showered upon the Israeli forces.[4]

At the time, the following was published in Israel's *Maariv* newspaper:[5]

> The Entebbe operation has caused a fight among the Jews of New York. While the Chabad Rebbe praised the operation several times and glorified the soldiers who risked their lives to save the abductees from the Air France flight in Entebbe, the rabbinical organization affiliated with the followers of Satmar came out with strong condemnation for those who praised the heretical military personnel.

As mentioned, the Rebbe claimed that the events were miracles; in one of many gatherings, the Rebbe was quoted as saying:

> We see in the revelation that this is the hand of God. God can also perform miracles by those who are not observant, as is recounted in several places in the Oral Torah.
>
> The merit of military personnel, who have chosen to put their lives in danger in order to save Jewish lives, is very great.

4. "Entebbe," chapter 10 in *Contemporary Halakhic Problems* (New York: Ktav, 1977), 2:226 .
5. Available at "Milḥemet Satmar VeLubavitch Ekev 'Mivtza Yonatan,'" Noaḥ Zvuluni, accessed June 28, 2021, http://www.ranaz.co.il/articles/article4854_19760829.asp.

> Their merit in this world, as well as in the World to Come, is guaranteed.

The Rebbe had strong words for those who disagreed with the way he understood the meaning of these events: "Mercy on those who do not see it as the hand of God.... Protests should be made [against those people]!" There is no doubt that the different attitudes toward the Entebbe operation exacerbated the ongoing tension between Chabad and Satmar.

Thus the extraordinary events of July 1976 resulted in different rabbinic responses which, in turn, led directly to halakhic rulings, as we will see below.

Blessings on Miracles and Salvation

She'asa Li Nes

On July 4, 2016, Prime Minister Binyamin Netanyahu visited Entebbe and participated in a ceremony to commemorate the fortieth anniversary of the operation. The Israeli newspaper *Yedioth Ahronoth* reported that at the ceremony a survivor of the 1976 hijacking made the blessing "*She'asa li nes bamakom hazeh,*" "[Blessed is He] who performed a miracle on my behalf in this place."

It would seem that the survivor's reciting a blessing was firmly based on the decisions of Rabbi Moshe Feinstein and the Lubavitcher Rebbe, who both declared the successful events of Entebbe "a clear miracle."

On Simḥat Torah (October 17), 1976, the Lubavitcher Rebbe asked a group of rabbis to give a ruling on two questions that were related to the operation. The first was whether or not a former hostage should recite this blessing upon returning to Entebbe.[6] On 24 Marḥeshvan (November 17), 1976, the committee of Chabad rabbis in Israel published a ruling that a blessing should indeed be recited. One of the rabbis who signed his name on the ruling was Rabbi Shlomo Zevin, a renowned *talmid ḥakham.*[7]

---

6. See *Iggerot HaKodesh,* 32:103, in footnote.
7. See "Mivtza Entebbe VeHaOlam HaTorani," Chabad of Israel, accessed August 2, 2021, http://www.chabad.org.il/Magazines/Article.asp?ArticleID=11956&CategoryID=2014.

A mishna in Berakhot (54a) mentions that a blessing is recited over miracles that occurred to our forefathers in the past. The gemara there derives the source of this halakha from Yitro who, upon meeting Moshe, blesses God for the miracles that happened to Moshe and the Israelites during the Exodus from Egypt. The gemara explains that there is a difference between a miracle which occurs to the masses and one that occurs to an individual; a blessing is recited by **all** for a miracle which affects the public collective, yet an individual whose life is saved by a miracle is also required to make a blessing. In the latter case, there is an argument among the *Rishonim* regarding the requirements for an individual's family to recite a blessing as well. While some suggest that only the children and grandchildren recite the blessing, others argue that all descendants are required to make the blessing.

Some *Rishonim* (the Ritva and others) prove from the continuation of the gemara that even for a miracle that occurs only to an individual, if the act has an element of *kiddush Hashem* (the sanctification of God's name), then all those who pass the area where the miracle took place are required to recite the blessing. We will explore the issue of *kiddush Hashem* later on.

The *Beit Yosef*, written by Rabbi Yosef Karo, quotes the Abudraham (Seville, fourteenth century), who maintains that these halakhot only refer to miraculous events that are truly supernatural. This would mean, for example, that if burglars do no harm to the people in the burglarized home, no blessing should be recited. In *Shulḥan Arukh* (end of *Oraḥ Ḥayim* 219), after quoting the opinion of the Abudraham, Rabbi Karo quotes those who disagree and concludes that in cases in which the miracle is not supernatural a blessing should be recited without *shem umalkhut*, i.e., omitting the names of God and the phrase "King of the Universe."

Interestingly, in *Shulḥan Arukh HaRav*, Rabbi Shneur Zalman of Liadi (founder of the Lubavitcher dynasty and the Chabad movement; 1745–1812) rules against this; he holds that a full blessing is recited for miracles both supernatural and natural.

Rabbi Bleich, in his article on this topic, understands that Rabbi Zevin and his Chabad colleagues obviously relied on this ruling, but he argues:

> Any follower of the Chabad movement, or one who consistently follows the opinions of *Shulḥan Arukh ha-Rav,* who may have been among the hostages in Entebbe, or whose parent or grandparent may have been among the hostages, may of course, follow the ruling of *Shulḥan Arukh ha-Rav* in this matter as well. Others would find it difficult to follow an opinion specifically rejected by the author of *Shulḥan Arukh* and by the vast majority of later authorities including *Magen Avraham,* Rabbi Elijah of Vilna and *Mishna Berura.*[8]

Obviously, the definition of what is considered a natural or supernatural miracle is crucial to our discussion, and the understanding of several *posekim* makes Rabbi Bleich's position unconvincing. Must a "real miracle" involve an unnatural act like the splitting of the Red Sea for it be considered a miracle? Rabbi Moshe Feinstein declares the events of Entebbe a clear miracle. Rav Ovadia, in his discussion regarding reciting Hallel on Yom HaAtzma'ut,[9] quotes the idea that the miracle of Purim is considered an unnatural miracle, even though there were no supernatural events that took place, thereby making relevant the recitation of the blessing of "*She'asa li nes bamakom hazeh,*" even though the miracle was not supernatural.[10]

Based on the preceding sources, there is room to argue that the survivors and perhaps even their children should recite the blessing upon a visit to Entebbe. If we see the Entebbe operation as an act of *kiddush Hashem,* perhaps every Jew who visits the site should make this blessing.

Birkat HaGomel

What about the recitation of *Birkat HaGomel*? The Gemara (Berakhot 54b) argues that there are four experiences which obligate a person to bring a sacrifice of thanksgiving to God after surviving danger. Today, this

8. Bleich, *Contemporary Halakhic Problems,* vol. 2, 230–31.
9. *Yabia Omer, Oraḥ Ḥayim* 6:41.
10. According to some opinions in the Gemara (Megilla 14a) the Megilla reading on Purim serves as the commandment of reciting Hallel. See Meiri ad loc., who holds that if one finds oneself on Purim without a Megilla, Hallel should be recited! Furthermore, the blessing *SheAsa Nissim* is recited while reading the Megilla.

halakha obligates such a person to recite a blessing of thanks, *HaGomel*. The Gemara refers to those who travel overseas or go through deserts, prisoners who have been released, and sick people who have been cured. While hostages in the Entebbe affair clearly fit these halakhic criteria and therefore are required to make a blessing, the question of whether or not the families of hostages are required to make the blessing as well is an important one.

Rabbi Ovadia Yosef has an entire responsum[11] regarding the hostages of Entebbe blessing *Birkat HaGomel*. He concludes that the survivors themselves should recite *HaGomel* but their families should not.

What about the soldiers involved in the operation? Are they obligated to recite *HaGomel*? While Chief Rabbi Shlomo Goren[12] argues that a soldier in such a situation must recite the blessing, Rav Ovadia argues that soldiers returning from war do not make this blessing, limiting the blessing to surviving the four specific dangers mentioned above.[13]

Rabbi Yehoshua Ben-Meir, the founding *rosh yeshiva* of Yeshivat Hesder Shevut Yisrael in Efrat, makes an interesting claim that *HaGomel* is only recited by individuals who are saved from danger and not in cases in which an entire community was saved. Soldiers, he maintains, are emissaries of the community and therefore are not considered individuals.[14]

Halakhic authorities debate the nature of miracles and the blessings that should be recited upon being rescued from death. These questions result from a certain theological approach: the understanding that the dramatic events that have occurred since 1948 were nothing short of miraculous.

11. *Yeḥaveh Daat* (Jerusalem: Hazon Ovadia, Porat Yosef, and Mekhon Yerushalayim Le-Ḥeker Yisrael, 1978), 2:25.
12. *Meshiv Milḥama* (Jerusalem: HaIdra Rabba, 1983–84), 2:134.
13. Yitzhak Yosef, *Yalkut Yosef* (Jerusalem, 1991), vol. 3, 119:28.
14. "Birkat HaGomel LaḤozrim MiPe'ilut Tzva'it," *Teḥumin* 1 (1979/1980): 349.

13

Operation Yonatan: The Raid on Entebbe, 1976

Can Prisoners Be Exchanged for Live Terrorists?

The events in Uganda in July 1976 were unfortunately not new to the Jewish people. In the previous decades – and in contemporary times – we have faced the same dilemma: Should one redeem prisoners at any cost? What price is considered reasonable?

Many articles and responsa[1] have been written referring to a mishna in Gittin (4:6) that states: "Captives are not redeemed [for] more than their actual value." This mishna explains that this halakha is because of *tikkun olam* (changing the world for the better); we must act responsibly for the entire nation of Israel and not necessarily think only

1. For a list of all responsa, see Michael Wygoda, "Ḥavot Daat," Ministry of Justice, accessed June 28, 2021, http://www.justice.gov.il/Units/MishpatIvri/HavatDaat/Pages/Shonot.aspx.

about the individual. We must consider the welfare of the community against the welfare of the captive.

The Gemara (Gittin 45a) gives two reasons for this ruling:

1. Preventing a "burden on the community," since collecting large sums of money to free a captive causes great financial strain on the community.
2. Discouraging extortion, since paying exorbitant sums of money in exchange for captives may lead to more kidnapping.

The *Rishonim* disagree about which of the above two reasons is the primary one. The practical consequence of this disagreement emerges in a case in which the captive's life is in danger. Would the mishna's decree hold up in the face of *pikuaḥ nefesh*? Although the first reason would not stand up to it, the second reason might.

Modern hostage situations like Entebbe raise an additional question within this millennia-old dilemma: Is the discussion of redeeming captives relevant to terrorist incidents?

REDEEMING HOSTAGES IN HALAKHA

In 1970, Rabbi Yitzchok Hutner (Warsaw/Brooklyn/Jerusalem, 1906–1980) boarded a plane which was hijacked and forced to land in Jordan. This might have been the first time since the kidnapping of the Maharam of Rothenburg (Meir ben Baruch; ca. 1215–1293) that the Jewish community debated the application of the rule referenced in the Tosafists,[2] that for a *talmid ḥakham* there is no limit to what ransom may be paid. Rabbi Hershel Schachter quotes Rabbi Yaakov Kamenetsky, who argues that what happened in Jordan is considered to be an act of war in the eyes of halakha and falls under the definition of *milḥemet mitzva*.

> Although generally in a case of *pidyon sh'vuyim* (rescue of captives) the Jewish community is forbidden to ransom a captive for an exorbitant sum, the ruling in the case of a great scholar is that he should be ransomed even for a sum that exceeds his

2. Gittin 45a, s.v. *DeLo*, and 58a, s.v. *Kol*.

> "worth." Thus, many Rabbis were of the opinion that every effort should be made to secure Rabbi Hutner's release. Rabbi Yaakov Kamenetsky dissented, however, arguing that the commandment of *pidyon sh'vuyim* only applies in peacetime, but surely not during hostilities, when the delivery of ransom money to the enemy would strengthen their position! He continued to explain that although a cease-fire existed at the time, the 1948 War of Independence had never really ended, for the Arabs' avowed goal to destroy the State of Israel and drive the Jews into the sea had never been renounced. In his view, although Israel was not then engaged in active battle, in the eyes of the halacha it was considered to be experiencing a mere lull in the ongoing original 1948 War of Independence.[3]

Similarly, Rabbi Yisrael Rozen (1941–2017), editor of the acclaimed series *Teḥumin,* wrote an article questioning the heavy price which Israel paid for the release of Gilad Shalit, an Israeli soldier taken captive in 2006. After quoting many articles that had been written throughout Israel's history of kidnappings, he concluded that one cannot use the gemara in Gittin as a reference in cases in which the ransom is not money but rather freeing live terrorists. His main argument was that the many cases discussed by the Gemara and by the rabbis in recent centuries regarding paying ransom to free captives all referred to questions of charity and the Jewish communities' monetary resources. None were challenged with dilemmas involving future dangers. In these cases, he argues that "halakha remains neutral and leaves room for tactical decisions to be made by the government."[4]

There have been two lengthy halakhic articles written and published specifically about what happened in Entebbe. However, there is a major difference between the two. One article, composed by Rabbi Shaul Yisraeli (Belarus/Israel, 1909–1995), a rabbinical judge and *rebbe*

---

3. Rabbi Hershel Schachter, "Land for Peace: A Halachic Perspective," *RJJ Journal of Halacha and Contemporary Society* 16 (Fall 1988): 72–95.
4. "Shiḥrur Shevuyim 'BiMeḥir Mufka' SheEinenu Kaspi," *Teḥumin* 30 (2009/2010): 100.

in Yeshivat Mercaz HaRav, discusses the halakhic implications which arose at the time. However, this article, which was published later in his book *Ḥavat Binyamin*, was written after the events took place. The second one, by Rabbi Ovadia Yosef, was written as the events were happening.

Rabbi Ovadia Yosef, who was Sephardi chief rabbi of Israel at the time, published an article in the journal *Torah SheBe'al Peh* entitled "Operation Entebbe in Halakha." The article was later published in his responsa collection *Yabia Omer*.[5] It is there, in an added footnote, that we learn that the responsum was actually written during the crisis; Rav Ovadia was planning to advise the government as to his conclusions:

> And when we were gathered together with the Torah sages to discuss this issue in terms of halakha, in the midst of the discussions, the prime minister, Mr. Yitzhak Rabin, came to us and informed us of the news that the IDF had already succeeded in killing the evil terrorists and their assistants in Uganda, and releasing the kidnapped Jews, and that they were on their way to the Land of Israel.

I have read testimonies[6] that other rabbis, Rabbi Shach and Rabbi Kanievsky (the Steipler), met during those days and created a halakhic ruling to be sent to the prime minister, urging him to go ahead with the prisoner exchange.

Endangering Lives to Save Hostages

Besides the famous discussion in Gittin about redeeming prisoners, Rav Ovadia discusses another question at great length: Is one permitted to put his life in danger in order to save others?

As it relates to our case, this question has two separate components: The first is whether or not the release of terrorists, which will definitely put other lives in danger, is permitted. The second asks whether soldiers are permitted to put their lives in imminent danger to save others.

---

5. *Ḥoshen Mishpat* 10:6.
6. See Uriel Banner, "Yaḥasam Shel Gedolei Yisrael LeShiḥrur Meḥablim LeHatzalat Ḥatufei Entebbe," *HaMaayan* 218 (Tammuz 2016): 23–35.

Rav Ovadia explains that this question is debated among the *posekim* and may even reflect an argument between the Babylonian Talmud and the Jerusalem Talmud. Rabbi Yosef Karo[7] cites the *Haggahot Maimoniyot* (based on the Jerusalem Talmud), which states that one is obligated to take a risk, even putting one's life in danger, to save others. Rabbi Karo explains that if the impending loss of life is certain (*vadai*), while the danger (*sakana*) to the would-be rescuer is subject to doubt (*safek*), the "certainty" of mortal danger to one's fellow takes precedence over the "doubtful" loss of one's own life. Rav Ovadia argues that normative halakha follows the Babylonian Talmud's opinion: one is prohibited to endanger one's own life to save others. Nonetheless, his conclusion is that under these circumstances, freeing terrorists for hostages is permitted since the danger to the hostages who face imminent execution is certain and immediate, while the danger to others as a result of the release of terrorists is merely doubtful.

Regarding the operation itself, the rabbis discussed its halakhic legitimacy. Under the special circumstances, where a potential alternative solution was to pay a ransom to free prisoners, two questions arose.

First, the rabbis asked: Normally a soldier may endanger his life in war. However, in our case, how can one justify putting the lives of soldiers and hostages in danger when an alternative "peaceful" solution exists? Freeing terrorists may (*safek sakana*) endanger lives but fighting terrorists is without doubt putting lives in direct danger (*vadai sakana*).

Another halakhic question mentioned by the *posekim* has to do with fighting a war on Shabbat. Even though the actual operation took place on Motza'ei Shabbat,[8] the preparations and flight to Entebbe occurred on Shabbat. The government hesitated in approving the mission. By Shabbat afternoon, the IDF army gave an order for the planes to make their way to the Sharm el Sheikh airfield. The operation was given the green light only afterward. Under the circumstances, was the IDF allowed to violate Shabbat?

---

7. *Beit Yosef, Ḥoshen Misphat* 426.
8. I remember listening to a soldier speaking to us in high school about reciting Havdala on the Entebbe airfield's runway. He told us that he made the blessing of *Meorei HaEsh* on the burning wreckage of the Ugandan air force.

Regarding the latter question, Rav Ovadia discusses the *heter* to fight on Shabbat. He mentions the gemara in Eiruvin 45a that discusses fighting bandits on Shabbat. The gemara differentiates between the purposes of the enemies attacking the city. If their aim is to steal money and property, then one may not violate Shabbat. However, if their goal is to kill Jews, then one must violate Shabbat and fight. Furthermore, if the city under attack is near the nation's border, Shabbat may be violated despite the absence of an immediate threat to life. The reason for this is that the conquest of border cities may ultimately result in loss of lives. The Rambam[9] rules that all Jews who are capable of doing so are obligated to help their fellow Jews in the besieged city.

Rav Ovadia then quotes Rabbi Yisrael Isserlin (Germany, 1390–1460), who rules that nowadays one may fight on Shabbat even if the ultimate motive of the enemy is to seize property because these attacks tend to turn quickly into acts of murder.[10] Rav Ovadia argues that besides the danger to the hostages, seizure of the airliner is considered an act of war. Were the hijackers allowed to succeed, it is quite possible that their initial success would have spurred them to further acts of aggression with more loss of life. Therefore, concludes Rav Ovadia, the war efforts, fighting, and rescuing may be done even on Shabbat.

Rabbi Yisraeli, for his part, also addresses the halakhic legitimacy of the operation. He explains that the operation is surely defined as a *milḥemet mitzva,* even though it includes a small group of soldiers and even though the war is conducted far away from home. On the other hand, he argues, in this unusual situation, the army had an option to hand over prisoners and pay the ransom. Even if this is considered putting others (Israeli citizens) in potential danger, fighting a war which also endangers soldiers and hostages is permitted and even required. Rabbi Yisraeli explains that the legitimacy of war is based upon the concept of *kiddush Hashem*. This idea, he explains, is based on the biblical verses

9. *Mishneh Torah, Hilkhot Shabbat* 2:33.
10. *Terumat HaDeshen* 156.

that indicate that the battles and wars against the nation of Israel are ultimately wars against God.[11]

The laws of *kiddush Hashem* have a special place in the halakhic hierarchy, overriding even the laws of *pikuaḥ nefesh*. Rabbi Yisraeli's argument is that fighting a war, which is obligatory, does not need to be based upon cold calculation regarding human life. The alternative in this case, to give in to the demands of the terrorists, even if it would be saving lives, would be an act of surrender and would bring disgrace and humiliation to our people which ultimately is a *ḥillul Hashem* (desecration of the name of God).

The IDF's surprise attack on Ugandan soil was an act of *kiddush Hashem*, according to Rabbi Yisraeli. He and Rabbi Ovadia Yosef agree, despite basing their halakhic reasoning on different considerations: Operation Yonatan was halakhically permissible, and the correct course of action under the circumstances.

11. For example, the war against the Midianites in Numbers 31 and David's battle against Golyat in I Samuel 17.

14

Peace with Egypt, 1977

May Land Be Traded for Peace?

On November 9, 1977, Anwar Sadat, president of Egypt, shocked the world by announcing his intention to go to Jerusalem and speak before the Knesset. He arrived ten days later and was formally greeted by the Israeli government. In his historic speech, he explained what brought him to his dramatic decision:

> After long thinking, I was convinced that the obligation of responsibility before God, and before the people, make it incumbent on me that I should go to the farthest corner of the world, even to Jerusalem, to address Members of the Knesset, the representatives of the People of Israel, and acquaint them with all the facts surging in me. Then, I would leave you to decide for yourselves. Following this, may God Almighty determine our fate.
>
> ... Any life lost in war is a human life, irrespective of its being that of an Israeli or an Arab. A wife who becomes a widow is a human being entitled to a happy family life, whether she be an Arab or an Israeli. Innocent children who are deprived of the

> care and compassion of their parents are ours, be they living on Arab or Israeli land. They command our top responsibility to afford them a comfortable life today and tomorrow.
>
> For the sake of them all, for the safeguard of the lives of all our sons and brothers, for affording our communities the opportunity to work for the progress and happiness of man and his right to a dignified life, for our responsibilities before the generations to come, for a smile on the face of every child born on our land – for all that, I have taken my decision to come to you, despite all hazards, to deliver my address.[1]

Prime Minister Menachem Begin responded similarly, noting that the people of Israel had always extended their hand in peace; it was the Arab nations that had rejected the plea for peace. Mr. Begin agreed that the visit's primary purpose was to end the state of war between the two countries. In his speech, he emphasized that his intentions were sincere:

> As free men, Mr. President, let us conduct negotiations for a peace treaty and, with the help of God, so we believe with all our hearts, the day will come when we will sign it, with mutual respect. Then will we know that the era of wars has ended, that we have extended a hand to one another, that we have shaken each other's hand, and that the future will be glorious for all the Peoples of the region. Of prime significance, therefore, in the context of a peace treaty is a termination of the state of war.[2]

However, unlike Begin, Sadat made it very clear that his people would demand a high price for any type of normalization between the countries.

---

1. The entire speech can be found at "Address of Egyptian President Anwar Sadat to the Knesset, November 20, 1977," accessed June 29, 2021, The Knesset, https://www.knesset.gov.il/description/eng/doc/Speech_sadat_1977_eng.htm.
2. Begin's speech can be found at "Menachem Begin Administration: Speech to Knesset Following Historic Speech by Anwar Sadat (November 20, 1977)," Jewish Virtual Library, accessed June 29, 2021, https://www.jewishvirtuallibrary.org/prime-minister-begin-speech-to-knesset-following-historic-speech-by-anwar-sadat-novemer-1977.

In his speech, he argued for a complete withdrawal from what he called "Arab-occupied territories." His conditions were stated bluntly:

> Any talk about permanent peace based on justice, and any move to ensure our coexistence in peace and security in this part of the world, would become meaningless, while you occupy Arab territories by force of arms. For there is no peace that could be in consonance with, or be built on, the occupation of the land of others. Otherwise, it would not be a serious peace.

Following the visit, both countries entered peace negotiations, brokered by the United States. Ultimately, the Egypt-Israel Peace Treaty was signed at the White House on March 26, 1979. The agreement was presented before the Knesset and, with a large majority of 95–18, accepted. The details of the deal included a full Israeli withdrawal from the Sinai Peninsula. At the date of the signing, there were over fifteen settlements in the peninsula, including the town of Yamit.

Although many Israelis supported the government's decision, there were others who felt that the price was too high and that by giving in to Sadat's demands, Israel was creating a dangerous precedent. As the time of evacuation drew closer, the movement against withdrawal became more passionate and dramatic. On April 19, 1982, when the IDF began to evacuate the city of Yamit, some of the residents, together with outside supporters, struggled with the soldiers. The evacuation ended with the residents and the protesters leaving the city while rending their clothes and declaring their undivided loyalty to the city.

HALAKHIC TOPICS IN LAND FOR PEACE

The outcome of these events left trauma and created a deep rift between different political movements within Israeli society. Similar dilemmas and questions were brought up in the religious world. While Rabbi Joseph B. Soloveitchik[3] and Sephardi Chief Rabbi Ovadia Yosef argued

3. In a letter to Chief Rabbi Avraham Shapira, Rabbi Lichtenstein cites the opinion of his father-in-law, the Rav. "Rabbi Yosef Dov Soloveitchik, *zt"l*, resolutely and vigorously asserted that there is no prohibition to hand over portions of the Land of Israel to

in favor of the agreement, granting the government full legitimacy to "trade land for peace," Ashkenazi Chief Rabbi Shlomo Goren and Rabbi Shaul Yisraeli were opposed.

Rabbi Tzvi Yehuda Kook was the most influential rabbinical figure in the opposing camp. On many occasions, he spoke harshly against any notion of "land for peace," both from a halakhic perspective and from a moral one:

> We have absolutely no right to relinquish control over any piece of the Land of Israel. We cannot do this, because we are not the only owners of the land. We are the emissaries of millions of Jews, not only the Jews of today, but the Jews who will come after us as well. A short while ago, an important Zionist activist told me that an old Russian woman approached him in Vienna and said, "Hold onto all parts of the Land of Israel for us. Do not relinquish a meter. Soon we will be coming." There is no man who is permitted to make territorial concessions on this land. Are these kilometers ours? Does someone own them? These kilometers belong to the millions of Jews in Russia and America and throughout the world no less than they belong to us. We are here as the representatives of the nation of Israel; we are not its owners without them. How can a person not feel ashamed by the thought of making do with a truncated state? No one has the right to relinquish lands which belong to the millions of Jews of all generations.[4]

---

the nations of the world when there are considerations of saving life, and moreover held that the definition of these considerations must take into account the views of military and political leaders." The quote is taken from Aharon Lichtenstein and Avraham Shapira, "A Rabbinic Exchange on the Gaza Disengagement," *Tradition* 40, no. 1 (Summer 2007): 49–70. Quotes by Rabbi Lichtenstein and Rabbi Shapira that are taken from this article are translations of their original letters.

4. Rabbi Kook's opinions on this topic can be found in numerous places. This declaration was published in *LiNetivot Yisrael: Kevutzat Maamarim* (Jerusalem: Menora, 1967). Similar quotes can be found in *Siḥot HaRav Tzvi Yehuda: Eretz Yisrael,* edited by Rabbi Shlomo Aviner (Jerusalem: Sifriyat Hava, 2005), 54, 138, and in the posters (*pashkevillim*) reprinted in the back of his book.

Relinquishing Land: Precedents

There are a few historical biblical precedents for handing over Israeli territory for the sake of the interests of the Jewish people. "Ḥiram, king of Tyre, had supplied Shlomo with all the cedarwood, cypress wood, and gold that he required, and in return, King Shlomo gave Ḥiram twenty towns in the region of the Galilee" (I Kings 9:11). Some argue that if Shlomo was permitted to give away towns in the Galilee as a token of friendship for services rendered, we too are permitted to give away sections of the Land of Israel for the sake of peace.

Rabbi Shlomo Goren mentions other precedents that disturb him ideologically, as these sources seem to indicate the legitimacy of negotiating land for national interests.[5] He quotes the midrash[6] about Avraham's agreement with the Jebusites regarding the purchase of Maarat HaMakhpela (the Cave of the Patriarchs). In this agreement, the midrash understands, Avraham "gave up" the right to conquer Jerusalem.

At the time of the destruction of the Temple, the Gemara teaches us that R. Yoḥanan b. Zakkai escaped the besieged city of Jerusalem (Gittin 56a). He negotiated with the Romans, offering a total surrender in return for saving the city of Yavneh with its *ḥakhamim*, or sages, thus ensuring the future of Jewish people. Rabbi J. David Bleich argues that this story serves as a powerful source proving that under certain circumstances, difficult and painful decisions can be made to preserve the life of the people at the expense of keeping a hold on the land:

> It is unthinkable to suppose that R. Yoḥanan ben Zakkai acted contrary to Halakha. The policies he advocated were clearly stamped with the imprimatur of Jewish values and tradition. It is only the analysis of the considerations upon which those policies were grounded that remains for our elucidation.
>
> R. Yoḥanan ben Zakkai was undoubtedly motivated by a desire to preserve Jewish lives. Continued resistance and warfare would assuredly have evoked repressive measures and resultant

5. *Torat HaMedina: Meḥkar Hilkhati Histori BeNosim HaOmdim BeRuma Shel Medinat Yisrael MeAz Tekumata* (Jerusalem: HaIdra Rabba, 1996), 91.
6. *Pirkei DeRabbi Eliezer* 36.

> loss of additional lives. Accordingly, he must have regarded any continuing obligation with regard to preservation of a Jewish homeland as suspended in face of danger. This can be explained on the basis of a number of considerations and, although the considerations are multiple in nature, they are not exclusive of one another.[7]

Rabbi Hershel Schachter, *rosh yeshiva* of RIETS, argues that this source has no relevance in our times:

> Surface examination of the two situations, however, reveals that they bear no basis for comparison. Whereas the Jews' revolt against the Romans was obviously doomed to failure, the war of the Israeli army today against the Arab insurgency is being conducted with moderate success. The Sanhedrin under Rabbi Yochanan ben Zakkai acted correctly by surrendering, for there is no mitzva to "stick out" a losing battle. This is quite dissimilar to the present situation in Israel; thus, it may be argued that it is incumbent upon them to continue to fight to the victorious finish, despite the possible tragic losses that may occur.[8]

The Prohibition Against Selling Land to Non-Jews

Those who oppose "land for peace" argue that the prohibition is biblical, based on *"Velo teḥonnem"* (Deut. 7:2), which can be translated as, "Do not give them a foothold in the land." This forbids us from relinquishing territory in the Land of Israel to non-Jews.[9] This law is mentioned by the Mishna (Avoda Zara 1:8) as a reason to prohibit selling houses in Israel

7. Rabbi J. David Bleich, "Of Land, Peace, and Divine Command," in *Contemporary Halachic Problems,* vol. III (New York: Ktav and Yeshiva University Press, 1989), 298–99.
8. Rabbi Hershel Schachter, "Land for Peace: A Halachic Perspective," *RJJ Journal of Halacha and Contemporary Society* 16 (Fall 1988): 77.
9. For a lengthy halakhic discussion on this prohibition see Rabbi Yaakov Warhaftig, "Lo Teḥonnem UMashma'uto BeYamenu," *Teḥumin* 2 (1980/1981): 193–212.

to non-Jews. Although most *posekim* understand that this prohibition is biblical, some argue that it is rabbinical in nature.[10]

There is a dispute among the rabbis as to whether this prohibition is limited to the seven Canaanite nations or whether it applies to all non-Jews.[11] Although the context of this prohibition seems to be referring to the seven nations, the *Tosafot* (medieval commentaries on the Talmud) explain that this is not the case; it applies to all idol-worshippers.[12] Many *posekim* understand that the prohibition is not limited to idol-worshippers and applies to all non-Jews.

Rav Avraham Yitzchak Kook was attacked for his support of the *heter mekhira* ("selling" the land of Israel to avoid the laws of *Shemitta,* the Sabbatical year). He was accused of transgressing the prohibition of selling land to non-Jews. In a responsum[13] explaining his leniency, he mentions that Rabbi Yoel Sirkis (*Bayit Ḥadash*; Poland, 1561–1640) limits the prohibition to idol-worshippers. Accordingly, as Islam is not halakhically considered idolatry, it is permissible to sell the land to Muslim Arabs.[14]

In fact, Rabbi Aharon Lichtenstein quotes the *heter* of "selling" land to Arabs during the *Shemitta* year as a reason for leniency in our case. In a response to Chief Rabbi Avraham Shapira (Jerusalem, 1914–2007), who opposes trading land for peace, Rabbi Lichtenstein writes:

> You open with the assertion that the evacuation is forbidden by Torah law because of the prohibition of *lo teḥonnem* [Deut. 7:2]? However, it is a matter of public knowledge that you permit the sale of land in the Land of Israel in order to cope with the problems of the Sabbatical year, and even encourage people to rely on this device. The problem of *lo teḥonnem* also arises in connection with this sale, and as is well known, leading halakhic

---

10. See Rabbi Yehuda Perlow's commentary on *Sefer HaMitzvot Shel HaRasag,* negative commandment 13.
11. See Warhaftig, "Lo Teḥonnem," 202, n. 16.
12. *Tosafot,* Avoda Zara 20a, s.v. *DeAmar.*
13. *Mishpat Kohen, siman* 63.
14. Professor Daniel Sperber proves that this opinion is based on an incorrect, censored text. See *Netivot Pesika* (Jerusalem: Rubin Mass, 2008), 63–70.

> authorities have discussed the issue since the days of Rav Kook, *ztz"l*. Among the arguments for leniency, it has been proposed that the prohibition only applies to the seven Canaanite nations, or, at the very least, that it is limited to idolaters, a category that does not include Muslims.[15]

The Commandment to Fight for the Land of Israel

The second main halakhic source that relates to this topic has to do with the understanding of the commandment of *yishuv Eretz Yisrael*, settling the Land of Israel. The Ramban understands that there is a positive commandment to live in the Land of Israel and that this commandment applies at all times, even when the Temple is not standing. In his commentary to the Rambam's *Sefer HaMitzvot*, he notes that this commandment includes the obligation to fight a war to conquer the land:

> This is what the Sages call obligatory war. And thus, they said in the gemara in Sota (44b): "Rava said: [With respect to] the wars [that] Yehoshua [waged] to conquer [the Land of Israel], all agree [that they were] obligatory. [With respect to] the wars [waged by] the House of David for territorial expansion, all agree [that they were] elective." And the formulation of the *Sifrei* is: "'And you possess it and settle in it' (Deut. 26:1) – by virtue of your possessing it, you shall dwell therein"...
>
> And from the fact that they said "The wars [that] Yehoshua [waged] to conquer," you understand that this commandment is fulfilled through conquest... [16]

The Rambam does not mention this commandment in his list, leading some authorities to believe that according to him there is no positive commandment today to dwell in the Land of Israel. However, many argue that the Rambam holds that it is a commandment to live in Israel, but due to "technical" reasons, he does not mention it in *Sefer HaMitzvot*.[17]

---

15. Lichtenstein and Shapira, "Rabbinic Exchange."
16. Ramban, *Commandments Omitted by the Rambam*, positive commandment 4.
17. See Goren, *Torat HaMedina*, 212–14.

Let us go back to the words of the Ramban. How far must one go to fulfill this commandment? When one is faced with a situation of *pikuaḥ nefesh*, can one endanger lives for this commandment?

Sefer HaḤinukh[18] explains that if someone has the opportunity to kill a member of the seven nations without endangering himself and fails to do so, he violates the commandment of destroying the seven nations. In his *Minḥat Ḥinukh*, Rabbi Yosef Babad (Poland/Ukraine, 1801–1874) disagrees with this remark. He points out that since in the normal course of the world, people are killed in battle, the Torah commands us to fight the seven nations, even if by doing so we endanger our lives. This idea becomes the fundamental principle of the argument that the laws of war take precedence over *pikuaḥ nefesh*.

Rabbi Chaim Jachter of Teaneck concludes:

> The argument for prohibiting exchange of land for peace combines the comments of the Ramban and *Minchat Chinuch*. It claims that the Torah obligates us to conquer *Eretz Yisrael* with force, so this *mitzvah*, by its very nature, entails risking our lives. We thus cannot surrender portions of *Eretz Yisrael* even if we are certain that it will save lives, for this would violate our obligation to conquer.[19]

As noted above, Rabbi Ovadia Yosef's opinion is that if an agreement would guarantee genuine peace between the Arab world and the nation of Israel, and if it would be supported by military experts, it is permissible to hand over parts of Israel. The ultimate factor is that *pikuaḥ nefesh* trumps the value of holding on to the Land of Israel. He uses a famous story to emphasize this point:

> People said to Rabbi Chaim Soloveitchik, during a conversation, that if this war [the First World War] would bring the redemption, perhaps it was worthwhile. Rabbi Chaim rebuked them and said, "It is better that many redemptions should be delayed from the

---

18. Commandment 425.
19. *Gray Matter*, vol. 2 (Teaneck, NJ: Jachter, 2006), 142.

> Jewish people than that one Jewish life should be lost. And so, if the question were to come before us, that by sacrificing one Jew the Messiah would come, of course we would rule that it is better for the Messiah not to come, and a Jew should not die. Does not *pikuaḥ nefesh* override every commandment in the Torah, including the Messiah and the redemption?"[20]

A Halakhic Question?

Those who oppose trading land for peace based on these halakhic arguments understand that the question here is similar to classic halakhic questions mentioned in the *Shulḥan Arukh*. Therefore, they relate to the problem as they would to any case in which a religious law stands in opposition to a specific action. Based on this logic, Chief Rabbi Avraham Shapira's ruling can be understood:

> Every order that is contrary to Jewish law and compels one to violate the words of the Torah holds no validity, is forbidden to fulfill and no person has the authority to deliver it. About such instances Rambam wrote, "It goes without saying that if an order of the king nullifies a commandment, then it is not listened to" (*Hilkhot Melakhim* 3:9). Anyone who violates this prohibition will not be exonerated, not in this world and not in the world to come.[21]

However, other opinions believe that our case in not a typical halakhic one. Rabbi Chaim David HaLevi argues that our topic cannot be measured using classic halakhic parameters; it is considered a meta-halakhic question that must be decided based on alternative parameters by the leaders and government of the time.

> This is the power of halakha, that it does not intervene in the details of the laws governing the state, and all it teaches are

---

20. Rabbi Ovadia Yosef, "Mesirat Shetaḥim MeEretz Yisrael BiMekom Pikuaḥ Nefesh," *Teḥumin* 10 (1988/1989): 47.
21. As quoted in Lichtenstein and Shapira, "Rabbinic Exchange."

fundamental principles. In my humble opinion, it seems exceedingly obvious that the guiding principle in all this is guaranteeing the security of the nation in every context of negotiations on the basis of a very broad understanding of the Torah's commandment, "And live by them" (Lev. 18:5). Therefore, the discussion regarding the return or retention of the territories must be based on a clear and simple principle – what is the best way to guarantee the security of the state, which is the preservation of the nation. This is a halakha that is not written, and it certainly does not stem from the law of *pikuaḥ nefesh*, but rather from simple logic.

We are left then with one clear and simple assumption: the decisive factor in this case is the preservation and security of the nation. Therefore, any government of Israel that comes to the conclusion that the surrender of territories will prevent wars and bloodshed, and in its wake bring true peace, is permitted – and even obligated – to do so. By contrast, a withdrawal that is liable to cause any kind of security risk is absolutely forbidden.[22]

A Question of Values

Finally, we will end the discussion with Rabbi Amital's argument that it is the government's right to make painful agreements with Arab nations in situations where the value of the Land of Israel comes into conflict with the value of the people of Israel:

> There is a hierarchy of values in Judaism, and anyone who fails to differentiate *bein kodesh lekodesh* (between one level of holiness and another) will end up unable to differentiate *bein kodesh leḥol* (between the holy and the profane), as we say in the Havdala prayer. The proper order is: the nation, the Torah, the land.... The interests of the nation of Israel certainly take precedence over the interests of the Land of Israel. [23]

22. "HaShalom VeHashlakhotav," *Torah SheBe'al Peh* 21 (1980): 39–51.
23. Rabbi Amital, "Meser Politi O Meser Ḥinukhi?" *Alon Shevut* 100 (5743): 42.

15

Peace with Egypt, 1977

Is One Permitted to Travel to Egypt?

The peace treaty signed between Israel and Egypt raises halakhic questions that relate to the Torah's ambivalence concerning the Egyptians. On one hand, the Torah teaches us: "Do not despise an Egyptian, for you lived as a stranger in his land" (Deut. 23:8). On the other hand, it prohibits Jews from living in Egypt. "[The king] must not acquire many horses for himself; he must not make the people return to Egypt to acquire more horses, since the Lord has told you: You must not go back that way again" (Deut. 17:16).

Does this prohibition apply in our days? Following the Yom Kippur War and the peace agreement with Egypt, Rabbi Yehuda Gershuni (Grodno/Israel, 1908–2000), a prominent *talmid ḥakham*, discussed this question and its relevance in times of war and times of peace.[1] Rabbi Ovadia Yosef, too, was asked whether reporters covering the peace talks

1. *Sefer Kol Tzofayikh: Berurim Hilkhati'im BeInyanim Shonim UViMeyuḥad BeBaayot HaOmdot KaYom Al HaPerek* (Jerusalem: Y. Gershuni, 1980), 439–45.

were permitted to travel to Egypt.[2] Rav Ovadia himself had lived in Egypt and served as a rabbinical judge there.

LIVING IN EGYPT, VISITING EGYPT, AND TRAVEL TO OTHER COUNTRIES

In modern times, our question also serves as an important precedent for issues such as dwelling in Spain after the expulsion and even visiting Germany after the Holocaust. The issue has been raised by a number of rabbis.

The Prohibition of Living in Egypt

Our rabbis teach us: "On three occasions, the Torah warns against returning to Egypt, yet the Jewish people violated this decree and each time were severely punished."[3]

First, on the shores of the Red Sea, Moshe says to the Jewish people, "Fear not! Stand firm and see the deliverance the Lord will bring you today. The Egyptians you see today, you shall never see again" (Ex. 14:13).

Second, we have the prohibition on the Jewish monarch – he "must not acquire many horses for himself; he must not make the people return to Egypt to acquire more horses, since the Lord has told you: You must not go back that way again" (Deut. 17:16).

Finally, when the Torah teaches us about potential curses that might fall upon the Jewish people, it states: "And the Lord will send you back in ships to Egypt, by a route that I told you that you would never see again" (Deut. 28:68).

As a result, many *posekim* understand that there is a prohibition against returning to Egypt. The Rambam's position is accepted by many: "It is permitted to dwell anywhere in the entire world except for the land of Egypt."[4] However, we find that throughout the centuries,

---

2. *Yeḥaveh Daat,* 3:81.
3. Y. Sukka 5:1 and *Mekhilta Parashat Beshallaḥ.*
4. Rambam, *Mishneh Torah, Hilkhot Melakhim* 5:6.

Jewish communities were established in Egypt, and many prominent rabbis, including the Rambam,[5] Radbaz, and Rav Ovadia, lived there.

As a result, some dismiss these verses as biblical prohibitions, and instead see them as temporary or conditional laws. Rabbeinu Baḥya ben Asher (Spain, 1255–1340) writes that since the Egyptians were known and famed to be immoral people, the Jews at the time were warned to distance themselves, but the establishment of communities in Egypt proves that the prohibition is temporary.[6]

Other rabbis, who accept the prohibition as the Rambam does, are very troubled by this question and suggest several explanations, which end up limiting the prohibition. Many of the halakhic limitations are connected to the reasons for the halakha.[7] Rabbi Eliezer ben Shmuel of Metz (1115–1175) understands that the prohibition is limited to traveling **from** Israel **to** Egypt as this would be a direct insult to God, who took the Jews out of Egypt and brought them to Israel.[8] Rabbi Moshe ben Yaakov of Coucy, France (1200–1260), opines that the prohibition emerges from the immoral behavior of the ancient Egyptians. However, the Mishna (Yadayim 4:4) states: "Sanḥeriv, king of Assyria, has long since come up and mingled all of the nations." The ancient Egyptian natives have been replaced by others, so the prohibition should be lifted.[9]

As noted, the Radbaz lived in Egypt. In his commentary on the Rambam, he discusses our problem and quotes the Yerushalmi in Sanhedrin 10:8, which permits temporary return to Egypt for business or other non-residential purposes.[10] This opinion is mentioned by the

5. Rabbi Ishtori (Spain and Israel, 1280–1355) in *Kaftor VaFeraḥ*, chapter 5, reports that the Rambam signed his correspondence as "The person who daily violates three prohibitions." Many rabbis challenge this statement, as many doubt its authenticity. In the Rambam's letters that we have today there is no such signature.
6. Rabbeinu Baḥya, Deut. 17:16.
7. See Rabbi Moshe Taragin's article on the connection between the reasons for this halakha and the halakha itself, "Returning to Egypt," The Israel Koschitzky Torat Har Etzion VBM, February 9, 2016, https://etzion.org.il/en/shiur-18-returning-egypt.
8. *Sefer Yere'im* 309.
9. *Semag*, negative commandment 237.
10. He justifies the Rambam's presence by suggesting that he was forced to remain there, as he was the king's personal doctor. He then explains that he (the Radbaz) was justified in settling there since he built a yeshiva and taught Torah.

Rambam himself.[11] He thus explains that many Jews arrived in Egypt with the intention of staying temporarilly and ended up remaining there. His conclusion is that the actual prohibition would be violated only if a person moved to Egypt with the intention of living there. Based on this opinion, Rav Ovadia argues that reporters are permitted to travel to Egypt, as they have no intention of settling there.

Rabbi Avraham Yitzchak Kook has an original explanation. His understanding combines both elements of our prohibition: the land and the people. First, he quotes the Rambam himself:

> It appears to me that if a king of Israel would conquer the land of Egypt with the approval of the court, it would be permissible to settle there. The prohibition against returning was only given to individuals or to dwell there while it is under the rule of the non-Jews, for their behavior is more depraved than that of the peoples of other lands, as can be inferred from Leviticus 18:3: "Like the practice of the land of Egypt in which you dwelled you shall not do..."[12]

Rav Kook mentions that one can derive two *ḥiddushim*, novel ideas, from this halakha:

1. When the people of Israel conquer the land of Egypt, the *kedusha* of the Land of Israel enters the land, thus affecting the *tuma* (impurity) of Egypt. This change to the **land** has the power to lift the prohibition.
2. The prohibition of living in Egypt applies only to individuals; however, when entire communities move, it is permissible to live there. The rationale is based on the concern that the immoral behavior of the **people** of Egypt would have a negative effect on the Jewish people. This obviously is not true when entire communities reside there.

11. *Mishneh Torah, Hilkhot Melakhim* 5:8.
12. *Mishpat Kohen, siman* 145.

This of course can justify the practice of the Rambam and all Jewish communities that lived in Egypt. Rabbi Gershuni seems to suggest that the occupation of Egyptian territory by the Israeli army during the war might accordingly lift the prohibition.

The Ritva argues that the prohibition applies only at times when the Temple is standing and Jews live in Israel.[13] Rabbi Eliezer Waldenberg suggests that accordingly, since the establishment of the State of Israel, the prohibition might have resurfaced.[14] Rabbi Yehuda Gershuni disputes this idea. He questions whether the Ritva's argument is based on the people of Israel dwelling in Israel, even under the rule of others, or if it is based solely on Jewish sovereignty over their land.

It seems, then, that visiting Egypt today is permitted; settling there today would be prohibited due to the establishment of the State of Israel and the fact that one of the world's large Jewish populations is found in the Land of Israel.

Spain and Germany

As noted above, the question of Egypt serves as an important source for discussing new prohibitions against living in countries that have persecuted Jews. In Jewish history, two countries have stood out for committing horrible crimes against the Jewish people: Spain (1492) and Germany (the Second World War). Rabbinical literature contains discussions about whether to apply similar decrees against returning to live in these countries. Can the prohibition against going to Egypt serve as a precedent for similar decrees in modern times?

Rabbi Avraham Yitzchak Kook was asked if one is permitted to travel to Spain for business in modern times, and he responded by comparing this question to the prohibition against returning to Egypt:

> Concerning the issue of living in Spain, I have not yet found recorded that there was a *ḥerem* (excommunication) or vow made concerning this, but it is probably not more stringent than settlement in Egypt, which is not forbidden unless one plans to live

13. Ritva, Yoma 38a.
14. *Tzitz Eliezer* (n.p.: Waldenberg, 1985), 14:87.

> there permanently and not for the purpose of commerce with the intention of returning (from whence one came).[15]

Marc Shapiro explores the source of this "well-known prohibition" and concludes that there is no known source prohibiting dwelling in Spain.[16]

Rabbi Meshulam Roth (1875–1962), a rabbinical judge in Jerusalem, was asked if following the Holocaust, a new decree should be made prohibiting Jews to live in or even visit Germany. In his answer, he argues against this idea, using the Egypt prohibition as an example of a similar decree that is very difficult to follow:

> The prohibition of living in Egypt, which is a Torah prohibition, has had many difficulties being accepted by the public, and the rabbis have been forced to seek a dispensation to justify the presence of the communities there. This decree (upon Germany) is even more severe than the Torah's, because in Egypt the prohibition is only to settle permanently, but to visit is permitted. What you are asking is to prohibit even visiting! This is undoubtedly something that the public cannot withstand and will cause an obstacle and a violation of the Torah's honor.[17]

The prohibition on returning to Egypt, then, was revisited in modern times. Its application had to be adjusted not only to the needs of today's community vis-à-vis Egypt but also to other countries that may bear a halakhic similarity to Egypt.

---

15. Rabbi Avraham Yitzchak Kook, *Iggerot HaRaaya* 2:632.
16. "The Herem on Spain: History and Halaka," *Sepharad* 49, no. 2 (1989): 381–94. Shapiro writes that based on Rav Kook's *heter* for communities to live in Egypt, he would also permit communities to reside in Spain. See n. 25.
17. *Sefer Kol Mevaser: She'elot UTeshuvot* (Jerusalem: Mosad HaRav Kook, 1955), vol. 1, responsum 13.

16

The First Lebanon War, 1982

Was the Siege of Beirut Halakhically Permissible?

On June 6, 1982, Israel began a military operation in Lebanon to remove the threat of terrorists who were attacking Israel's northern border. The PLO (Palestine Liberation Organization), under the leadership of Yasser Arafat, was stationed in Beirut; it was responsible for these attacks, as well as for thousands of rocket attacks on the Galilee. The acts of terror targeted the State of Israel, but were directed at Israelis living abroad as well. It was an attempt to assassinate Shlomo Argov, Israel's ambassador to the United Kingdom, that served as the impetus for Menachem Begin to officially launch Israel's counterattack.

The operation, named *Shelom HaGalil*, Peace for the Galilee, eventually became the (First) Lebanon War. At the time, no one knew that the war would end up keeping Israeli troops in Lebanon for another eighteen years. After attacking the PLO – as well as Syrian and Muslim Lebanese forces – the Israeli military occupied southern Lebanon, eventually surrounding the PLO and parts of the Syrian army. Contained in west Beirut and under bombardment, the forces and their allies negotiated passage from Lebanon to Tripoli. The war officially ended in September 1982, with hundreds of IDF soldiers killed and thousands injured.

Initially, the country was supportive of the government's decisions, but certain events that occurred during the war raised many questions regarding the aims and military goals of the Israeli government. This war diverged from Israel's previous wars; from this point onward, Israelis became more cynical and less trusting about government decisions. In previous wars, Israelis had felt that there was no choice but to fight. In the past, there had been no doubt or question as to what the country was fighting for. However, in 1982, the feeling of some was that there was an alternative and that some of the battles could have been avoided.

But there were two specific events during the war that created major controversies within Israeli society. First was the siege of Beirut and its occupation, which had not been part of the operation's original plans. Second was the Sabra and Shatila massacre by Christian militants, which raised questions about Israel's role. In this chapter, we will discuss the halakhic responses to the siege of Beirut; in the next chapter, we will take a closer look at the tragedy in Sabra and Shatila.

THE SIEGE OF BEIRUT: PRECEDENTS AND HALAKHIC OPINIONS

The IDF's siege of Beirut eventually led to the PLO's evacuation and relocation to Tunisia. But what are the halakhic parameters of such a siege?

The Midrash mentions that during the war with Midian, a war of revenge against the Midianites who took part in Balak's plan to have Balaam curse the Israelites, a siege was laid, surrounding the city. R. Natan explains: "They left the fourth side open so that they might escape."[1] The Ramban derives from this midrash a positive commandment: in times of war, one must leave open one side of a siege for the enemy to escape. He explains the rationale:

> We are commanded, when we besiege a city, to leave one direction open so that if [the inhabitants] want to flee, they can do so. From this, we learn to act with compassion even toward our enemies at

1. *Sifrei,* Numbers 31:7.

> the time of war. It also has an advantage, as it allows an opening to flee as opposed to strengthening [their efforts] against us…
>
> This is a commandment for all time **in a non-obligatory war** [*milḥemet reshut*], and so writes Maimonides in his great code.[2]

The Ramban mentions that the Rambam agrees with him; however, there are two major differences between the two opinions. The Rambam writes in his code of law:

> When a siege is placed around a city to conquer it, it should not be surrounded on all four sides, but only on three. A place should be left for the inhabitants to flee and for all those who desire to escape with their lives, as it is written (Num. 31:7): "And they besieged Midian as God commanded Moshe."[3]

Unlike the Ramban, the Rambam does not mention this commandment in his *Sefer HaMitzvot*; moreover, it is unclear from the Rambam if this law applies to all types of war.

In his book *Meshekh Ḥokhma*, Rabbi Meir Simcha HaKohen of Dvinsk (1843–1926) explains the meaning behind their disagreement:

> The reason for the dispute is that the Ramban posits that just as there is an obligation to seek peace, similarly there is a necessity to minimize losses to life and to allow the inhabitants of the city to escape.
>
> However, the Rambam sees this all as part of the strategy of battle. If they are entirely surrounded, when they are in terror for their lives, fearing that they will fall to the enemy, they will defend themselves and be invigorated, as we have seen in many historical instances that as great as is the despair, so is the ensuing victory. However, this will not happen if they [the enemy]

---

2. Ramban, *Hasagot HaRamban Al Sefer HaMitzvot,* positive commandment 5.
3. *Mishneh Torah, Hilkhot Melakhim* 6:7.

> have a way to survive and save their lives; then they will just flee. In my humble opinion, the Rambam is correct.[4]

The *Sefer HaḤinukh* agrees with the Ramban, limiting the commandment to cases of *milḥemet reshut* only.[5] Rabbi Yosef Babad notes that according to the Rambam, the law applies even in a *milḥemet mitzva* (commanded war). The reason he gives for this is that the source of the rule is in the war of Midian, which was a *milḥemet mitzva*.[6] The explanation given in the *Meshekh Ḥokhma* also supports this reading of the Rambam. If the purpose of our law is only tactical, then should it not apply to all wars?

Rabbinic Debate: Rabbi Shlomo Goren vs. Rabbi Shaul Yisraeli

During the Lebanon War, the Israeli newspaper *HaTzofeh* published a letter written by Chief Rabbi Goren. In it, Rabbi Goren argued that based on Jewish law, a total siege on Beirut was forbidden.[7] Rabbi Shaul Yisraeli responded – also in *HaTzofeh* – that the siege on Beirut must be complete, asserting that there was no place to show mercy toward terrorists who wished to destroy us.[8] Both rabbis agreed that civilians must be allowed to leave the besieged area and that enemies may be prevented from entering the area (or bringing in supplies); their difference of opinion related only to militants who are under siege.

Rabbi Goren's Argument

First, Rabbi Goren argues that every war of the State of Israel falls under the halakhic definition of a *milḥemet mitzva*.[9] Thus all halakhot of war mentioned in the Rambam's code of law would apply to wars nowadays. The Lebanon War was a defensive war and thus obligatory.

---

4. *Meshekh Ḥokhma,* Num. 31:7.
5. *Sefer HaḤinukh,* commandment 527.
6. *Minḥat Ḥinukh,* ad loc.
7. Published in *Meshiv Milḥama,* 3:5.
8. His response was published in his book *Ḥavat Binyamin* (Kefar Darom: Torah VeHa'aretz Institute, 1991), 1:111–19.
9. See Rabbi Zevin in *LeOr HaHalakha* 64, who argues similarly, that all modern wars are categorized as mandatory wars. See also Chief Rabbi Herzog, *Heikhal Yitzḥak, Oraḥ Ḥayim* 37:3.

Regarding the specific law of laying siege, Rabbi Goren bases his opinion on the Rambam's rulings mentioned above. Like Rabbi Yosef Babad in the *Minḥat Ḥinukh,* Rabbi Goren claims that the law applies to all wars, even a *milḥemet mitzva*. He then sets out to prove than even the Ramban would agree that under the circumstances of the Lebanon War, there is an obligation to leave one side open. The Ramban states that this commandment only applies to a *milḥemet reshut,* such as a war to conquer new land. However, a *milḥemet mitzva,* such as a war against Amalek, against the seven nations of Canaan, or to defend Jewish lives, does not have such a requirement; thus, a full siege may be put in place. The Lebanon War is a defensive war and thus obligatory. If so, then according to the Ramban, the siege on Beirut must be complete. Nonetheless, Rabbi Goren argues that the Ramban is only referring to the first two types of mandatory wars (wars against Amalek and the seven nations of Canaan) in which we are obligated to kill every single person. This is why we may not allow people to escape a siege. However, a defensive war, as in our case, is similar to a *milḥemet reshut,* and the siege must allow people to escape.

The *Minḥat Ḥinukh* is troubled by this: if the source of the commandment is from the war against Midian, a *milḥemet mitzva,* how can one assert that it does not apply to a *milḥemet mitzva*? Rabbi Goren, following the Ramban, suggests that wars outside the Land of Israel automatically gain the status of *milḥemet reshut.* Therefore, the war against Midian was technically a *milḥemet reshut*. The Lebanon War, too, would thus be a *milḥemet reshut,* and the rule regarding sieges should still apply.

Lastly, Rabbi Goren compares the commandment to the law of the Torah, which requires that before we attack our enemies, we must attempt to establish peace first:

> No war, neither a *milḥemet reshut* nor a *milḥemet mitzva,* should be waged against anyone until they are offered the opportunity of peace, as Deuteronomy 20:10 states: "When you approach a city to wage war against it, you should propose a peaceful settlement."[10]

---

10. *Mishneh Torah, Hilkhot Melakhim* 7:1.

Rabbi Goren's understanding is that **both** commandments – proposing a peaceful settlement and leaving one side of a siege open – apply in all types of war; both are rooted in a humanitarian commandment, attempting to avoid unnecessary bloodshed.

Rabbi Shaul Yisraeli's Response

The Rambam, in formulating this rule in *Mishneh Torah,* writes that it applies when one besieges a city in order to conquer it. This implies that it only applies to a *milḥemet reshut,* when the war is to conquer new territory, but not to a defensive war, which would be a *milḥemet mitzva.* Thus, both the Rambam and the Ramban only apply the commandment of leaving one side of a siege open for escape to a *milḥemet reshut* – which the Lebanon War was not.

Regarding the *Minḥat Ḥinukh*'s claim that the source of our law is from the war of Midian which was a *milḥemet mitzva,* Rabbi Yisraeli explains that this war was historically unique; it is actually comparable to a contemporary *milḥemet reshut* in that there was no command to directly kill the enemy. Thus, an escape route was required.

Rabbi Yisraeli quotes the *Meshekh Ḥokhma,* seen above. He agrees that according to the Rambam, this rule is a military tactic; the best way to create a siege is to leave a side open so that fighters have an escape route and do not fight to the end.

Therefore, according to the Rambam, this rule only applies when the tactic is appropriate; but according to the Ramban, it applies in every *milḥemet reshut.*

Rabbi Yisraeli takes issue with Rabbi Goren's connection of the commandments to request peace (before launching a war) and leaving an escape route in a siege as similar humanitarian laws. To his mind, they are entirely unconnected. The former is to afford the enemy the chance to surrender and be subjugated under Jewish rule; only the latter is a humanitarian law.

Rabbi Yisraeli argues:

> The requirement to leave a fourth side open so that the enemy can flee is not relevant when our aim is to defeat and destroy the

> enemy. Why let them escape from our grasp...when they are in a beleaguered state? Is it so that they can regroup and remobilize against us?

The application of halakha to military situations was a new challenge for the Jewish state, one which modern rabbis carefully deliberated, looking at ancient texts and earlier theoretical discussions.

17

The Sabra and Shatila Massacre, 1982

What Is the Moral Responsibility of an Army for Atrocities Committed by Its Allies?

In the summer of 1982, during the First Lebanon War, a Lebanese Christian militia – related to what was known as the Phalange party – entered the refugee camps of Sabra and Shatila and murdered between 460 and 3,500 civilians, mostly Palestinians. The Phalangists, allies of Israel, had been ordered by the IDF to clear out PLO fighters from the villages. It was during this raid that the Lebanese soldiers committed the massacre.

Although it was clear from the very beginning that Israeli soldiers were not directly involved in the killings, questions regarding indirect responsibility were raised. When the scale of the massacre became public, Israelis were outraged, demanding that the government investigate the IDF's role. As a result of the tremendous pressure, the government appointed the Kahan Commission to examine the events that took place at the refugee camps.

Following a four-month investigation, the Kahan Commission concluded that "direct responsibility" rested with the Phalangists; no Israelis were deemed "directly responsible," although Israel was "indirectly responsible." Defense Minister Ariel Sharon was found to bear "personal responsibility" "for ignoring the danger of bloodshed and revenge" and "not taking appropriate measures to prevent bloodshed." It was recommended that he be forced to resign.

Anticipating world reaction, the committee added to the end of the report the following paragraph:

> We do not deceive ourselves that the results of this inquiry will convince or satisfy those who have prejudices or selective consciences, but this inquiry was not intended for such people. We have striven and have spared no effort to arrive at the truth, and we hope that all persons of good will who will examine the issue without prejudice will be convinced that the inquiry was conducted without any bias.[1]

THE RABBINICAL RESPONSE TO THE MASSACRE

The rabbinical world, both in Israel and abroad, voiced its opinion. Rabbi Joseph B. Soloveitchik, in a personal phone call to Prime Minister Menachem Begin, demanded a commission of inquiry to investigate Israel's failure to prevent the massacres.[2] Rabbi Yehuda Gershuni, a prominent Torah scholar, compared the events to the story of the king of Moav who sacrifices a human in the midst of battle:[3]

> And the king of Moav saw that the men of war were stronger than he and he took with him seven hundred men who drew

1. The report is published in John Norton Moore, ed., *The Arab-Israeli Conflict*, vol. IV, part II (Princeton, NJ: Princeton University Press, 2016), 1206–1300.
2. See Shalom Carmy's article, "Soloveitchik the Zionist," *First Things*, May 2018, https://www.firstthings.com/article/2018/05/soloveitchik-the-zionist.
3. His article appears in *Arakhim BeMivḥan Milḥama* (published by the Mizrachi family and friends from Yeshivat Har Etzion, 2002), 149–51.

> their swords, to break a way to the king of Edom, yet they were unable. And he took his firstborn who would reign after him, and brought him up for a burnt-offering on the wall. And there was great wrath upon Israel. (II Kings 3:26–27)

This verse seems to indicate that although Moav and Edom were fighting among themselves, the wrath is on the Jewish people. Could this story illuminate our discussion?

Rabbi Gershuni quotes the biblical commentator Rabbi David Kimhi (Radak; France, 1160–1235), who explains, in contrast with the common understanding, that it is actually the son of the king of Edom who is sacrificed by the king of Moav, rather than the prince of Moav. It is the king of Edom who is upset at the Jewish people for not saving his son. This explanation is backed up by Amos 2:1, which explicitly lays the blame of the human sacrifice on the people of Moav and not on the Jewish people: "So says the Lord: On account of Moav's three crimes and on account of the fourth, I will not forgive them: they immolated the corpse of the king of Edom down to lime." Based on this last verse, Rabbi Gershuni argues that God's anger at the killing of non-Jews by non-Jews is not directed at the Jewish people. He also points out how ironic it is that although it is the king of Moav who kills the prince of Edom, his father, the king of Edom, is angry at the Jews and not at the real killers.

In Yeshivat Mercaz HaRav, Rabbi Shaul Yisraeli delivered a speech condemning those who called for an inquiry into the massacre.[4] He argued that Israel should not be blamed for acts of murder committed by others. The debate in Hesder yeshivas (Religious Zionist yeshivas that combine Torah learning and military service) was charged. Soldiers from Hesder yeshivas served in the war, and many were among the casualties. In fact, Yehuda Katz of Yeshivat Kerem BeYavneh is still considered missing in action today, almost forty years later.

Both Rabbi Yehuda Amital and Rabbi Aharon Lichtenstein, the heads of Yeshivat Har Etzion, supported the call for an official inquiry

---

4. This is quoted by Rabbi Eliezer Melamed. See his article "Bosariyut Musarit Ve-Totzaoteha," Yeshivat Har Bracha, February 21, 2003, https://yhb.org.il/shiurim/revivim-1144/.

into the massacre. In an open letter to Prime Minister Menachem Begin which was published in *HaTzofeh*,[5] Rabbi Lichtenstein expressed his shock and bewilderment. He argues that although he believes Israel's involvement was accidental and unintentional, it is still considered a terrible sin. In the letter, he quotes numerous sources regarding the morality and ethics of warfare and murder. He focuses on the need for atonement even when blood is shed accidentally. He quotes the Rambam's explanation of the rabbinical saying that "an accidental sinner is called a sinner":

> For with regard to an inadvertent transgression, the transgressor carries a certain amount of culpability, for he should have checked and been careful. Had he examined the matter thoroughly and been careful in asking questions, he would not have transgressed. Since he did not take the trouble to examine and research the matter before acting, he requires atonement.[6]

Rabbi Lichtenstein mentions commandments that teach us the sensitivity to human life the Torah expects of us. He refers to the *ir miklat* (city of refuge) system. The Torah teaches us that a person who accidentally kills another must move to a city of refuge. What is the purpose of this commandment? It seems that the city acts as both a protection from the murderer's family and an act of atonement, repentance for the act of bloodshed:

> The chapters of the Torah that discuss cities of refuge, which were designated specifically for one who committed manslaughter and for whom exile is punishment and atonement wrapped up together, testify to the moral and religious alarm associated with inadvertent killing. And if this is true of the actual taking of

5. The letter was published in *HaTzofeh* on October 15, 1982. The letter was translated by Rabbi Alex Israel.
6. Rambam, *Mishneh Torah, Hilkhot Shegagot* 5:6.

> life, it is applicable, to a lesser degree, to anything relating to the value of human life, however minor.[7]

Another biblical commandment which raises the question of moral responsibility in cases of murder is *Egla Arufa,* the ritual when a dead body is found outside of a town. Here, again, Rabbi Lichtenstein explains the meaning of this commandment and its message in our days:

> "If someone slain is found lying in the open … and the identity of the slayer not known" (and it makes no difference if the victim is a Jew or not), the Torah obligates the elders of the court, the representatives of the community and nation, whose responsibility can only be indirect, to break the neck of a heifer as an atonement, and for the priests to call out: "Atone for Your people Israel." The Mishna asks: "Do we think that the court elders shed that blood?" It answers: "Rather, that no person came into town whom we let leave without food, that no person came into town whom we abandoned without escort."

Rabbi Lichtenstein mentions the element of *ḥillul Hashem* involved and why this reason itself should justify establishing an official investigation:

> Alongside that event, undoubtably the bizarre initial refusal to establish a state commission of inquiry to properly investigate the matter has cast a heavy shadow over us all, has lowered Israel's honor and caused a desecration of Heaven internationally; while domestically, it has aroused doubts and divisions. The need for such an inquiry is pressing, whether for national reasons – to clear our name in the international arena – or to remove the embarrassment shared by Jewish communities globally.

---

7. For a detailed explanation of the reasons of this commandment, see Rabbi Yonatan Grossman's article, "Masei: The Inadverent Murderer and the Cities of Refuge," trans. David Silverberg, The Israel Koschitzky Torat Har Etzion VBM, May 7, 2017, https://www.etzion.org.il/en/tanakh/torah/sefer-bamidbar/parashat-masei/masei-inadvertent-murderer-and-cities-refuge.

In an article dealing with morality and religion, Rabbi Lichtenstein discusses the story of Shaul's sin of not killing Agag, king of Amalek. He mentions that this question was previously discussed in his open letter:

> Why was it that King Shaul was punished for not killing Agag, king of Amalek? Was it simply for not having killed the last remaining Amalekite? I suggested that he was punished not just for sparing Agag, but because the fact that he refused to kill Agag placed in a totally different light his killing of all the other Amalekites beforehand.[8]

His answer touches upon the justification of shedding blood in war. In his explanation, he points out the crucial difference between immoral murder and legitimate war.

> Shaul had been commanded to take a whole people and kill them – and this is, morally, a frightful thing. The only justification lies in it being a response to an unequivocal divine command. Therefore, if Shaul had been motivated in his actions purely by fear of God, by obedience to the *tzav* [decree], then he should have followed the command to the letter. God didn't say, "Kill Amalek but spare Agag." Now, if he didn't kill Agag but killed everybody else, what does that indicate? It indicates that what motivated him in killing the others was not the *tzav* of God, but rather some baser impulse, some instinctive violence. And the proof is that he killed everyone, but spared his peer, his royal comrade. If that is the case, then Shaul was not punished for sparing Agag: rather, he had to be punished because of the Amalekites he did kill! Why? Because he killed them not purely due to a divine command (which is the only thing that can overcome the moral consideration), but rather out of military, diplomatic or political considerations.

---

8. The article "Being Frum and Being Good: On the Relationship between Religion and Morality" appears in *By His Light: Character aned Values in the Service of God* (Jerusalem: Maggid, 2016), 110.

Rabbi Lichtenstein explains that this idea is a fundamental principle of the philosophy of the Hesder yeshiva, which combines Torah and military service. He points out to the prime minister of Israel that the moral right of his students to fight in a war stems from the complete certainty that the leaders of our country are acting out of pure motivations.

> I believe with all my might – otherwise I would not be in a Hesder Yeshiva which combines Torah and military service – that when the moment comes, we need to serve God through aggression. But the need and the means need to be carefully weighed.
>
> My students are invested in the Rambam's attitude that a soldier who enters war does so with the awareness and feeling that he does so for the sake of God, and as for our struggle for Eretz Yisrael, this is most certainly the case. But the details need a fundamental examination. When I look into the faces of the young men, I am overwhelmed by the sense of mission that fills and animates them. I feel a sacred obligation, personally and nationally, not only to encourage and strengthen them but to assure them, as much as is possible, that they put their lives on the line for the sake of God – objectively and subjectively – and this, each and every day, in every waking hour, in each and every battle, when they are prepared to give everything.
>
> Dare we offer them less?

The Question of *Ḥillul Hashem*

As mentioned, Rabbi Yehuda Amital came out publicly with his demand for a full investigation of the massacre. In a statement he published to his students, he wrote:

> The Beirut massacre, which took place under the occupation of the Israeli military, has caused – beyond the ethical aspects, which cry out to the very heart of the heavens – a great *chillul ha-shem* in Israel and the other nations. We now stand four days before Yom Kippur, and my entire being quakes and trembles out of fear

> for the Day of Judgment, for as is known, Yom Kippur does not atone for the sin of *chillul ha-shem*.[9]

In an address weeks later in Yeshivat Har Etzion, Rabbi Amital explained that his protest was not only against those who opposed an investigation but also against those rabbis who had spoken in favor of continuing the war for the sake of liberating parts of the Land of Israel. He quoted one rabbi who argued that even if peace exists, we must declare a war for the purpose of liberating these portions of land which are part of the Land of Israel, for without them we are not a complete nation.

In his talk in front of his students, he explained his concern about the militant voices coming from within the Religious Zionist community:

> These words (of this rabbi) were spoken in the practical debate about invading Beirut, which according to IDF estimates would have entailed the risk of hundreds of losses on our side and terrible damage to the civilian population. Doubts regarding a military mission were raised by many, and yet the voice that was so certainly and decisively in favor of military action came from the representatives of Religious Zionism.
>
> What is the connection between the struggle for Yehuda and Shomron and the invasion of Beirut?...
>
> The fact that these ideas are peppered with verses, statements of *Ḥazal* and expressions borrowed from Rav Kook makes me shudder.[10]

Many of Rabbi Amital's students were confused by his response. Some saw his approach as an attack undermining the entire legitimacy of the war; some wrote him letters questioning his positions. It seems that one in particular challenged the severity of the prohibition of killing

9. The statement and the response to it appears in Elyashiv Reichner's biography of Rabbi Amital, *By Faith Alone* (Jerusalem: Maggid, 2011), 185–95.
10. The address was printed in the yeshiva's Torah journal as "Meser Politi O Meser Ḥinukhi," *Alon Shevut* 100 (1983): 34–54.

non-Jews.[11] In his response, Rabbi Amital quotes source after source proving that Jewish law prohibits the murder of any human being. He then mentions the terrible additional *ḥillul Hashem* inherent in the killing of non-Jews. This idea is found in the writings[12] of Rabbi Meir Simcha HaKohen of Dvinsk, when he explains why the Torah does not demand the death penalty for the murder of non-Jews as it does for the murder of Jews. Rabbi Meir Simcha lays out the reasoning for this law:

> Perhaps it is because...when a Jew kills a Noahide, aside from the sin of murdering, he is also guilty of an additional sin, which is the desecration of God's name. His sin is so severe that even death by the hands of man cannot atone for his sins; therefore, he can be judged by God alone.

The rabbinical response to the massacre in Sabra and Shatila was one that was born out of great crisis within the State of Israel, at a time when the religious public, like the greater public, looked to its leaders for answers.

11. "Mikhtav," *Alon Shevut* 100 (1983): 55–62.
12. *Meshekh Ḥokhma,* Ex. 21:14.

18

The Aliya of Russian Jewry, 1989

What Is the Religious Meaning of *Kibbutz Galuyot*?

The Russian Revolution in 1917 signaled a dark time for Jews in that region of the world. As the Soviet Union was formed and its policies put in place, Jews found themselves the victims of appalling treatment. In an attempt to destroy Judaism, the Soviet government prohibited religious activity such as praying and learning Torah. Even speaking Hebrew was forbidden. During those dark years, many Jews were arrested, exiled, and killed. Generations of Jews were raised without any exposure to Torah and commandments and devoid of any religious life.

The first wave of aliya from the USSR began in the 1970s. The Six-Day War created an awakening within people around the world, bringing them closer to their Jewish identity and pride. Jews in the Soviet Union sent letters to both local and foreign governments, demanding that they be allowed to make aliya to Israel. The Soviet government, thinking that allowing some Jews to leave the country would lead to both quiet in the Jewish community and a positive image in the West, gave its permission. Between 1969 and 1973, 163,000 Jews from the Soviet Union immigrated to Israel.

The fall of the Berlin Wall in 1989 and the official collapse of the Soviet Union in 1991 changed the world. After years of tension between the East and the West, the Cold War was over. The effect in the Jewish world was enormous. Seventy years of persecution had ended, and the Jews living in the former Soviet Union were free. As a result, a mass exodus began. Between the years 1990 and 2000, over a million Jews made their way to the State of Israel.

This time, however, the reasons for aliya were a bit different; the immigrants were not necessarily motivated by Zionist ideology. Many of those making aliya had intermarried, and hundreds of thousands of them were not considered Jewish by Orthodox standards. This aliya brought with it new challenges, which we will discuss below.

However, before we focus on the specific questions of this special wave of aliya, we will raise broader issues that have to do with the commandment of aliya to the Land of Israel.

THE RELIGIOUS MEANING OF *KIBBUTZ GALUYOT*

It is important to note that of all the miraculous events that have taken place in the past seventy-five years, *kibbutz galuyot* (the ingathering of the exiles) might be the most important, serving as an indication that biblical prophecies are materializing in our days. Rabbi Yoel Bin-Nun dedicates an entire book to this theme. In his introduction, he explains the uniqueness of this miracle:

> I see in *kibbutz galuyot* the greatest miracle in all of human history, because there is no other nation that has survived thousands of years after it was exiled from its country and returned to its land. Throughout Jewish history, the return to Israel was from as many as one hundred countries. However, in the distant past, the return – both in the times of the Exodus from Egypt and the Return to Zion from Babylon – came in each case from only one country.

> No other generation but ours has ever seen such a phenomenon. Over the past few decades, to this very day, the ingathering of the exiles has been taking place before our eyes. Thus, this is the ultimate proof of the truth of Torah and prophecy and for God's existence among us. There is no need for any other evidence; for it is staring us in the face, as the prophet exclaims: "For they will see with their own eyes the Lord's return to Zion" (Is. 52:8).[1]

In fact, a suggestion has been made to add a chapter of Psalms to our daily prayers making note of the miraculous phenomenon of the gathering of scattered Jews from around the world. Basing his view on the daily obligation to mention the Exodus from Egypt in our prayers, Rabbi Benayahu Bruner, a rabbinical judge and *rosh yeshiva* in Safed, argues that there is a similar obligation to mention the redemption occurring in our times.[2] The commandment to remember the Exodus from Egypt is mentioned in the Torah (Deut. 16:3): "So that you will remember the day that you left Egypt all the days of your life." There is a disagreement in the Mishna as to what this verse is referring to (Mishna Berakhot 1:5).

> We mention the Exodus from Egypt at night. R. Elazar b. Azarya said: Behold, I am almost a seventy-year-old man and I have not succeeded in [understanding why] the Exodus from Egypt should be mentioned at night, until Ben Zoma explained it from a verse, "So that you will remember the day that you left Egypt all the days of your life" – "the days of your life" refers to the days; "all the days of your life" refers to the nights.
>
> But the Sages say: "The days of your life" refers to this world; "all the days of your life" includes the days of the Messiah.

If the halakha follows R. Elazar b. Azarya (as it seems to, based on the fact that we do mention the Exodus from Egypt during both day and

1. Rabbi Yoel Bin-Nun, *Nes Kibbutz Galuyot* (Tel Aviv: Yedioth Ahronoth, 2011), 11.
2. "Hosafat Mizmor Hodaa BeTefilla Al Shivat Tziyon BaDor HaAḥaron," *Teḥumin* 38 (2017/2018): 461–69.

night), it might indicate that in the future, in the days of the Messiah, there will be no commandment to remember the Exodus from Egypt. The Gemara mentions that R. Elazar challenges the Sages' view with the following verse (Berakhot 12b):

> Behold days are coming, says the Lord, and it shall no longer be said, "As the Lord lives, who brought up the children of Israel from the land of Egypt," but, "As the Lord lives, who brought up the children of Israel from the northland and from all the lands where He had driven them" (Jer. 16:14–15).

This seems to argue that in the future we will not mention the miracles of the Exodus from Egypt, because the new miracles of the future redemption will be greater. Basing his view on the Mishna and the verses from Jeremiah, Rabbi Bruner suggests reciting chapter 126 of Psalms, which describes the return of the Jewish people to Zion.

The Commandment of Aliya Post-1948

Many halakhic authorities, from the talmudic period up until our days, argue about whether one is obligated to make aliya. Although most of the *posekim* follow the Ramban's assertion that aliya is a positive commandment and present at all times,[3] not all are convinced that there is an active obligation all of the time.

Some, like Rabbeinu Chaim of the *Baalei HaTosafot,* argue that at times when the journey is too dangerous there is no obligation to move to the Land of Israel;[4] some, like Rabbi Moshe Feinstein, argue that it is only recommended and not obligatory;[5] and some, like Rabbi Avraham Bornsztain of Sochaczew (1838–1910), believe that the obligation only applies to those who can make a living off the land.[6]

Rabbi Eliezer Waldenberg discusses the commandment of aliya before and after the founding of the State of Israel. He posits that

3. See Rabbi Eliezer Waldenberg, *Tzitz Eliezer* 7:48.
4. Ketubbot 101b, s.v. *Hu.*
5. *Iggerot Moshe, Even HaEzer* 1:102.
6. *Avnei Nezer, Yoreh De'ah* 454.

although the commandment applies, in his opinion, at all times, as of 1948, all the reasons given for not making aliya cease to exist. Moreover, the miraculous events taking place today[7] serve as catalysts for making aliya. He explains that the commandment of *yishuv Eretz Yisrael* (settling the Land of Israel) consists of two sub-commandments: one upon the individual and one upon the public. When the Temple was destroyed, the commandment upon the public was annulled. However, with the establishment of the state, the commandment to build a country and a national home for the Jewish people resurfaced. Therefore, he concludes, the commandment of aliya to the Land of Israel is today, more than ever, a commandment upon all of the Jewish people.

Birkat Sheheḥeyanu on Aliya

An interesting question was raised by the Sephardi chief rabbi of Israel, Rabbi Yitzchak Nissim (Baghdad/Israel, 1895–1981) regarding the recital of *Sheheḥeyanu* at the time of aliya.[8] The rationale is based on the rule that this blessing should be made whenever one fulfills a commandment for the very first time. In his responsum, Rabbi Nissim mentions other *posekim* who discuss this question, among them Rabbi Haim Palachi (Izmir, Turkey, 1788–1868) and Rabbi Yaakov Hagiz (Morocco, 1620–1674), who argue against reciting the blessing. Rabbi Hagiz's position relates to the question of two contradictory blessings that may be recited together. Halakha maintains that at certain times, when sad and happy events occur simultaneously, two blessings may be recited. A good example would be the death of a parent who leaves a large inheritance behind, when both *Sheheḥeyanu* and *Dayan HaEmet* are recited.[9] Similarly, Rabbi Hagiz argues that at the time of aliya to the Land of Israel, *Birkat HaGomel* is recited on the "miracle" of surviving the journey, together with the blessing of *Dayan HaEmet* and performing *keria* upon seeing the desolation of the land. He notes that the recital of *Birkat HaGomel* includes within it *Sheheḥeyanu*. Rabbi Nissim points out that one can derive from the words of Rabbi Hagiz that if not for *Birkat*

7. *Tzitz Eliezer* 7:48.
8. *Yayin HaTov* #47.
9. *Shulḥan Arukh, Oraḥ Ḥayim* 223:2.

HaGomel, Sheheḥeyanu would be recited. The logic behind this, Rabbi Nissim explains, is that *Sheheḥeyanu* is not necessarily a blessing recited on ultimate happiness, but rather upon experiencing a benefit. Making aliya, he argues, is surely considered a religious benefit.

Rabbi Mordechai Fogelman (1898–1984) of Kiryat Motzkin discusses this question as well.[10] He quotes an opinion which argues that the blessing of *Shehḥeyanu* has to do with a state of happiness. This opinion (written before 1948) holds that the Land of Israel is desolate and the Temple is in ruins, so surely no blessing may be recited under these circumstances. Rabbi Fogelman argues that, based on this argument, the blessing should indeed be recited today:

> The blessing of *Sheheḥeyanu* in our days for immigration to the State of Israel is an expression of joy and thanksgiving to God, who, following the Holocaust, has taken us from darkness to light, from enslavement to redemption, and brought us back to the land of our patriarchs and prophets.

Violating Shabbat for the Aliya of Soviet Jews

When the gates of the Soviet Union first opened, many were concerned that they might close at any moment. The prevailing feeling was that there was no time to spare; it was necessary to do everything possible to gather the Jews from these countries and encourage and help them to settle in the Land of Israel. After the dissolution of the Soviet Union, there was a profound feeling that without immediate action, many Jews would be lost to the nation. They had already been isolated from Jewish tradition for seventy years, and many had married non-Jewish spouses.

Rabbi Shaul Yisraeli was asked if under the circumstances, Shabbat could be violated for the purpose of aliya to the State of Israel.[11] Can documents and permits for former Soviet Jews be produced on

10. "Birkat HaAretz VeSheHeḥeyanu LeOlim Ḥadashim," *Torah SheBe'al Peh* 11 (1969): 55–60.

11. The article was printed in a special collection of articles dedicated to aliya from the former Soviet Union: "HaAliya MeRusya KeGidrei Pikuaḥ Nefesh," *Torah SheBe'al Peh* 32 (1991): 26–31; printed also as "Pikuaḥ Nefesh BeSakana Ruḥanit," *Teḥumin* 2 (1980/1981): 27–34.

Shabbat? If needed, can one drive? It is well known that if a life is in danger (*pikuaḥ nefesh*), one must violate Shabbat. But does this apply only to physical harm? Might it relate to spiritual harm to the "Jewish soul" as well?

Rabbi Yisraeli ties the question to an argument among the *Rishonim*: Rabbi Shlomo ben Aderet (Rashba; Spain, 1235–1310) addresses a case in which a Jewish girl is in danger of converting to Christianity, and asks whether Shabbat could be violated for the purpose of saving her. His answer: one may not sin for the purpose of saving others from sin. Therefore, in our case, it would be forbidden to violate Shabbat. Rabbi Yosef Karo,[12] after quoting the Rashba, points out that the *Tosafot* disagree, asserting that one is permitted to violate a "smaller" commandment for the purpose of keeping a "greater" one. Ultimately Rabbi Karo rules, following the *Tosafot,* that it is permissible to violate Shabbat to save a Jew from converting to Christianity.[13]

However, Rabbi Yisraeli explains that it is unclear how far this ruling extends. The *Taz* is of the opinion that when it comes to violating Shabbat for *pikuaḥ nefesh,* there is no difference between physical and spiritual danger.[14] However, Rabbi Avraham Abele Gombiner (the *Magen Avraham*; Poland, 1635–1682) disagrees and holds that this leniency is limited to cases in which the danger is clear, without any doubt.[15] Rabbi Pinchas Goldschmidt, the current chief rabbi of Moscow, discusses whether or not one can rely on Rabbi Yisraeli's *heter* and allow Soviet Jews to travel on Shabbat to the State of Israel.[16] His opinion, written in 1994, is that there is no guarantee that Soviet Jews leaving the country and immigrating elsewhere will be religious. Therefore, he concludes that the situation at the time does not justify violating Shabbat.

12. *Beit Yosef, Oraḥ Ḥayim* 306.
13. *Shulḥan Arukh, Oraḥ Ḥayim* 306:14.
14. *Turei Zahav, Oraḥ Ḥayim* 306:4.
15. *Magen Avraham, Oraḥ Ḥayim* 306:29.
16. "Aliya MeRusya BeShabbat," *HaMaayan* 34, no. 4 (Tammuz 1994): 1–4.

Setting aside the practical question of whether or not we should violate Shabbat, between the lines of these discussions one can sense a bigger argument regarding the importance of immigration to the State of Israel. It is obvious that Rabbi Yisraeli understands that aliya is not just a means to keep the Jewish people from assimilation; rather, it is a fulfillment of the biblical prophecy of the return of the Jewish people to their home.

19

The Aliya of Russian Jewry, 1989

Who May Be Buried in a Jewish Cemetery?

During the 1990s, the aliya from the countries of the former USSR included many Jews from assimilated families. Many of those who immigrated to Israel under the Law of Return were not halakhically recognized as Jewish, because, all too often, the father, not the mother, was Jewish. One of the most sensitive challenges that unfortunately became a practical question was the burial of these citizens who joined the IDF and were killed in the line of duty.

Orthodox Jewish custom is very particular about who is buried in a Jewish cemetery, limiting interment only to those who are halakhically recognized as Jewish. In the past, this question did not arise. While there were always soldiers in the IDF who were not Jewish – Druze, Bedouin, Circassian – their families and communities preferred for them to be buried in their own cemeteries, in keeping with their own traditions.

However, soldiers from families that immigrated from the former Soviet Union identify as Jewish. They speak Hebrew and are passionate Zionists. They risk their lives to protect the Jewish people – and, in our case, sacrifice their lives. Is there room to consider this when the question of burial arises? In other words, is the Israeli soldier who is not considered Jewish by Orthodox standards regarded as a non-Jew for the purpose of burial?

The mass aliya from the former Soviet Union brought with it many other questions and challenges, most of which have to do with conversion, yet the specific matter of burial serves as an example that reflects the unique challenge of this particular immigration. One infamous case began on August 6, 1996, when a sergeant in the IDF, Lev Pischov, fell in battle. As Lev's mother was not Jewish, the military chaplaincy decided to bury him at the far edge of the military cemetery in Beit She'an. This led to a public outcry, which forced the government to appoint a committee to decide on an official policy regarding the issue.

In recent years, many suggestions have been made about this delicate matter, including by politicians. Below we will study this topic, starting with the source of the prohibition of burying non-Jews alongside Jews.

BURYING A NON-JEW IN A JEWISH CEMETERY

The Mishna states that separate cemeteries were established for those executed by the court, depending on the severity of the method used for their punishment. "And they would not bury him [the executed person] in his ancestral plot. Rather, two graveyards were established [for] the court: One for those who were killed [by decapitation] or strangled, and one for those who were stoned or burned" (Mishna Sanhedrin 6:5). The Gemara explains that this is because one should not bury an evil person next to a righteous person:

> And why all this? Because a wicked man is not buried next to a righteous man. As Rav Aḥa bar Ḥanina says: From where [is it derived] that a wicked man is not buried next to a righteous man? As it is stated: "And it came to pass, as they were burying a man, that behold, they spied a raiding party; and they cast the man into the tomb of Elisha; and the man, he touched the bones of Elisha, and he revived and stood up on his feet" (II Kings 13:21)...
>
> Just as a wicked man is not buried next to a righteous man, so an extremely wicked man is not buried next to a less wicked

> man. [If so,] let them establish four graveyards. It is learned as a tradition [that there are] two graveyards. (Sanhedrin 47a)

This is the source for the custom in Jewish law that people should be buried next to those of similar religious stature, with the very pious separated from the less pious.[1]

Nevertheless, the rabbis argue about the status of this law. On one hand, the Rambam omits this law; on the other hand, others – like Rabbi Moshe Sofer – understood that this is a law given to Moshe at Sinai and accordingly has the status of a biblical law.[2] Similarly, Rabbi Avraham Yitzchak Kook claimed that because this law is derived from the prophet Elisha, it has the weight of biblical law.[3] Rabbi Yaakov ben Moshe Levi Moelin (Maharil; Germany, 1365–1427) deems the principle a more general custom with mystical connotations.[4]

Theoretically, the sources mentioned above prohibit burying a non-Jewish soldier in a Jewish cemetery. However, other sources indicate otherwise. The Gemara (Gittin 61a) states: "One sustains poor gentiles with poor Jews, and one visits sick gentiles with sick Jews, and one buries dead gentiles with dead Jews – on account of the ways of peace" (Gittin 61a). The Gemara's phrasing, "One buries dead gentiles with dead Jews," might be understood to mean that not only do we bury non-Jews, but we bury them with Jews in the same place. Rashi, anticipating an improper interpretation of this sort, explains: "But not in the graves of Jews; rather we tend to their funeral needs if they are found dead among Jews."[5]

Rabbi Nissim of Girona (the Ran) quotes the above opinion of Rashi and explains that although Rashi's language seems to imply that the obligation to bury non-Jews applies only when they are found together with Jews, this is not the case; rather the obligation to tend to their dead applies even when they are found dead by themselves. The

1. *Shulḥan Arukh, Yoreh De'ah* 362:5.
2. *Ḥatam Sofer, Yoreh De'ah* 341.
3. *Daat Kohen: Teshuvot BeHalakhot Shulḥan Arukh Yoreh De'ah, siman* 201.
4. Maharil, *Semaḥot* 10.
5. Gittin 61a, s.v. *Im meitei Yisrael.*

Ran, like Rashi, holds that according to Jewish law it is forbidden to bury them together.

As noted, the Rambam does not mention the law of not burying the righteous with the less righteous in *Mishneh Torah*. However, the obligation of burying the dead, both Jews and non-Jews, is found in numerous places in *Mishneh Torah*. While the phrase "to bury their dead in addition to the Jewish dead" is mentioned in *Hilkhot Melakhim* 10:12, it does not appear in *Hilkhot Avel* 14:12.

Rabbi Yoel Sirkis, the *Baḥ*, explains the meaning of this inconsistency:

> It seems that his use of the phrase "in addition to the Jewish dead" does not imply that if the non-Jew is found alone, we do not tend to the burial. Of course, even in the absence of Jewish dead, we bury a non-Jew…
>
> The Rambam's terminology, however, does give implicit permission in the case of a non-Jew found dead among Jewish dead. In such a case, the non-Jew may be buried in a Jewish cemetery. Even though we do not bury a non-Jew alongside a Jew… we may, however bury this non-Jew in our cemetery in the interests of peace.[6]

Rabbi Yehuda Shaviv, a prominent Torah scholar from Alon Shevut who passed away in late 2018, wrote an article on the topic, arguing that in delicate situations like this one, the soldiers should be buried in a Jewish military cemetery.[7] His arguments include the opinion of the *Baḥ* quoted above and several other claims:

1. As mentioned above, the source for separation in cemeteries today is learned from the custom to separate the wicked from the less wicked in killings mandated by religious courts. There are rare cases in halakha in which it is possible (as in the case of a person sentenced to death by a court) to determine who is

6. *Bayit Ḥadash, Tur Yoreh De'ah* 151, s.v. *Asur.*
7. "HaNe'ehavim BeḤayehem! UVeMotam?" *Teḥumin* 14 (1993/1994): 319–30.

righteous and who is not, and the degree of that righteousness. However, it is difficult – if not close to impossible – to make these determinations outside of the realm of capital punishment. Moreover, the soldiers who give up their lives for the Jewish people are surely righteous, and deserve their place in the World to Come.

2. When the rabbis of the Talmud enacted rabbinic decrees, they sometimes limited the scope of those decrees to avoid situations that might lead to the undermining of human dignity, *kevod haberiyot*. If our law of separation is only a custom (as the Maharil suggests), surely the respect we owe these fallen soldiers should permit us to bury them together with their Jewish comrades.

Rulings of IDF Chief Rabbis

Rabbi Shlomo Goren writes in his autobiography that when he served as the chief rabbi of the IDF, a British soldier who volunteered to fight for Israel in the War of Independence was killed in battle. When the question of where to bury him was raised, Rabbi Goren allowed his burial with the Jewish soldiers.[8] However, since Rabbi Goren was concerned that the family would want to place a cross on the grave, he chose to place the grave in a separate section within the cemetery.

In 1968, a similar question was raised regarding an officer in the IDF who was killed. The officer's mother was not Jewish, but his father was. Rabbi Goren quotes a talmudic source about R. Ḥanina b. Tradyon, one of the Ten Martyrs who was killed by the Romans for teaching Torah. The Romans wrapped him in a Torah scroll, piled bundles of twigs around him, and placed damp woolen cloths on him to prolong the agony of being burned to death.

> His pupils advised him: "Open your mouth, that the fire may enter and put an end to your sufferings."
>
> R. Ḥanina replied, "It is best that He who has given the soul should also take it away: no man may hasten his death."

8. Rabbi Shlomo Goren, *With Might and Strength*, trans. Miryam Blum, ed. Avi Rath (Jerusalem: Maggid, 2016), 167–68.

> ... Thereupon the executioner removed the wool and fanned the flame, thus accelerating the end, and then himself plunged into the flames. (Avoda Zara 18a)

The Gemara adds that a voice from heaven declared that the executioner (who was not Jewish) was welcomed together with R. Ḥanina to enter the World to Come.

Rabbi Goren concludes: "From all this, it is clear that even a foreigner who gives up his life for the people of Israel has a part in the World to Come, even if he does not convert to our faith. It seems that the same applies regarding burying him in a Jewish cemetery."[9]

During his tenure as chief rabbi of the IDF, Rabbi Yisrael Weiss proposed a solution to the problem. The solution was formulated in consultation with Rabbi Yosef Shalom Elyashiv, Rabbi Mordekhai Eliyahu, and Rabbi Ovadia Yosef. The proposed solution was the establishment of designated plots for non-Jewish casualties in the middle of the military cemetery.[10] The plot in this case is identical to the other plots and tombs in the cemetery, so that on entering the cemetery, one cannot notice any difference between the graves.

A later IDF chief rabbi, Rabbi Rafi Peretz, presented a slightly different solution:

> We in the rabbinate decided that the halakhic position would be that the burial of a Jew and non-Jew would be in the same cemetery (although there are different opinions). In the military cemeteries, the difference between the graves will be four cubits (about two meters). These two meters are "swallowed up" in the trees and other things.[11]

---

9. *Terumat HaGoren* (Jerusalem: HaIdra Rabba, 2005), 2:198.
10. For a summary of the solutions, see Eliad Avruch and Lilach Ben-Zvi, "Kevurat Ḥalalei Tzahal SheEinam Yehudim Al Pi HaHalakha," The Institute for Zionist Strategies, November 2015, http://izs.org.il/papers/BurialSoldiers.pdf.
11. From the minutes of the fifty-sixth session of the Knesset Committee on Immigration, Absorption, and Diaspora Affairs, January 30, 2014, https://main.knesset.gov.il/Activity/committees/Immigration/Pages/CommitteeAgenda.aspx?tab=3&ItemID=544877.

Halakhic authorities have made sure to recognize those Israeli soldiers whose status as Jews is called into question when it comes to burial. Although they have not converted to Judaism, these soldiers have a special connection to the Jewish people, and halakha takes this into consideration.

20

The Aliya of Russian Jewry, 1989

How Does Conversion Change with Today's *Kibbutz Galuyot*?

The *kibbutz galuyot* from the Soviet Union was truly miraculous. However, after seventy years of living behind the Iron Curtain, with minimal access to Jewish tradition, and after two thousand years of exile, it is not surprising that the *olim* (immigrants) brought with them many questions regarding their Jewish status. Many Jewish men arrived with wives who were not Jewish; as a result, their children were not considered Jewish by Orthodox halakhic standards. In many cases, even *olim* who were halakhically Jewish had difficulty proving it.

Dilemmas, challenges, and difficult questions regarding conversion have been discussed throughout Jewish history. However, the situation in this case was fundamentally different for a number of reasons: First, the number of people seeking to convert skyrocketed, requiring more personnel. Second, the motivations for converting were different than they had once been. Many of the immigrants were interested in becoming part of the Jewish community without the belief or practice. In other words, they were interested in becoming Israeli.

CONVERSION IN JUDAISM

There are many commandments in the Torah regarding the special way we must behave toward converts. We must love them; we must be kind and sensitive to them. But is there a commandment to convert a non-Jew?[1]

Rabbi Shimon ben Tzemach Duran, known as the Rashbatz, wondered why the great rabbis who compiled lists of all the 613 commandments omitted the commandment of conversion. He quotes the Gemara, which teaches us that once a potential convert shows seriousness in accepting the Jewish faith, we convert him immediately. The reason: "We do not delay [when it comes to a] commandment" (Yevamot 47b). This statement seems to indicate that there is a positive commandment for the court to assist non-Jews who are interested in joining the Jewish faith. While some argue that conversion is part of specific commandments, the Rashbatz disagrees: after arguing that the commandment of conversion should be listed separately, he contends that he does not see how this law could be included in the other commandments that appear on the lists.[2]

Rabbi Yehuda Gershuni attempts to answer the Rashbatz's challenge.[3] He seems to agree that there is a biblical commandment to convert non-Jews, but asserts that it might be included in the commandment to love God. He then quotes the Rambam, who explains what is included in the commandment of loving God:[4]

> The third commandment is that we are commanded to love God, i.e., to meditate upon and closely examine His commandments,

---

1. For a complete discussion of this topic, see Gad Eldad, "Tokef HaḤiyuv LeKabel Gerim," *Teḥumin* 18 (1997/1998): 210–18. Rabbi Shlomo Goren also holds that there is a commandment of conversion; see *Torat HaShabbat VeHaMoed* (Jerusalem: World Zionist Organization, 1982), 206–7.
2. *Zohar HaRakia* 28.
3. *Sefer Kol Tzofayikh,* 503–5.
4. *Sefer HaMitzvot,* positive commandment 3.

> His utterances, and His works, in order to understand Him; and through this understanding, to achieve a feeling of ecstasy. This is the goal of the commandment to love God.
>
> *Our Sages also said that this mitzva includes calling out to all mankind to serve God (exalted be He) and to believe in Him.* This is because when one loves a person, for example, one praises him and calls out to others to draw close to him. So too, if one truly loves God – through one's understanding and realization of His true existence – one will certainly spread this true knowledge to the ignorant and the foolish. [We see that this commandment includes spreading love for God to others] as the *Sifrei* states: "'You shall love God' (Deut. 6:5) – make Him beloved among the creatures as your father Avraham did, as it is written (Gen. 12:5), 'The people they had gathered in Haran.'"
>
> The meaning of this passage in the *Sifrei* is as follows: Avraham, as a result of his deep understanding of God, acquired love for God, as the verse (Is. 41:8) testifies, "Avraham, who loved Me." This powerful love therefore caused him to call out to all mankind to believe in God. So too, one must love Him to the extent that one draws others to Him. (Emphasis mine.)

Rabbi Yehuda Yerucham Fishel Perlow (Poland, 1846–1934) similarly suggests that the commandment of conversion is included in another one. Basing himself on the view of the Ri of Barcelona (Rabbi Judah ben Barzillai; Spain, eleventh/twelfth century), he claims that the acceptance of converts who truly desire to become part of the Jewish nation and keep the Torah is a commandment upon Jews and is part of the obligation to love the convert.[5]

This discussion is crucial; if there is a commandment on the Jewish people or on the court system to help those who wish to join the Jewish people, then we must offer assistance, guidance, and companionship.

5. Commentary of Rabbi Yehuda Yerucham Fishel Perlow to *Sefer HaMitzvot Shel HaRasag*, end of positive commandment 19.

Acceptance of the Commandments

As a result of the many conversions taking place in recent years, a severe disagreement within the religious community regarding the degree to which we should be stringent about the conversion process is taking place. The disagreement focuses on halakha's requirement of *kabbalat hamitzvot*, acceptance of the Torah's laws.[6] The Gemara quotes a *baraita* which states that a non-Jew who wishes to convert must accept the entire framework of Torah and commandments: "A gentile who comes to accept the words of the Torah except for one matter, he is not accepted. R. Yosei, son of R. Yehuda, says: Even one detail of rabbinic law" (Bekhorot 30b).

Accordingly, the conversion process mandates that the prospective convert accept observance of the commandments; failure to do so renders the conversion invalid. Although many opinions have argued that this is not clear-cut, it seems that the accepted practice has been to follow the ruling of Rabbi Yosef Karo, who distinguishes between ab initio (*lekhatḥila*) and ex post facto (*bediavad*).

> All matters of the convert – from informing them of the mitzvot and their acceptance of them, the circumcision, and the immersion – must be [performed] in the presence of three who are fit to judge and during the day. This, however, is only *lekhatḥila*, but *bediavad*, if [the convert] undergoes circumcision or immersion in the presence of two or at night ... this one is a [valid] convert and may marry a Jew. *However, when it comes to accepting the commandments, the conversion is invalidated* if this is performed not during the day or not in the presence of three [judges].[7] (Emphasis mine.)

6. For a complete discussion on this topic, see Rabbi Chaim Navon's article, "Acceptance of the Mitzvot as a Requirement for Conversion," The Israel Koschitzky Torat Har Etzion VBM, December 25, 2016, https://etzion.org.il/en/acceptance-*mitzvot*-requirement-conversion.
7. *Shulḥan Arukh, Yoreh De'ah* 268:3.

There is an argument among the *posekim* as to how to understand the position of the Rambam on this matter. On one hand, the Rambam explicitly writes in various places that the acceptance of commandments is indeed a prerequisite for conversion:

1. If he rejects even one thing, he is not accepted.[8]
2. If the non-Jew wishes to enter the covenant...and accept the yoke of Torah...[9]
3. Or if he should become a righteous convert and accept all the commandments.[10]

On the other hand, in the following law, he seems to imply that, *bediavad,* acceptance of the commandments is not an indispensable requirement for conversion:

> When a court did not check a [potential] convert's background and did not inform him of the mitzvot and the punishment for [the failure to observe] the mitzvot and he circumcised himself and immersed in the presence of three ordinary people, he is a convert. Even if it is discovered that he converted for an ulterior motive, since he circumcised himself and converted, he has departed from the category of non-Jews and we view him with skepticism until his righteousness is revealed.[11]

Many quote Sephardi Chief Rabbi Ben-Zion Uziel (1880–1953) as the sole opinion who seems to maintain that the prospective convert must be informed about commandments but is not necessarily required to commit to their observance, so that acceptance of the commandments is not required even *lekhatḥila:*

8. *Mishneh Torah, Hilkhot Issurei Bia* 14:8.
9. Ibid., 13:4.
10. Ibid., *Hilkhot Melakhim* 10:9.
11. Ibid., *Hilkhot Issurei Bia* 13:17.

> It is clear from all the above (sources) that we do not require of him to observe the commandments, and the court need not even know that he will observe them. For were this not true, converts would never be accepted, for who can guarantee that this non-Jew will be faithful to all the commandments of the Torah. We inform him about some of the commandments so that he may abandon [the conversion], if he so desires, and so that he not be able to say later that had he known, he would never have converted. This is *lekhatḥila,* but *bediavad,* the failure to inform him does not invalidate [the conversion]. We learn from all that has been stated that accepting the observance of the commandments is not an indispensable requirement for conversion, even *lekhatḥila.*[12]

"National" Interests

Rabbi Yisrael Rozen, founder of the Zomet Institute in Alon Shevut, which promotes the integration of halakha and technology, was appointed to head the Chief Rabbinate's conversion center. He served as director and as a rabbinical judge there during the years 1995–2011. He maintained that the practice in Jewish tradition has always been based on the understanding that without *kabbalat hamitzvot,* a conversion is invalid. In fact, he argued that Rabbi Uziel was misunderstood, and that even he did not claim otherwise.[13]

However, Rabbi Rozen also argued that at these special times of *kibbutz galuyot,* there is room for leniencies within the framework of halakha. For example, he quotes the opinion of the great Torah leader Rabbi Chaim Ozer Grodzinski (Lithuania, 1863–1940):

> It appears that this law – that if a non-Jew who wishes to become a convert accepts all the mitzvot except for a single detail of rabbinic law, we do not accept him – only applies where he stipulates that he does not accept [that one detail] and that it should be permitted to him by right. In such a case, we do not accept him, for conditions may not be attached to conversion, and there is

12. *Piskei Uziel* 65.
13. "Mediniyut HaGiyur BeYisrael," *Teḥumin* 36 (2015/2016): 319, n. 2.

> no half conversion. If, however, he accepts upon himself all the mitzvot, but he intends to violate [a certain law] to gratify his appetite, this is not regarded as a deficiency in his acceptance of the mitzvot.[14]

Rabbi Rozen argues that only if the courts realize, without any doubt, that the convert has no intention of keeping the commandments is the conversion invalid. However, if the convert claims to accept the commandments, the court has no reason to believe otherwise. Furthermore, he argues that the conversion process should not be adversarial; the judges of the rabbinical court have a responsibility to help converts enter the faith and not question their motives.

Other rabbis have similarly emphasized the issue of national responsibility and argued that the miraculous events of the return of the Jews to the Land of Israel should motivate us to find leniencies in order to aid immigrants who show an interest in joining the Jewish faith. Rabbi Shlomo Rosenfeld, *rosh yeshiva* of Shadmot Neria, writes that since the establishment of the State of Israel, mixed couples have arrived in Israel, and the waves of immigration from the former Soviet Union and Ethiopia have exacerbated this problem. Thus, it is appropriate to implement the principle of "There is a time to act for God" – extenuating halakhic circumstances call for special leniencies.[15]

Similarly, Rabbi David Bass, who is a rabbinical judge on the conversion court, writes that preventing conversion today creates assimilation; conversion has become a national responsibility, since the division of the nation is a threat to its existence. Leniency in conversion has become a way of caring for the spiritual future of the Jewish people.[16]

Other rabbis from the *ḥaredi* community have argued that there is no room for "national" ideology regarding conversion; as a result, they have questioned the legitimacy of the Religious Zionist courts.[17]

---

14. *Shut Aḥi'ezer* 3:26.
15. "Et Laasot LeGiyur Mishpaḥot Me'uravot," *Teḥumin* 17 (1996/1997): 223.
16. "Tokpo Shel Giyur Bediavad Im HaGer Eino Shomer Kol HaMitzvot," *Teḥumin* 23 (2002/2003): 187.
17. For a complete summary of the debate between the *ḥaredi* rabbis and the "nationalist" rabbis, see Rabbi Yosef Tzvi Rimon's article, "Modern-day Ashkenazi Psak regarding

National Identity

We have mentioned the importance of *kabbalat hamitzvot* as part of a convert's entering into the Jewish faith. However, specific actions are required for one to become Jewish. Basing his view on the Gemara, the Rambam describes the full process of conversion:

> For [all] future generations, when a non-Jew desires to enter into the covenant, take shelter under the wings of the Divine Presence, and accept the yoke of the Torah, he must perform circumcision, immersion, and the offering of a sacrifice.[18]

Accordingly, the Rambam says:

> Whether a convert is circumcised, but does not immerse himself; or immerses himself, but is not circumcised – he is not considered a convert until he performs both of these activities.[19]

Rabbi Joseph Soloveitchik understands that circumcision and immersion in a *mikve* symbolize the two main components of Jewish identity. He explains:

> The Torah relates that the Holy One concluded two Covenants with Israel. One Covenant was made in Egypt. "And I shall take you unto Me for a people, and I will be to you a God" (Exodus 6:7). The second Covenant was at Mount Sinai. "And he [Moses] took the book of the covenant … and he said: 'Behold the blood of the covenant which the Lord made with you in agreement with all these words'" (Exodus 24:7–8) …
>
> What is the essence of these two Covenants?… Just as Judaism distinguished fate from destiny in the realm of personal individuality, so it also differentiated between these two concepts

the Nullification of Conversion," in *Conversion, Intermarriage, and Jewish Identity*, ed. Adam Mintz and Marc D. Stern (Jerusalem: Urim, 2015), 261–91.

18. *Mishneh Torah, Hilkhot Issurei Bia* 13:1–4.
19. Ibid., 13:6.

> in the sphere of our national-historical existence. The individual is tethered to his nation with bonds of fate and chains of destiny. In accordance with this postulate, one can say that the Covenant of Egypt was a Covenant of Fate, and the Covenant of Sinai was one of destiny.
>
> What is the Covenant of Fate? Fate signifies in the life of the nation, as it does in the life of the individual, an existence of compulsion. A strange force merges all individuals into one unit. The individual is subject and subjugated against his will to the national fate/existence, and it is impossible for him to avoid it and be absorbed into a different reality. The environment expels the Jew who flees from the presence of God, so that he is awakened from his slumber, like Jonah the prophet, who awoke to the voice of the ship's captain demanding to know his personal national-religious identity.[20]

When explaining the meaning of the Covenant of Fate, Rabbi Soloveitchik stresses the importance of being part of the Jewish nation, feeling the pain and sorrow of the Jewish nation and sharing its fate. The motto of this covenant is: "All Israel are bound together (*ḥaverim*)" (Sota 37a). We are all persecuted – or we are all saved – together.

Rabbi Soloveitchik explains the second covenant as follows:

> What is the Covenant of Destiny? In the life of a people (as in the life of an individual), destiny signifies an existence that it has chosen of its own free will and in which it finds the full realization of its historical existence.

Here the motto is:

> The proclamation that "We shall do, and we shall hear" (Exodus 24:7) is the foundation of the Torah.[21]

20. *Kol Dodi Dofek* (New York: Yeshiva University, 2006), 52.
21. Ibid., 65–66.

Rabbi Soloveitchik later explains that circumcision symbolizes the Covenant of Fate, while immersion in a *mikve* symbolizes the Covenant of Destiny.

If we understand that fate relates to Jewish identity and destiny has to do with the religious side of Judaism, then the process of joining the Jewish family must be both in the realm of nationality and in that of religion. Thus, we could restate the Rambam's ruling as follows: a convert who wishes to be Jewish and not religious or vice versa is not fully Jewish. In the words of Rabbi Soloveitchik:

> A non-Jew who wishes to join the nation must take upon himself both covenants. He places himself in the ambit of Jewish fate and sanctifies himself for the acceptance of the Jewish destiny. The act of conversion involves associating oneself as a member of the people of the Covenants of Egypt and of Sinai. Keep this important principle in mind: there is no such thing as partial conversion. One cannot omit one *iota* of either of these two Covenants. Total devotion to the Jewish people – as a nation that God took to Himself in Egypt, with all its tribulations, suffering, responsibilities, and actions; and as a holy people that is itself consecrated, heart and soul, to the God of Israel and His halakhic and moral demands – is the absolute foundation of Judaism and hence is also the basis of conversion.[22]

This idea that joining the Jewish faith consists of first joining the Jewish nation may be proven from the questions we ask the potential convert. The motive for asking these questions is to investigate if the convert is committed to the faith. We attempt to discourage the potential convert by laying out the difficulties of the religion. The Gemara lists the questions:

> What did you see that [motivated] you [to] come to convert? Don't you know that the Jewish people at the present time are anguished, suppressed, despised, and harassed, and hardships are [frequently] visited upon them? If he says: I know, and I am

22. Ibid., 73–74.

> unworthy, [then the court] accepts him immediately. And [the judges] inform him [of] some of the lenient mitzvot and some of the stringent mitzvot, and they inform him [of] the sin [of neglecting the mitzva to allow the poor to take] gleanings, forgotten sheaves, and [produce in the] corner [of one's field], and [about the] poor man's tithe. (Yevamot 47a)

Note that the potential convert is not challenged with the laws of Shabbat or *kashrut,* but rather the commitment to Jewish national identity. When we give him a "taste of the commandments," the Gemara mentions *mitzvot bein adam leḥavero* (commandments between one Jew and another) rather than *mitzvot bein adam laMakom* (commandments between a Jew and God).

As noted, many of the immigrants from the former USSR who are not considered Jewish by Orthodox halakhic standards have joined the Covenant of Fate and the national identity of the Jewish people.

Is national acceptance without the acceptance of commandments sufficient? This idea has been raised by some authorities.[23] The commonly accepted ruling rejects this approach and promotes the combination of *kabbalat hamitzvot* and the acceptance of national identity. Still, the question remains: How can this element not be a major factor when one faces the challenges of conversion today? This is an issue that halakhic authorities in Israel will continue to address.

---

23. See Zvi Zohar and Avraham Sagi in *Giyur VeZehut Yehudit* (Jerusalem: Machon Shalom Hartman and Mosad Bialik, 1997), 186–87; and Michael J. Broyde and Shmuel Kadosh, "Review Essay: *Transforming Identity* by Avi Sagi and Zvi Zohar," *Tradition* 42 (2009): 84–103.

21

The Gulf War, 1991

May One Leave Israel in Times of Danger?

On August 2, 1990, Iraq invaded Kuwait. The world condemned the act and a strong international coalition formed, under the leadership of the US, against Iraq. On January 17, 1991, coalition air forces attacked Iraq. In response, Iraq fired missiles into Israel. Iraq had threatened to attack Israel with various types of weapons, including non-conventional ordnance, with the declared aim of destroying a significant part of the country. For the first time in Israel's history, the entire country faced a real threat of destruction by non-conventional weapons.

In view of the unprecedented danger to the home front, the Israeli government ordered the IDF to distribute gas masks to the entire population and instructed the public to prepare "safe rooms" for use in case an alarm was sounded. Israel became the first country since World War II to provide its entire population with gas masks and protection kits. Over the next month, approximately thirty-eight Scud missiles fell in nineteen missile attacks; each warhead was considered a potential chemical weapon. These missiles mainly hit the greater Tel Aviv region and Haifa. As sirens went off around the country, millions of Israelis ran to so-called safe rooms with their gas masks, fearing a chemical attack. Ultimately, no gas or chemicals were found in the missiles. While the attacks caused very few deaths, there was a lot of damage to property.

For the first time in Israel's history, the home front served as the main theater of hostilities; for the first time ever, the IDF devoted its main operational efforts to defending civilians and coordinating wartime activities between government offices and emergency services. Concerned that Arab coalition partners might abandon them, the US urged Israel not to actively engage in the war.[1]

Because of these attacks, many tourists and Jewish students from abroad left the country. A similar phenomenon had been witnessed during the Six-Day War, when some people fled the country. The question arose: Should civilians flee the city or not? Jewish students learning at the time in yeshivas debated whether to remain in Israel. Some, pressured by their parents, returned home. What is the halakhic approach to these dilemmas?

FLEEING ISRAEL IN THE FACE OF DANGER

Rabbi Hershel Schachter writes that in 1948, due to the dangers of the war, Rabbi Yitzchok Zev Soloveitchik (the Brisker Rav or Griz; Volozhin/Brisk/Jerusalem, 1886–1959) thought of moving to Switzerland. Rabbi Herzog tried to convince him that he should not leave the Land of Israel; there was no need to fear, he opined, since Jewish tradition relates that there will not be a third destruction. The Brisker Rav answered that he had a tradition from his father, too: when there is shooting, one flees.[2]

Theoretically, the Brisker Rav was correct. The commandment to live in the Land of Israel does not override *pikuaḥ nefesh*. This may be derived from the laws regarding leaving Israel. The Rambam permits leaving Israel for specific reasons:

---

1. Taken from Netanel Lorch, "The Arab-Israeli Wars," Israel Ministry of Foreign Affairs, accessed July 1, 2021, https://mfa.gov.il/MFA/AboutIsrael/History/Pages/The%20Arab-Israeli%20Wars.aspx.
2. *BeIkvei HaTzon* (Jerusalem: Beit HaMidrash DeFlatbush, 1997), 115–16.

> It is forbidden to leave the Land of Israel for the Diaspora at all times except to study Torah, to marry, or to save one's property from the gentiles. After accomplishing these objectives, one must return to the Land of Israel.
>
> Similarly, one may leave the Land of Israel to conduct commercial enterprises. However, it is forbidden to leave with the intent of settling permanently in the Diaspora unless the famine in the Land of Israel is severe.[3]

If one is permitted to leave Israel for the purpose of livelihood, then it is obvious that one may do so when one's life is in danger. On the contrary, we might argue that in the face of danger, one is actually obligated to flee and save oneself! Is one permitted to stay in a dangerous area?

The response may be found in the words of the Rambam following his permission to leave Israel at a time of terrible famine: "Though it is permitted to leave the Land of Israel under these circumstances, it is not pious behavior."[4] However, this conclusion presents a significant problem. If we were to adopt this position, would we encourage all citizens to flee the country every time a war or threat to the State of Israel occurs?

The answer is found within the distinction between the two components of the commandment to live in Israel.[5] The Ramban holds the position that there is a commandment at all times to live in the Land of Israel (*yishuv Eretz Yisrael*). In a lengthy passage, he elaborates:

> We have been commanded to take possession of the land that God gave our forefathers, Avraham, Yitzḥak, and Yaakov, and not leave it in the hands of other nations or in desolation…
>
> This is what the Sages called obligatory war…. And from what they said "Yehoshua's war of conquest," you understand that this mitzva is fulfilled through conquest…

3. *Mishneh Torah, Hilkhot Melakhim* 5:9.
4. Ibid.
5. See Rabbi Yaakov Ariel, *BeOhalah Shel Torah* (Kefar Darom: Torah VeHa'aretz Institute, 2003), vol. 4, chap. 11.

> And I say that the mitzva about which the Sages expanded greatly, namely, living in the Land of Israel, to the point that they said that anyone who leaves it and lives outside the Land [of Israel] should be regarded in your eyes as an idolater.... This is all part of this positive precept, for we have been commanded to take possession of the land and dwell in it. If so, it is a positive precept for [all] generations, binding upon every individual, even during the period of the exile.[6]

Many commentators have understood that this commandment includes two obligations: one for the individual and the other for the public.[7]

As the Ramban mentioned, the commandment to fight for the Land of Israel is included in the commandment of *yishuv Eretz Yisrael.* One is obligated to endanger his life for the conquest of the land. This commandment is obviously a commandment of the public. However, the individual who is commanded to settle the land might not be obligated to give up his life. This can be proven from the above halakha that states that at times of severe famine, one is permitted to travel abroad.

Chief Rabbi of Ramat Gan Rabbi Yaakov Ariel proves otherwise from this halakha. We have mentioned that the Rambam permits, even in times of danger, remaining in the Land of Israel. Rabbi Ariel questions the logic of this position. According to the laws of *pikuaḥ nefesh,* one is obligated to save one's own life; how does the Rambam permit remaining in Israel during a famine? His answer is that the commandment of the individual is connected to the national commandment of *yishuv Eretz Yisrael.* As noted, Jews are obligated to endanger their lives for the Land of Israel and this *heter* applies similarly when the individual fulfills the commandment.[8]

Rabbi Shaul Yisraeli also discusses the question. He concludes that it is prohibited to leave the Land of Israel when we are in a state of war. His reasoning is that the laws of war obligate all Jews to participate

6. Ramban, *Commandments Omitted by the Rambam,* positive commandment 4.
7. See Rabbi Eliezer Waldenberg, "Gidrei Ḥovat HaAliya VeHaHitnaḥalut BaAretz Im Kom HaMedina," *Torah SheBe'al Peh* 32 (1991): 111.
8. *BeOhalah Shel Torah,* vol. 4, chap. 11.

in the war effort. The Rambam mentions the different types of wars that are recognized as a *milḥemet mitzva* (an obligatory or commanded war). One of them is a war fought to deliver Israel from an enemy which attacks it.[9] All wars today in Israel fit this definition, and thus all are obliged to participate in defending the country.[10]

You Shall Not Be Afraid

The Torah teaches us that soldiers must not fear at times of war. The priests and the officers must enforce this law by warning the soldiers of this prohibition:

> When you go out to battle your enemies, and see horses and chariots, an army greater than yours, do not be afraid of them; for the Lord your God, who brought you out of Egypt, He will be with you.
>
> Before you engage in battle, the priest shall come forward and address the men. "Listen, Israel," he shall say to them, "this day you are going into battle against your enemies. Do not lose heart or be afraid, do not panic or dread them..."
>
> And further, "Is there a man here," the officers shall say to the men, "who is afraid or fainthearted? Let him go back home so that his comrades do not become fainthearted along with him." (Deut. 20:1–3, 8)

The Rambam understands that, aside from the prohibition of fearing the enemy, this commandment includes the prohibition of retreating from battle. He writes about the "obligation not to become frightened, nor to flee during battle."[11] In *Sefer HaMitzvot*, he quotes verses that back up his understanding:

> The Torah commanded us not to fear or become frightened of the enemy during war, nor to flee from them. Rather, we are obligated

9. *Mishneh Torah, Hilkhot Melakhim* 4:1.
10. *Eretz Ḥemda* (Jerusalem: Mosad HaRav Kook, 1984), 49–52.
11. Introduction to *Hilkhot Melakhim.*

> to overcome [our fear] and to stand firmly against them, as (Deut. 7:21) states: "Do not panic before them," and (Deut. 3:22) states: "Do not fear them."[12]

Does this commandment apply only to soldiers, or to civilians too? *Sefer HaḤinukh* understands that this commandment applies only to adult men, because only they are obligated to fight.[13] Rabbi Yosef Babad (the *Minḥat Ḥinukh*) questions this assertion; elsewhere he argues that women are obligated to fight in battle and therefore this law should apply to them.[14] It seems that according to both *Sefer HaḤinukh* and *Minḥat Ḥinukh,* the law applies only to soldiers in combat.

During the Gulf War, Rabbi Yaakov Ariel was the chief rabbi of Ramat Gan. He was asked whether or not civilians were permitted to leave the city and find refuge elsewhere. In his written response, he deals with this question as well as with the question regarding leaving the country altogether in times of danger. He mentions that the Ashkenazi chief rabbi of Israel, Rabbi Avraham Shapira, on his visit to Ramat Gan during the Gulf War, claimed that the Rambam in *Sefer HaMitzvot,* as mentioned above, deliberately quotes verses from the Torah that address all Jews directly, rather than soldiers only. He therefore concludes that the commandment applies to the entire nation of Israel.[15]

However, Rabbi Ariel questions this claim by comparing the Rambam's choice of verses elsewhere. In *Mishneh Torah,* when the Rambam describes the importance of showing no fear in the face of the enemy, he chooses verses that are recited to the soldiers as they prepare for battle:

> Once a soldier enters the throes of battle, he should rely on the Hope of Israel and their Savior in times of need. He should realize that he is fighting for the sake of the oneness of God's Name.

12. *Sefer HaMitzvot,* negative commandment 58.
13. Commandment 425.
14. *Minḥat Ḥinukh,* ad loc.
15. Rabbi Yaakov Ariel, "Azivat HaAretz UNetishat HaIr MeḤashash Sakana," *Teḥumin* 12 (1990/1991): 193–99.

> Therefore, he should place his soul in His hand and not show fright or fear.... Anyone who begins to feel anxious and worry in the midst of battle to the point where he frightens himself violates a negative commandment, as it is written (Deut. 20:4): "Do not lose heart or be afraid, do not panic or dread them."
>
> Furthermore, he is responsible for the blood of the entire Jewish nation. If he is not valiant, if he does not wage war with all his heart and soul, it is considered as if he shed the blood of the entire people, as [Deut.] 20:8 states: "Let him go back home so that his comrades do not become fainthearted along with him."[16]

This halakha and the source mentioned in it contradict Rabbi Shapira's conclusion and suggest that the prohibition applies only to soldiers.

Rabbi Ariel offers an answer which resolves the contradiction. His understanding is that the essence of the Torah's prohibition is the concern that fear at time of war will lead to despair and demoralization, which will, in turn, lead to defeat.

In times of war, the entire nation must stand strong against the enemy. The maintenance of national morale is a duty placed upon the individual whether or not that person is personally engaged in war. That explains why the Rambam quotes verses which warn the people that they must not fear the enemy. However, there is a more specific command to the soldier who actually fights the enemy, who is probably more likely to be frightened, as he directly engages the enemy.

Based on this understanding, Rabbi Ariel suggests that our question about civilians fleeing the city would depend on whether or not this would lead to despair among the people and the army. On the contrary, Rabbi Ariel argues, if all the people were to stay in the city and then be injured by missiles, this might lead to a greater feeling of despair. Thus, he concludes, if people wish to move to another city, they are permitted to do so. However, those who feel that their presence in the city will strengthen the morale of the community may remain even in the face of danger.

---

16. *Mishneh Torah, Hilkhot Melakhim* 7:15.

The question of risking one's life by staying in a specific city or within the State of Israel is one that has been addressed by modern halakhic authorities; while they rely on earlier rulings, they must modify their understanding of the dilemma to speak to the state and its wars.

22

Operation Solomon, 1991

What Is the Halakhic Status of the Ethiopian Jewish Community?

Ethiopian Jews (Beta Israel) have been arriving in Israel since the seventies, but it was a dramatic operation in 1991 that proved the state's commitment to this unique group of people. This operation, named Operation Solomon (*Mivtza Shlomo*), brought close to fifteen thousand Ethiopian Jews to Israel over thirty hours in a daring airlift that broke world records for the number of passengers on board one airplane (1,088). Eighteen airplanes from Israel's national airline, El Al, together with twenty-three Israel Air Force planes, participated in the greatest airlift in Israel's history. The operation was conducted in secrecy, as there was some concern that the Ethiopian Jews would be harmed by the rebels who were threatening to take over the country. That Friday night, as the secret operation began, I remember that my *rosh yeshiva* at Yeshivat Or Etzion, Rabbi Haim Drukman, announced in the *beit midrash* that *kibbutz galuyot* was underway at that very moment.

Prior to the operation, during the years 1977–1991, thousands of members of the Ethiopian community had made their way to Israel through Sudan. There they were met by representatives of the Jewish Agency who, together with members of the Mossad and the IDF, gathered them and transported them by air and sea to Israel.

There are quite a few theories regarding the Beta Israel community's presence in Ethiopia and its connection to the Jewish people.[1] One common theory is that they are descendants of the tribe of Dan, which was exiled from Israel among the Ten Tribes in the eighth century BCE. In any case, it appears that the community reached Ethiopia anywhere between the tenth century BCE and the destruction of the Second Temple. During the ninth century of the Common Era, a merchant by the name of Eldad HaDani appeared in Tunisia, claiming that he was from a Jewish community in Ethiopia. Rabbi Tzemah ben Haim, the Gaon of Sura (ninth century), accepted this narrative and endorsed his claim.[2] However, there were rabbis like Rabbi Meir of Rothenburg (Worms, Germany, 1215–1293), who expressed reservations as to the authenticity of the statements.[3]

During the following centuries, there were several encounters between the community and other rabbis and Jewish leaders. The great Italian scholar Rabbi Ovadia of Bertinoro (1445–1550) wrote in a letter from Jerusalem in 1488:

> I saw two of them in Egypt. They are dark-skinned...and one could not tell whether they keep the teaching of the Karaites, or of the Rabbis, for some of their practices resemble the Karaite teaching...

---

1. See Rabbi Menachem Waldman's book, *MeEver LeNahar Kush* (Tel Aviv: Ministry of Defence, 1989); he is an expert on this subject. Rabbi Sharon Shalom's book, *From Sinai to Ethiopia: The Halachic and Conceptual World of Ethiopian Jewry* (Jerusalem: Gefen, 2016), 61–72, has a summary of the community history.
2. The original letter of Rabbi Tzemah was printed in Italy in 1480. See Rabbi J. David Bleich, "Baayat HaḤavashim," *Or HaMizraḥ* 33, no. 3 (Nisan-Tammuz 1984/1985): 235–53, see pp. 235–38.
3. *Teshuvot Maharam Rothenburg* 193.

> but in other things, they appear to follow the instruction of the Rabbis; and they say they are related to the tribe of Dan.[4]

THE ETHIOPIAN JEWISH COMMUNITY IN HALAKHA

The question of the Ethiopian Jewish community's halakhic status is one that has been discussed in the past, but the existence of the State of Israel has made the debate more pressing; the status of the community within a Jewish state is an issue that must be addressed.

The Opinion of the Radbaz

The Radbaz is probably the first important *posek* to recognize the "Jewishness" of the Ethiopian community. In two separate responsa, the Radbaz addresses the status of the Beta Israel community.

In the first, he is asked for his opinion regarding the status of a woman from a town in Ethiopia that was attacked; the males were killed, while the women and children were taken captive. The woman in question, whose husband was presumably among the dead, was purchased as a slave by a Jew, who subsequently entered into a sexual liaison with her which resulted in the birth of a son. Two questions are raised regarding this case: Is the woman in question Jewish? If she is, then a second concern arises regarding the status of the woman's child – whether or not he is considered a *mamzer* (a person born of a forbidden relationship). The reasoning behind this assumption is that the community does not practice Jewish law and therefore no proper form of Jewish divorce could ever have been used. Thus, any form of divorce would not be halakhically recognized, and the children may be *mamzerim*.

Regarding the first question, the Radbaz states: "It is clear that she is of the seed of Yisrael, of the tribe of Dan."[5] Regarding the second, he rules that there is no validity to their marriages since marriage requires two halakhically acceptable witnesses. Radbaz compares the Beta Israel to the Karaites, who do not accept the Oral Torah and therefore are disqualified from serving as witnesses. Since a valid marriage does not exist, it follows that a bill of divorce for its dissolution is superfluous.

4. Avraham Ya'ari, *Iggerot Eretz Yisrael* (Ramat Gan: Masada, 1971).
5. *Shut Radbaz* 7:9.

Thus, there is no concern that the children are *mamzerim*. In light of these considerations, marriage to a woman from the Beta Israel community is permissible.

In a second responsum, the Radbaz is asked his opinion regarding a Jew who bought a slave from the Beta Israel community. Here again, the question is whether or not the person in question is Jewish. The Radbaz again argues that the community are to be considered Jewish (note the use of the term *Falasha* for Beta Israel, a term which is now regarded as offensive and inappropriate):

> With regard to the *Falasha* slave, since it has become clear that he is a Jew, this purchase is naught but the ransom of captives, not the purchase of a slave, and the obligation was incumbent upon all of Israel to redeem him.
>
> ...those Jews who come from the land of Kush are without doubt from the tribe of Dan, and since they did not have in their midst sages who were masters of the tradition, they clung to the simple meaning of the Scriptures. If they had been taught, however, they would not be irreverent toward the words of our sages, so their status is comparable to a Jewish infant taken captive by non-Jews... and even if you say that the matter is in doubt, it is a commandment to redeem them.[6]

There is no doubt that the Radbaz believes that these people are descendants of the tribe of Dan and are Jewish.

The Modern Approach to Ethiopian Jewry

In 1973, Rabbi Ovadia Yosef – then the Sephardi chief rabbi – ruled that the Beta Israel are Jews and should be brought to Israel. His reasoning was based in large part on the Radbaz.

> I have therefore come to the conclusion that the *Falasha* are the descendants of the tribes of Israel who emigrated southwards to Kush. There can be no doubt that the authorities who declared

6. *Shut HaRadbaz* 7:5.

> them from among the tribe of Dan investigated and examined the evidence thoroughly and reached this conclusion on the basis of the most reliable testimony and evidence. I too... have investigated and examined this matter thoroughly after the leaders of the community approached me...
>
> I have decided that, in my humble opinion, the *Falasha* are Jews who must be saved from assimilation. We should promote their immigration to the Land, educate them in the way of our holy Torah, and include them in the building of the Holy Land. Thus "the children shall return to their own border" (Jer. 31:16).[7]

Two years later, his opinion was confirmed by other authorities who made similar rulings, including Chief Ashkenazi Rabbi Shlomo Goren.[8]

It is important to note that Rav Ovadia's ruling was unprecedented in the history of the State of Israel; it was solely based on this decision that the government decided to apply the Law of Return in this case, ensuring the aliya of the entire community from Ethiopia.

However, not all rabbis are in complete agreement with the chief rabbis.[9] In June 1984, Rabbi Moshe Feinstein addressed the matter in a private letter to Rabbi Mordechai Tendler.[10] After quoting the Radbaz, Rabbi Feinstein argues: "However, for practical application of the law it is difficult to rely on this, for it is not clear if the Radbaz knew well the reality regarding them, nor is it clear whether up until our time their status has [remained the same and] not changed." It is therefore easy to understand why Rabbi Moshe Feinstein demands the following: "Regarding their Judaism, we must consider it a *safek* (doubt), and we must require of them true conversion before we permit them to marry within the Jewish community."

7. This letter appears in a footnote to the responsum printed in *Yabia Omer, Even HaEzer* 8:11.
8. *Torat HaMedina,* 172–207.
9. See Bleich, "Baayat HaḤavashim," 239, as well as "Black Jews: A Halakhic Perspective," *Tradition* 15, no. 1–2 (1975): 49–57.
10. This letter appears in Michael Corinaldi, *Ethiopian Jewry: Identity and Tradition* (Jerusalem: Hebrew University Magnes Press, 1998), 211. It was printed as "Ḥovat Kerovam Shel Yehudei Etiopiya," *Teḥumin* 12 (1990/1991): 98.

However, at the same time, he argues that the Jewish people have a responsibility toward this community:

> Nevertheless, even before their conversion, it is an active precept to save them from being drawn into a non-Jewish creed and from danger, as the law is for any Jew, for *safek nefashot lehakel* (a doubt involving saving lives is judged leniently), even though here the doubt is in their very status as Jews.
>
> One should also know that even if in practical application of the law they are not Jews, *nevertheless, since they think they are Jews and sacrifice their lives for their Judaism, we are obligated to save them.* (Emphasis mine.)

Rabbi Feinstein makes an interesting point, and although it is not directly relevant to our discussion, I find it important enough to mention. Practically speaking, Rabbi Feinstein believes that the members of the community should convert before arriving in Israel. Once the process is complete, Rabbi Feinstein emphasizes our commitment to them:

> If they have legally converted, as I have heard they are doing, we shall consider them like all Jews, and one must assist them and support them for all needs of livelihood, both physically and spiritually. And I suffered great anguish because I have heard there are those in Israel who are not drawing them close in spiritual matters and are causing, God forbid, that they might be lost from Judaism. *And it seems to me these people are behaving so only because the color of the Falasha's skin is black.* It is obvious that one must draw them close, not only because they are no worse than the rest of the Jews – *and because there is no distinction in practical application of the law because they are black* – but also because, one might say, they are *gerim* (converts), and are therefore included in the commandment "And you shall love the convert." (Emphasis mine.)

Israel's Ethiopian Jews: Halakha in Practice

Based on the above opinions, do the Ethiopian Jews require conversion? There seem to be three opinions regarding this question.

As we saw, Rabbi Moshe Feinstein and others argue that regular conversion is required.

A second opinion asserts that they must undergo a modified conversion (*giyur leḥumra)*, which is a ceremony involving immersion in a *mikve*, a declaration accepting Rabbinic Law, and for men, a symbolic re-circumcision. In an article printed in 1983, Rabbi Menachem Waldman quotes Rav Ovadia's ruling in which he recognized that the Beta Israel are Jewish. However, Rabbi Waldman mentions that in practice both chief rabbis, Rabbi Goren and Rabbi Yosef, required *giyur leḥumra* (the convert was required to follow the more stringent opinion and perform a conversion that included committing to observance and immersion).[11] In fact, during the 1970s and early 1980s, the Beta Israel were indeed required to undergo *giyur leḥumra*. Rabbi Sharon Shalom, a leader in the Ethiopian community today and graduate of Yeshivat Har Etzion, notes in his book that the *rashei yeshiva*, Rabbi Lichtenstein and Rabbi Amital, required that he and his friends perform *giyur leḥumra*.[12]

Lastly, in a second response to our question, written in 1985, Rav Ovadia argues explicitly that there is no need for conversion at all.[13]

Mamzerut Questions

If one follows Rabbi Feinstein, believing that Beta Israel are not Jewish from birth and require regular conversion, then questions of *mamzerut* are not relevant. However, if we assume that they are Jewish by birth, this becomes an issue, because halakhic marriage and divorce were not practiced within what is ostensibly a Jewish community.

Although the Radbaz clearly claims in both of the abovementioned responsa that the Beta Israel are descendants of the tribe of Dan, there appears to be confusion regarding his opinion on the question of *mamzerut*. The two responsa seem to contradict one another. In the first responsum, Radbaz refers to them as akin to Karaites, which means that they are disqualified to serve as witnesses. In the second responsum, he

11. "Daat Ḥakhmei Yisrael Al Yehudei Etiopiya ('HaFalashim')," *Teḥumin* 4 (1982/1983): 325–26.
12. Shalom, *From Sinai to Ethiopia*, 15.
13. *Yabia Omer, Even HaEzer* 8:11.

compares them to Jewish infants taken captive, in which case they may serve as witnesses; thus, their marriages would be valid and the problem of *mamzerut* would exist.

Chief Rabbi Shlomo Amar addresses this contradiction and assures us that the Radbaz does not hold that the tribe of Dan has a problem of *mamzerut*.[14] He quotes Rabbi Ovadia Yosef, who argues that the Radbaz and other *posekim* are not concerned with issues of *mamzerut*. Rav Ovadia asserts that the Radbaz retracted his opinion that the Beta Israel might be considered *mamzerim*, as there are many other doubts involved in this issue.

Rabbi Feinstein, who requires full conversion, agrees that even according to those who do not require conversion, there is no concern of *mamzerut*: In his letter, he states: "But in regard to practical application of the law, they are not *mamzerim* or the like, for the Radbaz mentions that many doubts apply to them."

The ingathering of Jews from all corners of the earth is truly one of the most miraculous events in Jewish history. In this case, the return of descendants of the Ten Tribes is a remarkable indication of the special times in which we are living and a fascinating example of halakha's development within the Jewish state.

14. "Yiḥus Olei Etiopiya," *Teḥumin* 23 (2002/2003): 343.

23

The Massacre at Maarat HaMakhpela, 1994

May One Take the Law into One's Own Hands?

The First Intifada lasted from December 1987 until the Madrid Conference in 1991; some date its conclusion to 1993, with the signing of the Oslo Accords. During this first Palestinian uprising, 172 Israelis were killed. In the Oslo Accords, Israel recognized the "right of the Palestinian people to self-determination." On the other side, Palestinian representatives recognized the State of Israel.

These accords created the Palestinian Authority and negotiations continued for a number of years, until the process ended after the failure of Camp David II in 2000, which led to the outbreak of the Second Intifada. During the Palestinian uprising, violent clashes erupted throughout Yehuda, Shomron, and Gaza. As the main emergency doctor of the Ḥevron area, American-born Dr. Baruch Goldstein was involved in treating victims of Arab-Israeli violence during those years. On December 6, 1993, Mordechai Lapid and his son Shalom Lapid were killed by terrorists in Ḥevron. Goldstein, a close friend of the family, arrived at the scene and tended to the victims.

On Purim morning, February 25, 1994, at five in the morning, Goldstein entered Maarat HaMakhpela and opened fire, killing 29 Muslims and wounding another 125, among them children. During the massacre, he was overcome, disarmed, and beaten to death.

The vast majority of Israeli society condemned the massacre, voicing shock and dismay. Prime Minister Yitzhak Rabin denounced Goldstein. In the Knesset, he declared:

> You are not part of the community of Israel.... You are not part of the national democratic camp which we all belong to in this house, and many of the people despise you. You placed yourself outside the wall of Jewish law.... We say to this horrible man and those like him: you are a shame on Zionism and an embarrassment to Judaism.[1]

Opposition Leader Binyamin Netanyahu stated: "This was a despicable crime. I express my unequivocal condemnation."

THE RABBINICAL RESPONSE TO THE MASSACRE

Although most rabbis came out vehemently against Goldstein, there were a few who failed to do so. Both chief rabbis of Israel voiced strong condemnation of the attack. Sephardi Chief Rabbi Eliyahu Bakshi-Doron declared: "I am simply ashamed that a Jew carried out such a villainous and irresponsible act." His Ashkenazi counterpart, Rabbi Yisrael Meir Lau, called it "a desecration of God's name."[2]

Rosh Yeshivat Har Etzion Rabbi Aharon Lichtenstein composed a letter to his colleagues at other Hesder yeshivas:

---

1. Quoted in Clyde Haberman, "West Bank Massacre: The Overview; Rabin Urges the Palestinians to Put Aside Anger and Talk," *New York Times*, March 1, 1994.
2. Quotes taken from "Statement by Ambassador Gad Yaacobi of Israel to the United Nations," Israel Ministry of Foreign Affairs, accessed July 1, 2021, https://mfa.gov.il/MFA/InternatlOrgs/Speeches/Pages/Ambassador%20Yaacobi%20to%20the%20UN%20Security%20Council%20on%20t.aspx.

> Therefore, I must vigorously protest against what transpired last night before all of Israel and the entire world. A person, whatever his previous merits may have been, departed this world while engaged in an act of awful and terrible slaughter, *tevah ayom ve-nora*, and thereby, beyond the crime itself, desecrated the name of Heaven, trampled upon the honor of the Torah and *mitzvot*, soiled and sullied the image of *Kenesset Yisrael*, and endangered the future of [Jewish] settlement in Yehudah, Shomron, and Gaza. This man won praise and honor in the yeshiva of his hometown, in Kiryat Arba, and was eulogized "*ke-halakha*," with full ceremonial honor, by her *Rosh Yeshiva*.
>
> Woe to the ears that hear this! But, if it has been decreed that we must hear it, at least there should be a clear protest which expresses not just disassociation, but also disgust and shock. We must do so, not to protect our public image, but to preserve our self-image.[3]

Rabbi Dov Lior, *rosh yeshiva* of the Nir Hesder yeshiva in Kiryat Arba, responded to the letter and defended his position; he had delivered a eulogy for Goldstein in his yeshiva. His central approach was that although he did not necessarily support the massacre, he felt it was appropriate to honor other periods and acts from Goldstein's life:

> Indeed, I eulogized the late Baruch Goldstein (may *Hashem* avenge his blood), who was lynched by the non-Jews in the Cave [of Makhpela]. A Jew who is killed because he is a Jew must certainly be called *kadosh*, a holy martyr, just as we refer to the *kedoshei ha-Shoa*, the holy martyrs of the Holocaust, without investigating their previous conduct. How much more so in this case, for we knew him intimately as God-fearing and compassionate, as one who loved humanity and saved lives.

3. Aharon Lichtenstein, Avraham Kurzweil, Shmuel Haber, and Dov Leor, "A Rabbinic Exchange on Baruch Goldstein's Funeral," *Tradition: A Journal of Orthodox Jewish Thought* 28, no. 4 (Summer 1994): 59. Quotes from this article are translations of the authors' original letters.

> Even if someone holds the opinion that his final act was improper, *lo haya ke-shura*, why should he not be entitled to a eulogy *ke-halakha*? In my eulogy, I intentionally did not address the deed itself, but rather his personality and his achievements, and I did not take a public position on the deed itself.[4]

In his response, Rabbi Lior attempted to understand the context that had led Goldstein to commit the massacre:

> I marvel that great Torah sages, lovers of Israel, are quick to judge an individual without knowing the background and circumstances in which he acted and which compelled him to act. Perhaps this was a situation of "his heart coerced him" (T.B. *Shevuot* 26a), for he was the first to see the spilling of blood in the area; people died before his eyes, and (he) also (heard) the cry "Slaughter the Jews! (Atbah al-Yahud!)" on Purim night and (saw) the disgrace of the Jewish people. All these together, I assume, caused him to do this extreme deed.
>
> I repeat that my purpose in these remarks is not to formulate a conclusive judgment, but rather to judge favorably, *le-lammed zekhut*, as we are commanded to judge our fellow Jews favorably [*Avot* 1:6].
>
> I hope the honorable rabbi will understand the spirit of my words, which are said in pain and distress, and may *Hashem* bind up His people's wounds [Isaiah 30:26].

In a second letter, responding to the *rashei yeshiva* of Yeshivat Hesder Karnei Shomron, Rabbi Lichtenstein protested the silence of all other *rashei yeshiva,* not only in face of the massacre, but also in the face of Rabbi Lior's description of Goldstein as a holy martyr:

> Thus, the question begs to be asked: Why were you silent then? Why was no protest heard from those in our community, *mi-pi anshei shelomeinu,* who champion your political views, against the

4. Ibid., 61.

> tribute given in a *yeshivat hesder* to (as Rabbi Leor wrote in his response to me) "the late Baruch Goldstein (may *Hashem* avenge his blood), who was lynched by the non-Jews in the Cave [of Makhpela]. A Jew who is killed because he is a Jew must certainly be called *kadosh,* a holy martyr, just as we refer to the *Kedoshei Ha-Shoa,* the holy martyrs of the Holocaust, without investigating their previous conduct"?
>
> Was this the time for the enlightened scholars, with impeccable foreheads, without slivers and without beams, perhaps even foreheads adorned with *tefillin,* to be silent and still?[5]

Rabbi Lichtenstein goes on to explain:

> Even as we are astonished by the silence relating to the tribute expressed in tears and eulogy, we must likewise question the inaction within our own yeshivot in regard to the killing itself. I do not suspect my colleagues, God forbid, of giving a seal of approval to the occurrence, even after the fact. But the reluctance to take a public position, in and of itself, calls for inquiry; it has caused moral and public damage to both our immediate and our broader community.
>
> The Chief Rabbis, *shlita,* have said their piece; Rabbi Menachem Eliezer Shach and Rabbi Ovadia Yosef have issued, however belatedly, vigorous statements. In the religious-national camp, however, several of the elder statesmen who are accustomed to take positions and issue protests on the occasion of much less significant events were struck mute.
>
> This fact has given rise to a variety of questions, and many have reached the sad conclusion that "since they are silent, presumably, the rabbis are content" (Gittin 56a).[6]

As mentioned in the above quotes, besides the transgression of "*Lo tirtzaḥ,*" "You shall not murder," according to many, this murderous

5. Ibid., 62.
6. Ibid., 63.

act also involves *ḥillul Hashem*. Previously we have discussed this idea, regarding the massacre performed by the Phalangists during the First Lebanon War at Sabra and Shatila. This idea is found in the writings of Rabbi Meir Simcha HaKohen of Dvinsk. He explains why we find that the Torah does not demand the death penalty for the murder of non-Jews as it does for the murder of Jews. Rabbi Meir Simcha lays out the reasoning for this law:

> Perhaps it is because when a Jew kills a Noahide, aside from the sin of murdering, he is also guilty of an additional sin, which is the desecration of God's name. His sin is so severe that even death by the hands of man cannot atone for his sins; therefore, he can be judged by God alone.[7]

VIGILANTE MURDERS IN THE 1930S AND THE RABBINICAL RESPONSE

This was not the first time in the history of our country that partisan acts of murder were committed against the Arab population by vigilantes. During the Arab riots prior to the establishment of the State of Israel, at the time that the Jewish community in Israel (Yishuv) was under daily murderous attacks, certain individuals responded by killing random Arabs within their towns and communities.

In 1937, both chief rabbis, Rabbi Yitzhak Herzog (Poland/Land of Israel, 1888–1959) and Rabbi Yaakov Meir (Land of Israel, 1856–1939), in the name of the Torah, condemned any acts of revenge and called on the Jewish population to show restraint (*havlaga*).[8] In July 1938, in a gathering called by heads of the Yishuv, the chief rabbis called for further restraint. Rabbi Ben-Zion Uziel (who would become Sephardi chief rabbi the next year) explained that "*Lo tirtzaḥ*" is an unconditional law.[9] Killing is only permitted for the sake of saving a life. Additionally, he

7. *Meshekh Ḥokhma,* Exodus 21:14.
8. See Eliezer Don-Yehiya, "Dat UTeror Politi: HaYahadut HaDatit UPe'ulot HaTagmul BiTkufat HaMeoraot," *HaTziyonut* 17 (1993): 162–63.
9. Appears in Binyamin and Ya'akov Peterzeil, *Negged HaTeror* (Jerusalem, 1939), 68–69.

quoted a verse in the Torah written in the context of the Torah's laws of providing cities of refuge for unintentional killers.

> "So that innocent blood is not shed, bringing bloodguilt upon you, in the land that the Lord your God is giving you as a possession" (Deut. 19:10). This law teaches us not only that it is prohibited to murder and spill innocent blood, but that it is prohibited to spill blood in the holy Land of Israel, which becomes impure when it is soaked with blood. This act puts a stain on the name of Israel and on its honor.

In a declaration which appeared in the newspaper *Haaretz* in July 1939, Rabbi Herzog and the newly appointed Sephardi Chief Rabbi Uziel said the following:

> God forbid, no one of the Jewish faith should even think of performing acts of revenge and acts of murder against innocents. God forbid that the current situation (of Jews being killed) should bring us to act against the Torah and commit murder, which would desecrate not only the name of Israel but also the entire operation of national renewal here in the Land of Israel.[10]

In 1938, the chief rabbi of Tel Aviv, Rabbi Moshe Avigdor Amiel (Belarus/Land of Israel, 1883–1946), protested the sporadic attacks on Arab civilians by Jews who were responding to the Arab attacks on the Jewish population. The Yishuv called for *havlaga* (restraint). Rabbi Amiel's objection was not only to the attacks themselves but also to the reasons given by the Yishuv:

> I object to the term *havlaga,* which indicates that the prohibition of shedding the blood of Arabs is based on the need to "restrain" ourselves, while this is really forbidden because of the prohibition of "*Lo tirtzaḥ.*" It is an incomparable moral degradation to justify the sinfulness of murder simply because it is ineffective.

10. "Kriat HaRabbanut HaRashit," *HaOlam,* July 14, 1938.

> In my opinion, even if we knew that by these acts of murder, we would bring about complete redemption, we must reject this "redemption" with both hands, and not be redeemed by blood.
>
> Moreover, if we succeed in capturing a number of Arabs who have committed murder, but we have a doubt, one in a thousand, that there is an innocent among them, we must not harm them, lest the innocent suffer as well.[11]

RABBINIC RESPONSES TO VIGILANTE MURDER IN THE STATE OF ISRAEL

These earlier rabbinic protests are reflected in the opinions of today's rabbis. However, in our day, there is also a well-established government, responsible for the safety and security of its citizens, in the mix.

In 2010, Rabbi Shlomo Aviner of Beit El strongly condemned the suggestion that there are those who permit the killing of another human being in the name of the Torah:

> I do not believe that there is a rabbi who has permitted the murder of Arabs. Perhaps he expressed such an idea as figurative hyperbole, but even by doing so he violated the dictum of "Sages, be careful with your words" (Avot 1:11). If, however, it should become clear, God forbid, that a rabbi gave a practical ruling to do such a thing, it would become retroactively clear that that rabbi, with all of his importance, is unworthy of the title *moreh horaah*, teacher of the law.[12]

He adds that any vigilantism is even more severe a sin in our days:

> (Nowadays) we have an army and a police force who risk their lives day and night for the nation's security, and it is they, and no one else, who are appointed by the entire nation to fight the enemies of our people. No private individual is entitled to engage in anti-Arab terrorism, to weaken the government and to perform,

---

11. "Issur 'Lo Tirtzaḥ' Klapei Aravim," *Teḥumin* 10 (1988/1989): 148.
12. *BeAhava UVeEmuna, Nitzavim-Vayelekh* 5770, #175.

> in the name of the nation, any act whose repercussions will be felt by the entire nation.
>
> Let us rid ourselves of the desecration of God's name inherent in such painful, insulting questions.

During the First Intifada, Rabbi Yaakov Ariel discussed halakhic questions that came up during those challenging times.[13] In one article, he argues that although the IDF admits that it does not have the power to completely enforce law and order throughout the land, that does not give authority to civilians to take the law into their own hands. He obviously permits self-defense but emphasizes the responsibility on the community – in this case the IDF – to handle the war against our enemies.

The murder of innocent worshippers by Baruch Goldstein was a shock to the entire country and called for a response by the rabbinic authorities. Vigilante justice has always been forbidden in halakha; today's rabbis agree that it has no place in the Jewish state.

13. "Hagana Atzmit (HaIntifada BeHalakha)," *Teḥumin* 10 (1988/1989): 61–75.

24

Prime Minister Rabin's Assassination, 1995

What Is the Status of a Head of State?

Yitzhak Rabin was born on March 1, 1922, in Jerusalem. As a member of the Palmach, he fought in the War of Independence (1948). Rising through the ranks of the IDF, he was appointed Chief of the General Staff (1964) and oversaw Israel's victory in the Six-Day War (1967). He then served as ambassador to the United States for five years. In 1974, after the resignation of Golda Meir, Rabin became prime minister. In 1992, Rabin was reelected prime minister on a platform embracing the Israeli-Palestinian peace process. He signed several historic agreements with the Palestinian leadership as part of the Oslo Accords as well as a peace treaty with Jordan. In 1994, Rabin won the Nobel Peace Prize.

On November 4, 1995, as he was leaving a rally in Tel Aviv supporting the peace process, he was gunned down by Yigal Amir, a political extremist. Rabin's assassination shocked the Israeli public and much of the world. He was buried on Mount Herzl on November 6, 1995, in a ceremony attended by many world leaders.

It is clear why the assassination shocked the entire country much more than the murder of a private citizen would have. The killing of

Israel's prime minister was an attack on the entire country and a threat to the unity of its people. As the murder was committed by a religious Jew (Amir had been a student at Yeshivat Hesder Kerem BeYavneh and Bar-Ilan University), there were many who were troubled by the connection between religion and political radicalism.

HOW SHOULD THE ASSASSINATION BE COMMEMORATED RELIGIOUSLY?

In the decades since the assassination, many suggestions have been made regarding the fitting way to mark the event. The Knesset passed the Rabin Memorial Law in 1997, making his yahrzeit, 12 Ḥeshvan, a national day of remembrance.

Some have proposed holding a day of fasting and prayer, similar to the custom of commemorating the political murder of Gedalia ben Aḥikam, who served as the governor of Yehuda immediately after the destruction of the First Temple. His assassination by Jewish rivals in approximately 582 BCE marked the end of Jewish autonomy for generations. The Fast of Gedalia is observed annually on the first weekday after Rosh HaShana. The Fast of Gedalia emphasizes that, even after the physical destruction of the Temple, it was the killing of a Jewish leader which led to the end of Jewish sovereignty, the essence of the destruction. Fasting on the day of Rabin's murder would deliver a similar message in our days: violence and murder will ultimately lead to destruction, God forbid.

Below we examine the halakhic status of the Israeli government and its prime minister and the meaning of mutiny and rebellion against them. Obviously, in the background of this dilemma is the reality that the State of Israel is a secular one, and it does not operate under a halakhic system. The first question we will deal with is the following: What is the place of a Jewish state in halakha and the religious world? There are different approaches to this question; we will present three.[1]

1. See Uri Dasberg, "Medina Yehudit – Shalosh Gishot," *Shana BeShana* (1998): 241–52.

The King in the Bible

We will begin with the law in the Torah that seems to indicate that there is a positive command to appoint a king (*melekh*):

> When you enter the land that the Lord your God is giving you, and have taken possession of it and settled in it, should you say, "I will set a king over me, like all the surrounding nations," **you shall set over you a king** whom the Lord your God chooses. The king you set over you must be one of your own people. You may not set a foreigner over you, who is not your brother. (Deut. 17:14–15)

It is therefore puzzling that God is upset with the request for monarchy in the days of Shmuel (as is the prophet himself):

> And all the elders of Israel gathered ... and they said to him ... "Appoint a king for us to govern us like any other nation." When they said, "Give us a king to govern us," **the idea displeased Shmuel**, and Shmuel prayed to the Lord. And the Lord said to Shmuel, "Heed the voice of the people in all they say to you. For it is not you they have rejected – **it is Me they have rejected, from reigning over them.**" (I Sam. 8:4–7)

The *Tanna'im* debate this contradiction and offer different answers:

> R. Yehuda said: But it is a commandment from the Torah for them to request a king over themselves, as it is written, "You shall set over you a king." So why were they punished for this in the days of Shmuel? Because it was too early for them to ask.
>
> "Like any other nation" – R. Nehorai said: They did not ask for a king for any other reason but so that he would institute idolatry, as it is written (I Sam. 8:20), "So we, too, will be like all the other nations. Our king shall govern us and go out before us and fight our battles."[2]

2. *Sifrei, Devarim* 156; appears similarly in Sanhedrin 20b.

However, there is an alternative approach, which contends that within the Bible we find two separate arguments, one for and one against the entire notion of kingship.[3] These are not necessarily contradictory; rather, they emphasize the ambivalence of the matter.

Appointing a king is a sensitive issue, as it may be seen as a direct challenge to God's kingship in this world. On the other hand, from a pragmatic, practical perspective, government is a necessity required to prevent anarchy. We may add to this suggestion a third biblical source which suggests a new approach to the question of whether kingship is a good idea. In this source, we find that the king of Israel is somewhat a reflection of God's kingship:

> And they ate and drank before the Lord on that day with great joy, and they crowned Shlomo the son of David a second time, and they anointed [him] to the Lord as ruler and Tzadok as priest. And Shlomo **sat on the throne of the Lord** as king instead of David his father, and he prospered, and all Israel obeyed him. (I Chr. 29:22–23)

This passage indicates that the throne of the Davidic dynasty reflects the kingship of God in this world.

Thus, in the Bible we find three very different attitudes toward the idea of establishing a monarchy:

1. In Deuteronomy, we have a positive approach, suggesting the functional side of government.
2. In Samuel, we have a negative approach, warning us that every type of human kingship is a threat to the kingship of God.[4]
3. In Chronicles, we have an understanding that kingship in Israel reflects God's kingship in the world.

---

3. My good friend Dr. Assaf Malach wrote an article on this theory, "Bein Rosh HaShana LeYom HaAtzma'ut," *The Jewish Statesmanship Center*, accessed August 2, 2021, www.statesmanship.org.il/he/המכללה-למדינאות/item/919 -בין-ראש-השנה-ליום-העצמאות-ד-ר-אסף-מלאך-. Many of the ideas mentioned here are based on his article.
4. When Gidon the Judge is approached by the people and offered kingship, he claims that any form of kingship by humans is a challenge to God's kingship; see Judges 8.

Views of the *Rishonim*

In the medieval period, we find similar ideas and approaches among the *Rishonim*. The great biblical commentator Rabbi Yitzhak Abrabanel (Lisbon/Venice, 1437–1508) is radically critical of the idea that appointing a monarch is a positive command. He understands that the Torah is merely suggesting that if the people are interested in appointing a king, then they must act upon the Torah's detailed instructions for doing so:

> When the Torah says, "When you come to the land...and you say: 'Let us appoint a king over ourselves like all the nations around us,'" *this does not constitute a commandment at all.* God does not command that they say this and request a king (as the Ramban has explained). Rather, this is foretelling the future. It means, after your settlement in the chosen land, the conquest and all the wars, and after the division [of the land]...*I know that you will be ungrateful and say of your own volition,* "Let us appoint a king over ourselves," not out of necessity to fight the nations and occupy the land, for it will have already come under your occupation, but rather to render yourselves equivalent to the nations that crown kings over themselves.[5] (Emphasis mine.)

In his commentary, he mentions the disadvantages of creating a monarchy.

However, from the reading of the Rambam's description of the king of Israel's responsibilities, one senses a very different approach. Not only does the Rambam list the appointment of a king as one of the 613 mitzvot, he also explains as follows:

> In all matters, his deeds shall be for the sake of heaven. His purpose and intent shall be to elevate the true faith and fill the world with justice, destroying the power of the wicked and waging the

5. Commentary on Deuteronomy. Translation taken from Rabbi Elchanan Samet, "What Is the Torah's Ideal Political System?" The Israel Koschitzky Torat Har Etzion VBM, accessed December 28, 2021, https://etzion.org.il/en/tanakh/torah/sefer-devarim/parashat-shoftim/shoftim-what-torahs-ideal-political-system.

> wars of God. For the entire purpose of appointing a king is to execute justice and wage wars as I Samuel 8:20 states: "Our king shall govern us and go out before us and fight our battles."[6]

While reflecting on the Davidic king's messianic task, the Rambam writes:

> If a king will arise from the House of David who diligently contemplates the Torah and observes its commandments as prescribed by the Written Law and the Oral Law like David, his ancestor; who compels all of Israel to walk in (the way of the Torah) and rectify the breaches in its observance, and who fights the wars of God, we may, with assurance, assume him to be *Mashiaḥ* [Messiah] .... He will then improve the entire world, motivating all the nations to serve God together...[7]

In the works of the Rabbi Nissim ben Reuven of Girona we find a middle ground, an approach that argues that kingship serves a secular purpose, maintaining law and order.[8] He explains that the Torah requires government in order to prevent anarchy. The king of Israel has no responsibility for Torah observance and religion. The reason that Shmuel is upset at the people for requesting a king is that they want the king – and not the religious leadership – to judge the people.

Modern Views on the King

In the past century or so, it seems that the argument has continued. As Zionism arose as a political movement, beginning in the late nineteenth century, the place of the "king" became tied to the Jewish state. In the works of the Satmar Rebbe and other rabbis who opposed Zionism, there is no religious value to a secular state. Rabbi Samson Raphael Hirsch (Germany, 1808–1888) argues that statehood has never been

6. *Mishneh Torah, Hilkhot Melakhim* 4:10.
7. Ibid., 11:4.
8. *Derashot HaRan* #8.

a Jewish ideal in and of itself; it should be understood as a means for applying religious ideals:

> In the wilderness Israel received the Torah, and thus, in the wilderness, without land or soil of its own, it became a nation.
>
> It [the Jewish people] received, therefore, the gifts of a land and of statehood, not, however, as an end unto itself, but solely as a means for carrying out the Torah.[9]

Rabbi Joseph B. Soloveitchik sees worth in a Jewish state, as he believes it contributes to the values of the Torah. He recognizes that government and sovereignty have religious weight. In his lectures, he explains why he chose to "cross the lines" and move over to the Mizrachi movement:

> First, we were the first to explain that the establishment of the State has halakhic significance, since by its means we shall be able to fulfill the commandment of possessing and settling it. We said, this commandment is fulfilled not only by building up the country economically, but also by our sovereignty there. The existence of the State of Israel and the fact that Jews and not Englishmen determine aliya; that Jews and not Arabs are the political masters in the country; and that a Jewish government, police force and army exist, is the greatest possible fulfillment of the commandment of settling in *Eretz Yisrael.*
>
> ...Our movement understood this and welcomed the State's existence as a fundamental religious value within our scale of values. True, we are not always happy with certain actions and tactics of the government. But this does not detract from the importance of the State of Israel as the instrument for the realization of possessing the land. We know that the government is not itself the State. Governments come, and governments go, rulers come and rulers go, but the land – and the State, we hope to God – remain forever. Only our movement expressed itself

9. Rabbi Samson Raphael Hirsch, *The Nineteen Letters*, trans. Bernard Drachman (Jerusalem and New York: Feldheim, 1969), letter no. 8, pp. 59–60.

> unequivocally for the State of Israel and granted it halakhic status.[10]

Rabbi Avraham Yitzchak Kook may have been the first to refer to the future Jewish homeland as "the State of Israel." In his writings, he seems to disagree directly with the words of Rabbi Hirsch, as it is clear that he foresees the State of Israel not just as a means for bringing the Jewish people together, but rather as the Throne of God in this world:

> The nation is not the highest level of happiness for humankind. This can certainly be said about most regular countries whose value is not more than a large mutual insurance pact. Ideals, which are the crown of human life, are irrelevant and beyond their purview.
>
> This is not the case with a nation whose foundation is idealistic. A nation in which the highest content is embedded into its very being. This type of nation offers the highest happiness for the individual and it is the highest level on the ladder of satisfaction.
>
> **And this nation is our nation, the State of Israel. It is the foundation of God's Throne in the world,** and all its desire is that God will be one and His Name one. This is truly the highest happiness.[11]

Rav Kook's understanding of the meaning of a Jewish state is similar to the Rambam's view of kingship. However, the Rambam's view on the legitimacy of the king of Israel is not clear. On the one hand, he writes that a king must be established by a prophet, but may be from any tribe of Israel;[12] elsewhere he mentions that a king of Israel must be a descendant of Shlomo.[13] Nevertheless, he notes that the establishment of the Hasmonean dynasty is part of the miracle of Ḥanukka, even

10. *The Rav Speaks*, 137–38.
11. "Orot Yisrael," *Orot* (Jerusalem: Mosad HaRav Kook, 1963), 6:7.
12. *Mishneh Torah, Hilkhot Melakhim* 1:8.
13. *Sefer HaMitzvot*, negative commandment 362.

though it was neither established by a prophet nor were its members of the Davidic line.[14]

It appears that the Rambam recognizes several models of Jewish kingship.[15] The ideal king of Israel, whom the Rambam refers to as *melekh hamashiaḥ*, is from the tribe of Yehuda. However, even a Jewish leader from another tribe, or one not appointed by a prophet, has religious value. Furthermore, it is possible that the Rambam values Jewish kingship and government as the essence of the commandment of settling the Land of Israel.

Mitzvat Yishuv Eretz Yisrael

The Ramban writes that there is a positive commandment to settle in the Land of Israel.[16] Many rabbis are troubled by the fact that the Rambam does not list this commandment himself in his *Sefer HaMitzvot*. Rabbi Yitzhak de Leon (Spain, fifteenth century) explains that the commandment only applies in the era during which the Jews reside in the Land of Israel, and it will only be reinstated in Messianic times.[17] Rabbi Avraham Bornsztain suggests that the Rambam includes *yishuv Eretz Yisrael* in the commandment of destroying the Seven Nations. Using the same logic, Rabbi Hershel Schachter argues that "it would appear that the simple explanation for the Rambam's omission of this commandment is that he views it as identical to that of appointing a king, which he already enumerated elsewhere."[18] This view understands that settling the Land of Israel is not just a "technical" commandment of living in the land but rather a means establishing sovereignty over it.[19]

---

14. *Mishneh Torah, Hilkhot Ḥanukka* 3:1.
15. See the article by my father, Rabbi Binyamin Tabory, in "Malkhut Yisrael UMalkhut Beit David," *Daf Kesher* #118, Tevet 1987, http://gush.net/dk//1to899/118daf.htm. Also see Ya'akov Blidstein, *Ekronot Mediniyim BeMishnat HaRambam* (Ramat Gan: Bar-Ilan University, 1983), 31–39; Rabbi Elyakim Krumbein, *Afikei Yehuda: A Volume in Memory of Rabbi Yehuda Gershuni* (Jerusalem: Ariel, 2005), 214–26.
16. Positive commandment 4.
17. *Megillat Esther* on *Sefer HaMitzvot.*
18. "Land for Peace: A Halachic Perspective," *RJJ Journal of Halacha and Contemporary Society* 16 (Fall 1988): 82.
19. See Rabbi Itamar Warhaftig's article, "Hakamat HaMedina KeMitzva," *Teḥumin* 18 (1997/1998): 421–32. He maintains that the establishment of the State of Israel is a

Rabbinic discussions of monarchy in Israel have included a variety of understandings of the imperative to set a king over the nation; some halakhic authorities even tie the king to the commandment of settling the land. Israel's current government and its leader are viewed by some as akin to the biblical king. Thus the prime minister may in fact represent Jewish kingship. Prime Minister Rabin's assassination, then, can be seen as much more than an attack on an individual leader; it is an attack on the monarchy, on *malkhut Yisrael,* an entity that has both religious and civic standing.[20]

commandment, based on our claim that sovereignty is the essence of the commandment to live in Israel.

20. Rav Kook claims that the duly elected government of Israel has the status of a *melekh* (*Mishpat Kohen, siman* 144:14–17).

25

Operation Defensive Shield, 2002

What Acts Are Permitted on Shabbat During Military Operations?

The Second Intifada, which began at the end of September 2000, was a difficult period for the Israeli public, particularly on the home front. During these deadly months, over 1,100 Israelis were murdered and over 8,000 were injured. Many attacks were carried out by suicide bombers who blew themselves up on buses, in restaurants, and in public areas.

Travel became a terrifying experience for Israelis at the time. Simple daily tasks like riding the bus to work became stressful, filled with anxiety and fear. Palestinian terrorists were responsible for the lynch of two Israeli soldiers in Ramallah, the suicide attack at the Dolphinarium in Tel Aviv where twenty-one young people were massacred, and the attack at the Sbarro restaurant in Jerusalem which killed fifteen, among them a family of five.

On March 27, 2002, the first night of Pesaḥ , a Palestinian terrorist entered the Park Hotel in Netanya during the Seder and blew himself up. In the massacre, 30 were killed and 160 were injured, making it the deadliest terror attack ever to take place in Israel. So many deaths and injuries on a night celebrated by Jews as the holiday of freedom stunned Israel and the entire Jewish world. That night, following the attack, the Israeli government decided to take control over the Palestinian cities that had been handed over to the Palestinian Authority under the Oslo Accords. In his address to the Knesset, Prime Minister Ariel Sharon stated the aims of this operation, named *Ḥomat Magen* (Defensive Shield):

> The government of Israel has thus decided to instruct the I.D.F. and other security forces to embark on Operation Defensive Shield, which has one goal: uprooting the terrorist infrastructure which Arafat built to continue attacking us.
>
> I.D.F. soldiers and officers have been given clear orders: to enter cities and villages which have become havens for terrorists; to catch and arrest terrorists and, primarily, their dispatchers and those who finance and support them; to confiscate weapons intended to be used against Israeli citizens; to expose and destroy terrorist facilities and explosives, laboratories, weapons production factories and secret installations. The orders are clear: target and paralyze anyone who takes up weapons and tries to oppose our troops, resists them or endangers them – and to avoid harming the civilian population.[1]

On Friday morning, March 29, Israel called up twenty thousand reservists, the largest mobilization since the First Lebanon War. During these highly emotional days, the IDF successfully took over the cities which were harboring terrorists. The goals of the operation were achieved, reducing terrorist attacks by 50 percent.

1. Delivered at Knesset on April 8, 2002; see "Text of Speech by Sharon to Israeli Parliament," April 8, 2002, New York Times, https://www.nytimes.com/2002/04/08/international/middleeast/text-of-speech-by-sharon-to-israeli-parliament.html

It was Erev Shabbat, Ḥol HaMoed Pesaḥ, when my entire tank battalion was drafted, and I found myself preparing tanks for battles together with my comrades that Friday night. Our *tzav shemoneh* (emergency call-up) had come in during the week between *Parashat Tzav* and *Parashat Shemini*. That night, I made Kiddush at the tank depot, on a bottle of wine I had remembered to bring with me from home.

Below I focus on the events during the operation and halakhic challenges that arose at the time. Most of the questions discussed are unique to army life. This type of question is part of the new language of halakha developed through the years since the establishment of the IDF. In his autobiography, Rabbi Goren, who was the first chief rabbi of the IDF and later chief rabbi of the State of Israel, explains the challenges he faced with the establishment of the IDF and his appointment as its chief rabbi:

> One thing that is important to realize is that the Torah's *halakha* and the *mitzvot* that are practiced today all have an unbroken tradition from the time of the Sanhedrin and the Second Temple, from the Men of the Great Assembly, the Tanaim and Amoraim, the Savoraim, the Geonim, the early and later halakhists, until modern times. All these laws and traditions are condensed into the *Shulḥan Arukh*, which explains almost every detail, large or small, concerning the observance of Shabbat and the Holidays, how to *daven* and how to put on *tefillin*, how *tefillin* are made, and all the kosher food laws, etc.
>
> On the other hand, we have no parallel tradition concerning life in a Jewish army. For two thousand years, we did not have our own army. We do not know which laws, among all the *mitzvot* in the *Shulḥan Arukh*, are binding upon soldiers in the army. Does the army have a special *Shulḥan Arukh*? Are there special dispensations? If so, what are these dispensations? There is no tradition in these matters and no writings concerning them. There did not exist a *Shulḥan Arukh* for Jewish soldiers.
>
> I knew that upon accepting the position as the chief rabbi of the army, I would have to create something out of nothing – I would have to write and compile a "military *Shulḥan*

> *Arukh*" without having any traditions from which to compile such a guide. I would have to gather hints from here and there, a grain here and a grain there, from the Bible, from the Written Law and the Oral Law, from all sorts of sources and from the Midrash. I would have to gather one grain to the next and create a whole mass from which we could learn how to conduct ourselves, how to keep the Torah in the army, and what is the Torah's application in the army, during wartime and during peacetime. I would have to develop solutions for each issue that arose, because we had no unbroken tradition of a religious lifestyle in a military setting. There would be questions related to the *halakhot* of Shabbat, kashrut, and many other types of issues, and they would require halakhic rulings. This was a tremendous challenge.[2]

TANK MAINTENANCE ON SHABBAT

During Operation Defensive Shield, I was approached by my commanding officer, who asked me to give rulings on halakhic matters that had come up. He was appointing me unofficial chaplain of our platoon, he said; whatever decision I made, he would follow.

Weekly tank maintenance is normally conducted on Thursdays; however, due to the usage of the platoon's tanks throughout the week, this could only be done on the coming Shabbat. This maintenance includes tightening the screws of the wheels as well as oiling and cleaning the cannon and various other parts of the tank. Adjusting the sights of the cannon is also required. Are all of these actions permitted on Shabbat?[3]

Pikuaḥ Nefesh on Shabbat

The obvious method to resolve this question is to determine whether these tasks may be classified as *pikuaḥ nefesh,* life-saving activity, which should be permitted on Shabbat. The truth, however, is a little more

2. Rabbi Shlomo Goren, *With Might and Strength: An Autobiography,* trans. Miryam Blum (Jerusalem: Maggid Books, 2016), 177–78.
3. In his book *Halakha MiMekorah: Tzava* (Jerusalem: Sulamot, 2000), Rabbi Yosef Tzvi Rimon mentions a similar question that came up during the operation. In his case, the question was about repairing a tank that was out of commission. See 1:307–8.

complicated. Even if the situation constitutes *pikuaḥ nefesh,* the question remains whether it is better to perform these acts *beshinui* (in an irregular manner) or not. It must be noted that the acts of maintenance included in our case would not be performed in the heat of battle.

Let us take a moment to consider why, as mentioned in earlier chapters, the Gemara permits violating Shabbat in life-threatening situations. The Gemara suggests possible sources and concludes that this is derived from the verse: "Keep My statutes and laws, for by them a person shall live; I am the Lord" (Lev. 18:5). The Gemara derives from this verse that "'by them a person shall live,' and not die by them" (Yoma 85b).

The *Rishonim* argue about the extent of such a principle. A classic question when halakha allows us to perform an act which is normally forbidden is whether the prohibition is considered *hutera* (allowed, i.e., suspended) or *deḥuya* (pushed off, i.e., overridden). If the former is the case, there is no need to worry about the prohibition in the given circumstance; if the latter is the case, we must still minimize the violation.

Some understand that other prohibitions are merely suspended in the face of danger (*deḥuya*), while in the case of Shabbat, they are waived completely (*hutera*). Rabbeinu Asher quotes Rabbi Meir of Rothenburg, who argues that for a sick person all medical treatment which violates Shabbat is permissible and there is no reason to try to lessen the violation.[4] This seems to indicate that any prohibition of Shabbat is *hutera* – suspended – in cases of *pikuaḥ nefesh.*

The Rambam lists the actions which may be performed on Shabbat for a woman giving birth:

> When a woman is in the process of childbirth, her life is considered in danger and the Sabbath laws may be violated on her behalf. A midwife may be called from a distant place, and the umbilical cord may be cut and tied.
>
> If she requires a light when she cries out because of labor pains, a candle may be lit for her. [This leniency is granted] even if she is blind, because light has a calming influence even if she does not see.

4. Rosh, Yoma 8:14.

However, the Rambam limits these actions. He opines that if possible, they should all be done *beshinui*:

> If she needs oil or the like, it may be brought for her. *If possible, the items that are brought should be brought in an uncharacteristic manner*; for example, a friend should bring a utensil tied in her hair. If this is not possible, it may be brought in the ordinary manner.[5] (Emphasis mine.)

The above ruling would seem to indicate that the Rambam believes that Shabbat is *deḥuya* – overridden – in cases of *pikuaḥ nefesh*. The idea of violating Shabbat in an irregular or backhanded way can only be understood if, under the circumstances, the prohibition of performing labor on Shabbat still exists.[6] Performing labor on Shabbat *beshinui* would be a rabbinical violation rather than a biblical violation.

Another support for this theory, that the observance of Shabbat is suspended rather than overridden, is the Rambam's choice of words when he permits performing labor on Shabbat in cases of *pikuaḥ nefesh*:

> The [laws of] the Sabbath *are pushed off in the face of a danger to life*, as are [the obligations of] the other commandments. Therefore, we may perform – according to the directives of a professional physician of that locale – everything that is necessary for the benefit of a sick person whose life is in danger.[7]

The Rambam here uses the term *deḥuya,* which implies that although saving a life takes priority, the prohibitions of Shabbat have not been lifted entirely. Accordingly, Rabbi Yosef Karo understands that this is the Rambam's ruling.[8]

---

5. *Mishneh Torah, Hilkhot Shabbat* 2:11.
6. See Rabbi Shmuel Ariel, "Asiyat Melakha BeShinui BeShabbat, BiMekom Tzaar O Hefsed," *Teḥumin* 31 (2010/2011): 80–96, who discusses the law of *shinui* on Shabbat.
7. *Mishneh Torah, Hilkhot Shabbat* 2:1.
8. *Kesef Mishneh,* ad loc. See Rabbi Ovadia Yosef, *Yeḥaveh Daat,* 4:30, in which he debates the Rambam's ruling.

The *Maggid Mishneh* (Rabbi Vidal of Tolosa; Spain, late fourteenth century) explains that the Rambam differentiates between a woman giving birth and a critically ill person. He points out that the Rambam does not mention performing the violation of Shabbat for sick people *beshinui*. He therefore posits that the Rambam's ruling is that Shabbat is *hutera*, overridden, in cases of critical illness.[9]

Nonetheless, Rabbi Moshe Isserles still argues that, if possible, one should perform the forbidden labor on Shabbat for a sick person *beshinui*.[10]

Applying the Principles to Maintenance

In a response to Rabbi Mayer Lichtenstein (at the time a yeshiva student serving in the army) regarding turning on the engines of tanks in Lebanon due to freezing temperatures, deputy chief rabbi of the IDF Rabbi Avraham Avidan argued that the custom is to follow the Rema; when possible, violating Shabbat should be done *beshinui*.[11]

Some of the actions I was asked about when serving in Operation Defensive Shield require violating biblical commandments on Shabbat; based on the above discussion, we would be required to perform the tasks *beshinui* (if possible) or find a way to make them a rabbinical violation.

Rabbi Shlomo Goren discusses oiling a gun on Shabbat and cleaning a cannon after it has been fired. His conclusion, after discussing the matter with "army specialists," is that it is possible to change the regular method of the cleaning process, reducing the level of labor performed from a biblical prohibition to a rabbinical one. His advice is to pour the oil directly into the cannon and then to clean the barrel with the cleaning rod rather than pouring the oil on the cleaning rod directly, which would be a biblical violation of *melabein* (soaking).[12]

Rabbi Goren's ruling is about a cannon that has been used enough times for soot to accumulate. But this was not the situation in our case, and therefore due to the forbidden labor of *seḥita* (squeezing), I thought

9. *Maggid Mishneh, Hilkhot Shabbat* 2:11.
10. *Oraḥ Ḥayim* 328:12.
11. *Shabbat UMoed BeTzahal* (Jerusalem: Yeshivat Shaalvim, 1990), 87.
12. *Meshiv Milḥama,* 2:105.

we could skip this task this one time. When it came to other actions like tightening the screws, I believed that these were essential and therefore should be performed the regular way.

I have mentioned that Rabbi Goren believes that the *heter* of fighting a war on Shabbat is not based on *pikuaḥ nefesh*, but rather on the verse in Deuteronomy 20:20 (see chapter 11).[13] This source is parallel to the claim that in life-threating situations, the prohibition against certain labor is suspended on Shabbat.

If we apply this ruling to our case, no *shinui* would be required. From my experience, this is one of the more difficult questions that faces the Israeli soldier: What is the halakhic status of a routine state of *pikuaḥ nefesh* within the army?

Rabbi Goren discusses talking on the army radio on Shabbat.[14] Although the usage of a radio for military purposes would be permitted on Shabbat based on the special *heter* of fighting on Shabbat, he still recommends that one should try to speak differently than one does on a weekday.[15] All our behavior and the way we act on Shabbat, he reasons, should differ from regular weekdays, including the way we dress, eat, and even speak.

Rabbi Yitzchak Kaufman, author of a book about halakha in the army, discusses cases that are similar to ours. He makes a distinction: not all treatments done for the upkeep of the tank on a regular weekday have the same importance. He uses the halakhic terminology of *hiddur* – that which enhances the act, but is not essential to it. This type of maintenance, he states, is not allowed.[16]

Based on all the above, it is my understanding that work on the tank which includes vital maintenance may be done on Shabbat – but, if possible, it should be done *beshinui*.

---

13. Ibid., 1:88–91.
14. Ibid., 1:344–46.
15. Ibid., 1:348.
16. *HaTzava KaHalakha*, 219.

Unloading Tank Equipment on Shabbat

My commanding officer had another question for me at the time, one that related to the removal of the equipment from a tank on Shabbat, including all ammunition, explosives, and guns. My officer explained that one of the tanks had to be transported Sunday morning, at first light. Unloading the tank's equipment could only be done in daylight, due to the delicate articles that had to be unloaded; thus, we could not perform the unloading on Motza'ei Shabbat.

In this case, the answer was much simpler. Had it been operationally necessary, unloading the tank would have obviously been permitted. However, asking a few simple questions, I verified that there was no chance that a tank-carrier driver would arrive at first light. I thus convinced the officer that the task could be done Sunday morning. When dealing with any halakhic questions in the army, one must be aware of all the facts; a thorough understanding of the reality is essential before a ruling is issued.

26

The Disengagement from Gush Katif, 2005

May a Synagogue Be Destroyed?

In the summer of 2005, 8,500 Jewish settlers from Gush Katif were forced to leave their homes and towns. Gush Katif, the Israeli name for a cluster of seventeen Jewish settlements in the southern Gaza Strip, is often used colloquially to refer to all twenty-one of the Jewish settlements in Gaza. During the same summer, four Jewish settlements with a total of about seven hundred residents in the northern Shomron were also dismantled.

This move was part of the Disengagement Plan, which meant evacuating all Israeli military and civilians from the Gaza Strip. The decision made by Israel's government, under Prime Minister Ariel Sharon, to disengage from Gaza was extremely controversial, and it created a great rift in Israeli society.

On February 16, 2005, the Knesset passed the plan by a vote of 59–40, with five members abstaining. An amendment proposing a referendum was defeated 72–29. Thousands of Israelis had joined the struggle against the decision, arguing that there were many faults in the decision-making process. Ultimately, Sharon refused to hold a national referendum and decided to go ahead with the plan although many people within his own party disagreed with him (the Likud split 19–17 in favor of the plan).

The residents of Gush Katif were notified in advance of the evacuation, but many of them did not voluntarily leave their homes; some did not even pack up their belongings. They would have to be removed by Israeli military and police.

On August 15, the forcible evacuation of the Gush Katif settlements began. The evacuation lasted one week; by August 22, the last residents had been evicted. All public buildings, as well as industrial buildings, factories, and greenhouses which could not be dismantled, were left intact. The greenhouses, in their prime, produced 320 tons of vegetables annually and exported produce worth half a billion shekels. The original plan was for the settlers to sell these greenhouses – involuntarily – to the Palestinians.

On August 28, the IDF began dismantling and transferring Gush Katif's forty-eight-grave cemetery. The dead were given second funerals, with the families observing a one-day mourning period. The transfer was completed on September 1.

Originally, the Israeli cabinet had planned to destroy all of Gush Katif's synagogues, but the government caved in to pressure from rabbis who opposed the decision and eventually reversed its decision. Most of the synagogues were destroyed by Palestinian mobs immediately after the evacuation.[1] Abu Abir, a member of the Popular Resistance Committees terrorist organization, commented: "The looting and burning of the synagogues was a great joy.... It was in an unplanned expression of happiness that these synagogues were destroyed."[2]

In 2007, it was reported:

> The ruins of two large synagogues in Gush Katif, the evacuated Jewish communities of the Gaza Strip, have been transformed

1. "Maher MeHaTzafui: HaPalestinim Hetzitu Et Batei HaKnesset," ynet, September 12, 2005, https://www.ynet.co.il/articles/0,7340,L-3140761,00.html.
2. Aaron Klein, "Synagogues Now Terror Firing Zone," ynet, February 27, 2007, https://www.ynetnews.com/articles/0,7340,L-3370395,00.html.

> into a military base used by Palestinian groups to fire rockets at Israeli cities and train for attacks against the Jewish state, according to a senior terror leader in Gaza.[3]

On September 12, 2005, the IDF completed its withdrawal from the Gaza Strip.

THE DISMANTLING OF A SYNAGOGUE IN HALAKHA

Many halakhic questions regarding the disengagement were discussed by rabbis at the time. These discussions were collected and published by Rabbi Yehuda Zoldan, himself a resident of Gush Katif, in a book titled *Shevut Yehuda VeYisrael.* Yeshivat Har Etzion published a collection of articles, *BiSe'arat HaAkira,* on theological and ethical issues related to the terrible events which took place in the summer of 2005.

In this chapter, we discuss the rabbinical debate concerning whether the army should have dismantled and demolished the synagogues or left them to be destroyed by the Palestinians. Although many rabbis voiced their opinions against the operation as a whole and were ignored, in the case of the synagogues, the government actually took the rabbinical rulings into account.

Former Ashkenazi Chief Rabbi Avraham Shapira published a halakhic ruling regarding the government's plan. He reiterates his well-known opinion that Jewish law forbids handing over any part of the Land of Israel to other nations. However, this time he addresses our dilemma as well. Rabbi Shapira disagrees with the planned destruction of the synagogues. He declares:

> A soldier or police officer that harms the holy items of Israel and, God forbid, destroys heavenly articles and holy accoutrements such as Torah scrolls, phylacteries, mezuzot – whether it is done within the context of the evacuation transgression or not – he is desecrating the holy articles of Israel and violates the command *lo taasun ken laHashem Elokeikhem* (Deut. 12:4).

3. Ibid.

> One who destroys an object in a synagogue is like someone who destroys a stone in the Sanctuary [of the Holy Temple] (Mordekhai, *perek Benei haIr; Magen Avraham* 152:6). There is an absolute prohibition for every soldier and every policeman to take part in the destruction of a synagogue and a study hall. And within that prohibition is the prohibition of destroying vessels belonging to the synagogue, for they are like the synagogue itself (*Be'ur Halakha* 152). Woe to him and woe to the soul of a soldier or policeman who takes part in this sin.[4]

This ruling is based on the understanding that there is a biblical prohibition against destroying houses of prayer. We therefore must study this halakha.

Kedushat Beit HaKnesset

The Torah (Deut. 12:1–4) states:

> These are the statues and ordinances that you shall keep to perform in the land which the Lord God of your fathers gives you to possess all the days that you live on the earth. You shall utterly destroy from all the places where the nations, that you shall possess, worshipped their gods, upon the lofty mountains and upon the hills, and under every lush tree. And you shall tear down their altars, smash their monuments, burn their *asherim* with fire, cut down the graven images of their gods, and destroy their name from that place. You shall not do so to the Lord your God.

The final verse is understood as a prohibition: one may not destroy that which is associated with God's name. However, the Gemara differentiates between two different types of religious articles. In the group named *tashmishei kedusha* (articles of sanctity) the Gemara includes items like mezuzot, tefillin, and Torah scrolls. In another group, named *tashmishei mitzva* (articles used in the performance of a commandment), the Gemara lists examples like lulav, tzitzit, and shofar.

4. Lichtenstein and Shapira, "Rabbinic Exchange": 49–70.

The *nafka mina* (practical halakhic difference) between the two groups is the question of what is to be done with the articles when they become redundant and one wishes to be rid of them. While *tashmishei kedusha* need to be buried in the ground, *tashmishei mitzva* may be thrown out:

> The Sages taught [in a *baraita*]: Articles [used in the performance] of a commandment may be thrown out [after use. Although these items were used in the performance of a commandment, they are not thereby sanctified. However], articles [associated with the] sanctity [of God's name, even after they are no longer used,] must be interred [in a respectful manner]. And these [items] are [considered] articles of a commandment: a sukka; a lulav; a shofar; and tzitzit. And these [items] are [considered] articles of sanctity: cases of [Torah] scrolls; tefillin; and mezuzot; and a container for a Torah scroll; and a cover for tefillin; and their straps. (Megilla 26b)

Based on the teachings of Rabbi Soloveitchik, Rabbi Hershel Schachter explains the principle behind this halakha.[5] The halakhic concept of *kedusha* has to do with the Torah itself. It is through the connection to Torah that certain people, places, and articles receive a status of sanctity. All articles like mezuzot and tefillin mentioned before have *kedusha* because they carry the words of the Torah on their parchment.

What is the halakhic status of a synagogue? The Ramban understands that a synagogue's status is similar to an article of a commandment, like a lulav or shofar. Rabbi Nissim of Girona disagrees, stating that the Sages compare the *kedusha* of a synagogue to articles like tefillin or mezuzot.[6]

However, there is a third possibility: that the *kedusha* of a synagogue involves a biblical prohibition. Rabbi Eliezer ben Shmuel of Metz understands that certain biblical laws regarding the Temple apply to synagogues as well:

5. *Eretz HaTzvi* (New York: Yeshiva University Press, 1992), 88–94.
6. Ran on Rif, Megilla 8a.

> "And you shall revere your God" (Lev. 19:32) – this includes the command that when a person enters the Temple, a synagogue, or a house of study, one must treat the place with awe and respect, as it is written: "Keep My Sabbaths and revere My Sanctuary" (Lev. 19:30).
>
> We have learned that the synagogue and the house of study are called *mikdash,* as it is mentioned in the *baraita*: "'I will desolate your temples' – 'your temples' includes synagogues and study halls." We therefore derive from here that when the Torah commands us to respect the Temple, it means respecting the synagogues as well.[7]

This seems to be the opinion of the Rambam as well. Referring to the prohibition of destroying the Temple, the Rambam understands that this biblical ruling applies to synagogues as well:

> [This prohibition is] not to destroy the Temple, **synagogues,** or study halls; and similarly, not to erase any of [God's] sacred names, nor to destroy any sacred texts, as (Deut. 12:2–4) states: "You shall surely destroy.... Do not do this to the Lord your God."[8]

It is clear from both sources that there are certain similarities between the Temple and a synagogue. Rabbi Soloveitchik explains that according to the above understanding that *kedusha* has to do with the Torah, the Temple and a synagogue have the same source of *kedusha,* as they both serve as a home for the Torah.[9] Accordingly, the question regarding destroying a house of prayer is a *maḥloket* between *Rishonim*; while the Ramban and Rabbi Nissim believe that it is a rabbinical prohibition, the Rambam understands that its source is biblical.

Rabbi Aharon Lichtenstein questions Rabbi Shapira's ruling. He challenges it by mentioning that, as we have established, there are those

7. *Sefer Yere'im* 409.
8. Rambam, Introduction to *Mishneh Torah,* negative commandment 65.
9. See *Shiurim LeZekher Abba Mori* (Jerusalem, 1982/1983), 1:171.

who hold that the nature of the prohibition is only rabbinical, thus allowing us to take other factors into consideration:

> You determine as obvious that whoever demolishes part of a synagogue building or its accessories violates a biblical prohibition. This appears to be the position of Rambam, as noted in his enumeration of the mitsvot (though this point is omitted both in *Sefer ha-Mitsvot* and in the *Mishneh Torah*, as has been discussed at length by the *Aharonim*). But many *Aharonim* have suggested that according to some *Rishonim* this is no more than a rabbinic prohibition, especially according to those who maintain that the very sanctity of a synagogue is a rabbinic decree, but perhaps even according to those who deem the synagogue's sanctity to be Torah law, insofar as the Gemara only mentions demolition of the stones of the Sanctuary or of the Temple courtyard, or burning consecrated wood; and minor sanctuaries, i.e., synagogues, were not explicitly added. Do you ignore these opinions because you accept as obvious the view of the *Sefer Yere'im* that the sanctity of a synagogue is by Torah law? Or that even if the sanctity of the synagogue building itself is only by a rabbinic decree, demolishing a synagogue is forbidden by Torah law, because it is intended for Divine service, and its destruction is thus an insult, as it were, against God – this being precisely what is forbidden according to a close reading of the verse, "You shall not do this to the Lord, your God" [Deut. 12:4 and *Sifri*]?

Rabbi Lichtenstein explains why halakhically there is good reason to argue that the demolition should be performed by Israel's own security forces: the fear of the *ḥillul Hashem* which would occur as a result of the Palestinians' desecration of our holy houses of prayer. It is well known that, in the past and in the present, the Arabs living in Israel and the world have not shown respect toward Jewish holy sites.

> From a purely halakhic perspective, if there is no third alternative (for example, agreement regarding the fate of the synagogues after they are transferred, similar to what is stated in Megilla 27b

> regarding the sale of a synagogue), and there exists a reasonable danger that if they remain standing they will turn into mosques, in which will be sounded words of incitement and blasphemy against God and His anointed one – is it preferable to destroy them – and especially so that "they tell it not in Gath" and "the daughters of the uncircumcised rejoice" [I Sam. 1:20]? Or perhaps, out of fear of violating the prohibition of demolishing a synagogue, mentioned by His Honor, it is preferable to abstain and do nothing (*shev ve-al ta'ase*), despite the emotional difficulty of witnessing desecration, which, especially in this area, encourages a scorched earth policy?

Rabbi Yaakov Ariel, who was the founder of the Hesder yeshiva in the city of Yamit (later relocated to Gush Katif), wrote a responsum about our question and ruled, like Rabbi Shapira, that under these circumstances, it is forbidden to destroy the synagogues.[10] In his responsum, he explains that the issue in question is whether it is permissible to commit a sin to prevent a more severe sin from being committed. He quotes a responsum of Rabbi Yaakov ben Yosef Reischer (Austria, 1661–1733) regarding a similar dilemma. The question before him was about old Jewish manuscripts buried in a cemetery which non-Jews were digging up and using as toilet paper. Rabbi Reischer argued that in this case it was permissible to burn the articles of sanctity (an act that is normally prohibited), as this would prevent a greater desecration from taking place.

The question before us is whether these issues are comparable. In other words, what is the greater desecration? Jews destroying their synagogues or non-Jews doing it?

The Gemara discusses ways to annul the *kedusha* of a synagogue. If the seven councilmen of the town gather before the public and decide to sell a synagogue, they are permitted to do so, and the *kedusha* is annulled (Megilla 25b). In his responsum, Rabbi Ariel discusses the status of the towns of Gush Katif and whether their council has authority and ownership over their synagogues. In his conclusion, he explains that even if it were possible to technically annul the *kedusha* of the synagogues, if

10. "Harisat Batei HaKnesset Shel Gush Katif," *Teḥumin* 26 (2005/2006): 23–36.

the world were to see Jews destroying synagogues, this would create a major *ḥillul Hashem*. He therefore concludes that the synagogues should be left intact, even if we know that the Palestinians will destroy – and even desecrate – them.

We will end with the hope expressed in the prophecy of Amos (9:15): "And will plant them on their land, and never again will they be uprooted from the land which I gave to them, says the Lord your God."

27

The Second Lebanon War, 2006

May a *Kohen* Fight in War?

In May 2000, after eighteen years, the IDF pulled out of southern Lebanon. As a result of the withdrawal, Hezbollah spread its forces in the area and continued its terror attacks against Israel. In July 2006, Hezbollah terrorists attacked Israeli forces on the border, killing three Israeli soldiers and kidnapping two.

Israel responded with airstrikes on Lebanese infrastructure. These clashes led to an Israeli ground invasion of southern Lebanon. The IDF called up thousands of reservists, and thus began the Second Lebanon War. Hezbollah attacked Israel with barrages of rockets, targeting civilian population centers. Israeli soldiers called to battle displayed heroism; Roi Klein's act of courage shook the country when, seeing a grenade, he threw himself on it to save his soldiers with a cry of *Shema Yisrael.*

The fighting ended, after thirty-four days, on August 14. In the conflict, Israel lost 121 soldiers and 44 civilians.

In the beginning, the war was supported by a wide and strong consensus among the Israeli population. However, as time went by and the number of casualties rose, the support dwindled and turned into fierce criticism of the government and even the IDF for not being prepared for the conflict. The reservists, some claimed, were ill-equipped;

the forces lacked proper training. Over the course of a year and a half, from September 2006 to April 2007, an official investigation by the Winograd Commission found fault in the army and government's conduct before and during the war.

After the war, my father, Rabbi Binyamin Tabory, was approached by one of his students who had served. This soldier, who was a *kohen*, had found himself in a complicated position. His commanding officer was killed in action, and the soldiers were informed that there would be no helicopter evacuation. The soldiers would have to carry their officer on a stretcher. This soldier was part of a small group (of approximately eight) given the order to carry the officer's body to a safe area.

Normally a *kohen* would avoid coming into contact with a dead body unless the situation was considered *pikuaḥ nefesh*. However, in this case, although there were enough soldiers to carry the stretcher, the soldier felt a need to participate with his comrades-in-arms, paying his last respects to his commanding officer. Should this have been permitted?

KOHANIM IN WARTIME: SELECTED HALAKHIC ISSUES

Kohanim serving in combat raise many questions. While I will not give a halakhic ruling in this chapter, I will share thoughts and dilemmas connected to this question.[1]

The History of *Kohanim* at War: The Tribe of Levi

Are *kohanim* obligated to fight in war? The Rambam writes that the *kohanim* are exempt from serving in the army:

> Why did the Levites not receive a portion in the inheritance of *Eretz Yisrael* and in the spoils of war like their brethren? Because they were set aside to serve God and minister unto Him and to instruct the people at large in His just paths and righteous judgments.... Therefore, they were set apart from the ways of

1. My father told me that when he mentioned this question to Rabbi Hershel Schachter, the response was that under these very specific circumstances, it is permitted. I understand that he is referring to the fact that this entire story occurred during battle, which, as we explained in past chapters, may be a reason for certain leniencies.

> the world. They do not wage war like the remainder of the Jewish people.[2]

Some commentators question the source of this halakha.[3] Rabbi Shimon Federbush, chief rabbi of Finland, expresses his surprise as it seems to be an explicit verse in the Torah.[4] In the beginning of Numbers, Moshe counts the people of Israel from every tribe. However, regarding the tribe of Levi, Moshe is commanded:

> Only the tribe of Levi you shall not number, and you shall not reckon their sum among the Israelites. But you shall appoint the Levites over the Tabernacle of the Testimony, over all its vessels and over all that belong to it; they shall carry the Tabernacle and they shall minister to it, and they shall encamp around the Tabernacle. (Num. 1:49–50)

Rabbi Federbush quotes commentaries on the Torah that point out that the purpose of the census is to prepare for war; thus, the tribe of Levi is not counted along with everyone else, as its members are exempt from fighting. Although these sources seem to indicate that the entire tribe of Levi is exempt from fighting in war, there are other sources which seem to indicate that *kohanim* do indeed serve. For example, one mishna lists all those who are released from military service (Sota 43a). The Torah releases from military service any soldier who has betrothed a wife but has not yet married her. The mishna rules that a *kohen* who betrothed a divorcee is not exempt from the fighting. Surely, the commentators note, this proves that *kohanim* fight in Jewish wars!

Therefore, suggest the *posekim*, either the Levites participate in the war efforts but not in combat itself, or, although they are exempt, it is permissible for them to volunteer to fight.[5]

2. *Mishneh Torah, Hilkhot Shemitta* 13:13.
3. See *Beit David*, vol. 1, #38.
4. *Mishpat HaMelukha BeYisrael* (Jerusalem: Mosad HaRav Kook, 2005), 194.
5. See Rabbi Eliezer Waldenberg, *Sefer Hilkhot Medina*, 2:3; also see Federbush, *Mishpat HaMelukha BeYisrael*, 195. See also Rabbi Shemaryahu Arieli, *Mishpat HaMilḥama* (Jerusalem: Rubin Mass, 1971), 37–43.

Kohanim and Impurity

During World War I, the British government turned to UK Chief Rabbi Joseph Herman Hertz (1872–1946) and asked his opinion regarding drafting *kohanim* to the British Army.[6] The assumption was that the *kohanim* could not participate in a war, as *kohanim* are not allowed to come into contact with dead bodies except those of close relatives or those found abandoned by the side of the road (*meit mitzva*).

Rabbi Hertz permits the draft, offering several reasons why the prohibitions of impurity (*tuma*) for a *kohen* do not apply in war:[7]

1. A soldier killed in battle is considered a *meit mitzva*.
2. The Hasmoneans, who were all *kohanim* yet went to war, provide a historical precedent.
3. The Torah specifically mentions those who are exempt from fighting in war but does not mention *kohanim*.

Those who disagree with Rabbi Hertz argue that the special halakha of *meit mitzva* applies only in unique circumstances and cannot be applied to every death in war.

Rabbi Shemarya Menashe Adler (1869–1959), a *talmid ḥakham* who emigrated from Poland to England, argued vehemently with Rabbi Hertz's justifications.[8] He ultimately agreed with Rabbi Hertz's conclusion, though he gave different reasons for his ruling. Rabbi Yitzhak HaLevi Herzog (who at the time was rabbi of Belfast and would later be Israel's Ashkenazi chief rabbi), also elicited Rabbi Adler's ire; Rabbi Herzog had argued in a newspaper article that the government should not draft *kohanim*.[9]

Meit Mitzva and *Kohanim*

The Mishna teaches us that although a *kohen gadol* (high priest) may never touch the dead, in a case in which he is the only one who can bury

6. See Rabbi Shlomo Zevin, *LeOr HaHalakha*, 58–59.
7. *The Jewish Chronicle*, April 14, 1916.
8. *Mareh Kohen* (Warsaw, 1923), chap. 147.
9. *The Daily Express*, May 24, 1916.

the dead, he is obligated to deal with the dead body, for the commandment of burying the dead overrides his prohibition against becoming impure: "A high priest and a Nazirite may not become impure for their relatives but may do so for an abandoned dead body."[10] The Gemara understands that this only applies if there are no other people around who can perform the commandment.

In some cases, the definition of a *meit mitzva* can be expanded and applied appropriately. In the Gemara, R. Ḥiyya claims that on the day that R. Yehuda HaNasi died *battela kedusha* (holiness was annulled; Ketubot 103b). The *Tosafot* mention that one of the *Rishonim*, Rabbi Chaim Kohen, understood that this passage permitted *kohanim* to touch the dead.[11] He reads the gemara as *battela kedushat kehuna* (the holiness of priesthood was annulled). "If I had been alive at the time of the death of Rabbeinu Tam," proclaimed Rabbi Chaim, "I would have become *tamei* [impure; to attend his funeral]." His reasoning is that great people – *tzaddikim* or even national leaders – have the status of *meit mitzva* for the purpose of allowing *kohanim* to become *tamei*.

I mention this source as an example of how the principle of *meit mitzva* may be applied to include a larger group of people than just one random dead body. However, it is difficult to automatically apply the concept of *meit mitzva* to all soldiers who fall in battle.

In I Kings 2, we read how Benayahu the *kohen* killed Adoniyahu. Rabbi David Kimhi, in his commentary (to I Kings 2:23), questions how a *kohen* came into contact with the dead. His answer: a *kohen* is permitted to fight in war and touch the dead. In his commentary on II Samuel 23, he adds that Pinḥas, who was a *kohen*, was also allowed to fight against Midian; when it comes to war against our enemies, the Torah does not differentiate between Israelites and *kohanim*.

Most *posekim* hold that the laws of impurity for a *kohen* still apply in modern times;[12] however, there are those who disagree. The Raavad argues that *kohanim* in our days are permitted to touch the

10. Mishna Nazir 7:1; for the source of this law, see the Gemara, Nazir 47b.
11. Ketubbot 103b, s.v. *Oto.*
12. *Shulḥan Arukh, Yoreh De'ah* 369:1; Rambam, *Mishneh Torah, Hilkhot Avel* 3:1.

dead because everyone is impure today.[13] His understanding is that since a *kohen* is already impure, there is no prohibition for him to continue being so.[14]

Birkat Kohanim

Some *posekim* are concerned about allowing *kohanim* in combat, as once they take a human life, they will no longer be eligible to recite *Birkat Kohanim* (the priestly blessing). In the Gemara, R. Yoḥanan prohibits a *kohen* who killed another person from reciting *Birkat Kohanim* (Berakhot 32b). The source for this halakha is found in the prophet's words: "And when you spread out your hands, I will turn My eyes away from you…your hands are covered in blood" (Is. 1:15). This verse implies that if a person's hands are "covered in blood," i.e., if he has killed another human being, God will ignore the blessing he proclaims by outstretching his hands. The rabbis understood from these words that a *kohen* who killed another person should not recite *Birkat Kohanim*, because his blessing would not be accepted. Rabbi Yosef Karo rules that this law applies even in the case of accidental killing;[15] however, some *posekim* argue that in the case of an accidental death, the *kohen* may recite the blessing if he repents.[16]

What is the halakha regarding a soldier who kills intentionally in battle? This question was brought up by the *posekim* mentioned earlier in the discussion of drafting *kohanim* during World War I. Rabbi Shimon Sofer (1850–1944), grandson of the *Ḥatam Sofer* and chief rabbi of the Hungarian city of Eger (Erlau), discusses whether the returning

13. The *posekim* argue whether he permits today touching the dead (Rav Akiva Eger) or holds that that there is still a prohibition today.
14. Other *Rishonim* disagree and maintain that this is only permitted when the *kohen* is actually in a state of *tuma*, e.g., when he is in contact with one of the seven dead relatives whom he is required to become *tamei* to. Based on this idea, some suggest that *kohanim* who wish to study medicine may do autopsies provided they are in a state of constant *tuma*. See Rabbi Shlomo Goren, *Torat HaRefua* (Jerusalem: HaIdra Rabba, Mesoret LaAm, 2000/2001), 256.
15. *Oraḥ Ḥayim* 128:35.
16. See Rema, ad loc.

soldiers from World War I are permitted to recite *Birkat Kohanim*. He concludes that it is allowed for two reasons:

1. In wartime, one does not know with certainty if he has killed an opposing soldier.
2. In wartime, the killing is done under duress (*be'ones*),[17] so that it is neither accidental nor intentional.

Rabbi Ovadia Yosef discusses this question specifically regarding IDF personnel who kill the enemies of Israel during battle.[18] First, he argues there is a *maḥloket* among the *posekim* as to whether this law applies to the killing of non-Jews as well as to Jews. Second, he quotes *posekim* who argue that a *kohen* may perform *Birkat Kohanim* after taking a human life while under duress. An Israeli soldier who fights to protect the Jewish people has fulfilled a commandment; he is in a better position than a *kohen* who has killed under duress. Thus, concludes Rav Ovadia, the *kohen* may recite the blessing.[19]

Rabbi Hershel Schachter quotes Rabbi Joseph B. Soloveitchik, who believes that the halakhic question is not so easily resolved.[20] When discussing this halakha, the latter cites God's words to David.

> "My son," David said to Shlomo, "I set my heart upon building a House for the name of the Lord my God. But the word of the Lord came to me, saying, 'You have shed much blood and waged mighty wars – you will not build a House for My name, for you have shed too much blood upon the earth before Me. Now a son has been born to you; he will be a man of peace. I will give him rest from all his surrounding enemies, for Shlomo will be his name, and I will grant peace and calm to Israel in his time. He will build a House in My name.'" (I Chr. 22:7–10)

---

17. *Hitorerut Teshuva* (Jerusalem: Mekhon Ḥatam Sofer, 1973/1974), 4:11.
18. *Yeḥaveh Daat*, 2:14.
19. See Rabbi She'ar Yashuv Cohen, "Nesiat Kapayim Al Yedei Kohanim Loḥamei Milḥamot Yisrael," *Teḥumin* 6 (1984/1985): 31–44.
20. *Nefesh HaRav*, 132.

The simple reading of this passage is that it is referring to the blood of the enemies of Israel, yet God still prevents King David from building the Temple.

Indeed, the idea that spilling blood leaves a stain on a person even when it is done with permission or even as a commandment is mentioned in several other sources. After Pinḥas kills Zimri and Kozbi, God declares (Num. 25:11–13):

> Pinḥas son of Elazar son of Aharon the priest has allayed My rage against the Israelites. Because he was passionate on My behalf among you, I did not destroy the Israelites in My own passion. Therefore, say this: I grant him My covenant of peace. For him and for his descendants, it shall be a covenant of everlasting priesthood, because he was passionate for his God and made atonement on the part of the Israelites.

In their commentaries, both the *Ḥizkuni*[21] (Hezekiah ben Manoah; France, thirteenth century) and Rabbi Naftali Tzvi Yehuda Berlin[22] (the Netziv; Russia/Poland, 1816–1893) explain that although Pinḥas had done the right thing, a covenant of peace was required to ensure that the stain of the killings would not affect his soul.

While the issues that arise regarding *kohanim* and war have been and will be addressed at length by halakhic authorities, may we be blessed with David's words from Psalms 29:11: "May the Lord give strength to His people; may the Lord bless His people with peace."

---

21. In his commentary on Num. 25:12. He cites R. Yoḥanan's ruling and explains that God reassures Pinḥas that he will still be able to serve as a *kohen* because he acted "in the name of Heaven."
22. *Haamek Davar,* beginning of *Parashat Pinḥas.*

28

The Second Lebanon War, 2006

May a Soldier Eat Non-Kosher During War?

During the Second Lebanon War, Israeli troops found themselves on Lebanese soil, required to carry out their mission without basic equipment. Some soldiers were ordered to either carry army rations, which was difficult, or to forage in the villages. Soldiers reported that in some cases they had to arrange food for themselves. One of my colleagues, a reservist captain in an elite unit, described to me how his unit baked pitas and cooked rice in an Arab village using local facilities.

A serious question arose regarding non-kosher food. Obviously, in a situation of *pikuaḥ nefesh*, one is permitted and even required to eat non-kosher food; however, there are sources in halakha that indicate that there is a unique leniency in wartime for doing so.[1]

1. Over the course of the State of Israel's many wars, this question has been addressed and discussed again and again. See Rabbi Shilo Refael in *Mishkan Shilo* (Jerusalem: Mosad HaRav Kook, 1995), 303–9; and Matan Glidai, "Heter Maakhalot Assurot BeMilḥama," *Teḥumin* 27 (2006/2007): 399–407.

THE *HETER* TO EAT NON-KOSHER FOOD IN WARTIME

The Torah mentions that when the Jewish people enter the Land of Israel, they will be allowed to eat from the spoils of war:

> When the Lord your God brings you into the land that He swore to your ancestors Avraham, Yitzḥak, and Yaakov that He would give to you, a land with great and goodly towns you did not build, houses full of all good things that you did not provide, hewn cisterns you did not hew, and vineyards and olive groves that you did not plant – and you eat and are satisfied... (Deut. 6:10–11)

The Rambam understands that these verses are referring to all wars and serve as a source for permitting non-kosher food in wartime:

> When the army's troops enter the territory of non-Jews, conquering them and taking them captive, they are permitted to eat meat from animals that died without being ritually slaughtered or which were terminally ill, and the flesh of pigs and similar animals, if they become hungry and can only find these forbidden foods.
>
> Similarly, they may drink wine used in the worship of idols. This license is derived by the Oral Tradition, which interprets "full of all good things" as pigs' necks and the like.[2]

However, the Ramban disagrees, reading these verses as referring only to when the Jewish people enter the Land of Israel. In his commentary on the verses mentioned above, he writes:

> According to the opinion of our Sages, our verse alludes further to their dispensation that while engaged in the conquest of the Land, it is permitted to eat those good things filling the houses. Even if there are items in those houses that are prohibited for consumption by the Torah, such as pigs' necks; or if one finds vineyards that are planted with forbidden mixtures of crops or olive trees that are *orla* [the biblical prohibition of eating from a

2. *Mishneh Torah, Hilkhot Melakhim* 8:1.

> tree's fruit within its first three years], it is similarly permitted to eat those grapes or olives...[3]

He then quotes the Rambam's ruling mentioned above and argues with his opinion:

> But this is not sound! For it is not only for the reason of saving a life or avoiding hunger that eating such things was permitted during wartime; rather, even after they captured the great and bountiful cities and they settled in them, the Torah permitted them to eat the spoils of their enemies. Furthermore, this law was not said regarding all soldiers, but only in the land that God swore to our forefathers to give to us, as is explicit here in the passage.

It seems that there are three points that the Rambam and the Ramban disagree on:

	Rambam	**Ramban**
To what situations does the *heter* apply?	All wars	Only war in the days of Yehoshua when entering the Land of Israel
To whom does it apply?	Soldiers at wartime	All the people entering the land
When does it apply?	Only in a situation in which people are hungry	Even when there is no hunger involved

3. Translation taken from *Ramban Commentary on the Torah* (New York: Mesorah Publications, 2008).

Rabbi Yitzchok Zev Soloveitchik attempts to explain the dispute.[4] The Rambam, he says, understands that the Torah's *heter* is based on war, while the Ramban understands that it is the food itself (the *ḥeftza*, or object) which is permitted at the time of entry to the Land of Israel. This explanation justifies the Rambam's application of the *heter* to soldiers only, as well as the reason this law applies to all wars; however, it does not necessarily explain why the Rambam limits the *heter* to situations when the soldiers are hungry.

The *posekim* understand that any discussion as to whether or not this law would apply today is based on the Rambam's opinion. However, Rabbi Yosef Babad feels that our halakha would apply, even according to the Ramban, to all wars in which the Land of Israel is occupied by Israeli forces.[5]

The Rationale for Non-Kosher Food in Wartime: *Bediavad* or *Lekhatḥila*?

Rabbi Yosef Karo points out that it is obvious that the Rambam's *heter* is not limited to soldiers who are starving, because in that case *pikuaḥ nefesh* would override the prohibition of eating non-kosher food.[6] However, Rabbi Naftali Tzvi Berlin understands that the *heter* for all soldiers to eat non-kosher food is based on the well-known principle of *pikuaḥ nefesh*. In his Torah commentary, he writes: "Being stringent concerning [non-kosher] food in wartime can bring [a soldier] close to danger."[7]

This idea may be used to explain the Rambam's rationale. It may be true that soldiers are able to "survive" physically by eating basic food, but in wartime, soldiers need to be in top form, both spiritually and physically. One cannot afford to wait for a situation of *pikuaḥ nefesh* to allow the soldiers to eat non-kosher food. In this context we can quote the famous phrase "An army marches on its stomach," which emphasizes the importance of nutrition for the military.[8]

4. *Ḥiddushei HaGaon Rabbeinu Ḥayim,* Ḥullin 17a.
5. *Minḥat Ḥinukh* 527:6.
6. *Kesef Mishneh, Hilkhot Melakhim* 8:1.
7. *Haamek Davar,* Deut. 6:10.
8. This explanation does not clarify why the Rambam permits wine which was poured in the service of idolatry, as such a serious prohibition would not be discounted for

However, there is an alternative explanation for this halakha. It is possible that this unique halakha is a special *heter* given by the Torah for wartime, based on the assumption that such a period requires desperate, radical measures. This explanation would probably lead us to the conclusion that this *heter* is not ideal, but rather *bediavad*.

To understand this possibility, we will mention a similar *heter* in wartime, *eishet yefat to'ar*. This law, under specific circumstances, permits soldiers to engage sexually with captives during wartime and marry them. The rabbis understand that this *heter* is not *lekhatḥila*, but rather based on the principle of "The Torah spoke only in response to the evil inclination" (Kiddushin 21b). The Rambam mentions this law together with the halakha permitting non-kosher food in wartime. "Likewise, he may have intercourse with a non-Jewish woman if he is overwhelmed by his desire."[9] The Rambam's comparison indicates that both are only to be applied *bediavad*.

Furthermore, the connection between these halakhot is proven by the Rambam's words regarding a person who had relations with a non-Jewish maid. Addressing this issue, the Rambam proclaims: "It is definite that according to the law of the Torah he must divorce this maid, for the Torah is relating itself to the evil inclination the same way it permits non-kosher food..."[10]

It thus seems quite likely that the Rambam's *heter* for non-kosher food is based primarily on "The Torah spoke only in response to the evil inclination."

The Application of the *Heter* in the Past

Rabbi Yisrael Meir Kagan (the *Ḥafetz Ḥayim*; Russian Empire, 1839–1933) wrote the first halakhic work for Jewish soldiers, *Maḥaneh Yisrael*. His audience was made up of Jewish draftees in the army of Czarist Russia. In his book, he strongly opposes the idea of eating non-kosher food

pikuaḥ nefesh. See the rest of the Netziv's commentary, in which he addresses this question.

9. *Mishneh Torah, Hilkhot Melakhim* 8:2.
10. *Teshuvot HaRambam* 154.

during military service.[11] He argues that one can survive without eating non-kosher meat. He also encourages the Jewish communities to open their homes to the soldiers and offer them kosher food.

During World War II, Chief Rabbi Herzog was asked whether the soldiers of the Jewish Brigade were allowed to eat non-kosher food. In his responsum, he quotes the above sources and argues that even according to the Rambam's opinion, there is no room for leniency.[12] His reason is that the Rambam's *heter* applies only in a war conducted completely by Jews; however, in World War II, Jewish soldiers were only part of a coalition fighting a global war. He then adds a significant remark that should be noted: although World War II was not a "classic" Jewish war, Rabbi Herzog argues, it was still important to participate in it, as the enemy was a cruel one aiming to destroy the Jewish people.

Rabbi Avraham Avidan, deputy chief rabbi of the IDF, addressed a question which came up during the First Lebanon War. He was asked by soldiers whether they were allowed to eat the fruits and vegetables growing in the local villages of Lebanon. Although his responsum deals with different questions than ours (the main question is theft), he does mention our halakha. He quotes the above view of Rabbi Yosef Karo in the *Kesef Mishneh* as well as Rabbi Yitzchok Zev Soloveitchik's explanation of the Rambam, and he concludes that these opinions lead us to the ruling that the special needs of war permit soldiers to eat non-kosher food even if they are not in life-threatening situations.

In his book, Rabbi Mordechai Halpern, an expert in medical ethics and a former IDF chaplain, discusses a situation in which an elite unit that was deep behind enemy lines found a warehouse of non-kosher food. In this specific case, the soldiers had their own army rations with them. Would they still have been allowed to eat the non-kosher food?

First, he mentions that this question exists only according to the Rambam's opinion. According to the Ramban, the rule does not apply today. This fact makes our question a *maḥloket* between *Rishonim*. The matter is of biblical nature. In cases in which we face a halakhic dilemma due to a *safek* (doubt), the rule is to follow the more stringent opinion

11. *Maḥaneh Yisrael* (Warsaw, 1881), chap. 23–25.
12. *Heikhal Yitzḥak, Oraḥ Ḥayim* #42.

for biblical issues. This itself is reason to prohibit eating the non-kosher food. However, Rabbi Halpern argues that even according to the Rambam, it would be prohibited; he understands (as explained above) that the Rambam's *heter* is only *bediavad*. He thus concludes that, according to all opinions, the soldiers are not allowed to eat the non-kosher food unless they are in a situation of *pikuaḥ nefesh*.[13]

However, in the year 2006, after the Second Lebanon War, because of its special circumstances, he added a note to this article:

> All of the above is true regarding eating the food when the war is over; *however, during the fighting itself*, we should follow the words of Rabbi Naftali Tzvi Yehuda Berlin that any stringency regarding [*kashrut* of] food might create a life-threatening situation!

Let us end with the words of the Rambam describing the Messianic future: "In that era, there will be neither famine nor war, neither envy nor competition, for good will flow in abundance and all the delights will be as freely available as the dust. The pursuit of the entire world will be solely to know God."[14] May these days come soon.

13. *Refua, Metziut VeHalakha* (Jerusalem: HaMakhon Al Shem Dr. Shlesinger LeḤeker HaRefua Al Pi HaTorah Leyad HaMerkaz HaRefui Shaare Zedek, 2011), 137–42.
14. *Mishneh Torah, Hilkhot Melakhim* 12:5.

29

Operation Cast Lead, 2008

Who Is Exempt from Going to War?

In the summer of 2005, Israel withdrew its military and civilians from the Gaza Strip, as we discussed at length in chapter 26. The hope was that this would bring an end to terror attacks against both Israeli soldiers and Israeli citizens, but they persist to the current day. The attacks have included thousands of rocket attacks against Israeli towns and cities, mostly against those bordering Gaza.

Between 2006 and 2008, following the withdrawal, clashes between Israel and the militant group Hamas continued. During these years, Hamas constantly attempted to kidnap Israeli soldiers. In fact, many tunnels dug for that purpose have been exposed and destroyed by the IDF. In June 2006, Hamas attacked an Israeli force which was stationed by the border. In the attack two IDF soldiers were killed, and a third, Gilad Shalit, was taken captive. Internal political and military clashes between the Palestinian Authority (helmed by Fatah) and Hamas led to Hamas's takeover of the Gaza Strip in June 2007.

Israel does not recognize Hamas as a legitimate authority, seeing it as a terrorist group guilty of the murder of innocents. Israel's response has been to besiege Gaza, limiting Hamas's ability to arm itself with more rockets. On December 24, 2008, over sixty rockets were fired from the Gaza Strip on Israeli towns. Three days later, Israel launched Operation Cast Lead, which continued until a ceasefire was agreed upon in January 2009.

Israel's ground forces entered Gaza on January 3. On January 5, the IDF began operating in the densely populated urban centers of Gaza. Hamas responded by intensifying its rocket and mortar attacks against civilian targets in southern Israel, reaching the cities of Beer Sheva and Ashdod.

At the time, the following story shook up many Israelis and became a legend. Lieutenant Aharon Karov, a paratrooper and officer whose unit was deployed to the Gaza front, was married the day his unit was called up; a few hours after his wedding night, he found himself fighting in Gaza. On January 13, he was critically wounded in an explosion, and it was doubtful whether he would survive. After a miraculous and difficult period of rehabilitation, Aharon recovered from his injuries and had a child. His father, Rabbi Ze'ev Karov, *rosh yeshiva* of the Karnei Shomron Hesder yeshiva, was interviewed the day his son was critically injured. In his emotional, moving words, he quoted the mishna which states that for a *milḥemet mitzva* (commanded war), even the bride and groom must leave their own wedding to fight for the Jewish people.

THE COMMANDMENT TO FIGHT IN A WAR

The Rambam lists three types of *milḥemet mitzva*: "The war against the seven nations who occupied the Land of Israel, the war against Amalek, and a war fought to assist Israel from an enemy which attacks it."[1] The first two examples are wars in which fighting is required to fulfill a commandment, i.e., killing Amalek and killing the seven nations (positive commandments 187 and 188 in his *Sefer HaMitzvot*). Settling the Land of Israel may be a commandment as well (see chapter 14). However, in the third case – defending Israel from enemies – what exactly is the commandment?

1. *Mishneh Torah, Hilkhot Melakhim* 5:1.

One possibility is that the Rambam is referring to the commandment of "Do not stand by while your neighbor's life is in danger" (Lev. 19:16), which the Sages understand as the source of the duty to save a fellow Jew's life. However, there is great difficulty in this suggestion, because in war, one puts one's own life in danger, possibly sacrificing it to save others, which seems to lie beyond the scope of "stand[ing] by." Therefore, it seems unlikely that this law serves as the basis for the commandment of fighting a defensive war.

Rabbi Yair Kahn, of Yeshivat Har Etzion, suggests that this commandment is referring to the natural elementary right of survival that every individual and every nation possess.[2] Responding to others' threats using defense or offense is based on the basic human right to live and to exist. There is a well-known rule in Judaism: "Rise to kill whoever comes to kill you" (Sanhedrin 72a). This rule, which legitimates self-defense, is similarly based on the above logic. The Gemara discusses the Torah's permission for a homeowner to kill a perpetrator who breaks in during the night (Sanhedrin 73a). The Torah states: "If a burglar is caught tunneling in, and is struck and killed, there is no bloodguilt on his account [and it is permissible to kill him]" (Ex. 22:1). The Gemara explains that the license to kill the burglar is based on the rule of "Rise to kill whoever comes to kill you," as the Torah permits people to protect themselves.

While the common understanding is that this is the source for the rule, the Meiri suggests an alternative option.[3] He quotes midrashic sources which connect our rule to wars that take place in the Bible. He refers to the war that Moshe conducts against the Midianites as a response to their attacks against the Jews (Num. 31). It is this case, argues the Meiri, that proves that the Torah recognizes the right given to a person to fight back against those who wish him or her harm.

Rabbi Natan Tzvi Friedman (1914–1993), a neighborhood rabbi in Bnei Brak, suggests that we need two separate sources, one to provide legitimacy for the individual and one for the community, or *tzibbur*.[4]

---

2. "Ki Tavo Milḥama BeArtezkhem," in *Ma Ahavti Toratekha*, ed. Yitzhak Recanati and Shaul Barth (Alon Shevut: Yeshivat Har Etzion, 2004), 46–61.
3. Ad loc.
4. "Din Rodef LeMeḥablim," *Shana BeShana* (1972): 143–48.

EXEMPTION FROM PARTICIPATING IN WAR

After we have established that it is a commandment to defend and protect a fellow Jew, we may discuss who is obligated and who is exempt from this commandment. It is important to note that there are two possible levels of exemption. An exemption from fighting does not necessarily exempt one from participating and helping in war efforts. The Torah mentions several groups of people who are exempt.

The Tribe of Levi

The Torah states that when conducting a census, the tribe of Levi is not counted as all other tribes are: "You shall not count the tribe of Levi, nor take a census of them among the Israelites" (Num. 1:49). The simple understanding is that the census is for military purposes; as the *kohanim* and Levites do not fight in the army, there is no need to count them.[5]

It seems that this is the source of the Rambam's ruling:

> And why did not Levi partake of the patrimony of the Land of Israel and its spoils with his brethren? Because he was set apart to serve God, to worship Him, and to teach His just ways and righteous ordinances to the masses. As it is stated, "They shall teach Yaakov Your ordinances and Yisrael Your law." Therefore, they have been set apart from the ways of the world: *they do not wage war like the rest of Israel,* nor do they inherit or acquire unto themselves by physical force. They are, rather, the Lord's corps.[6] (Emphasis mine.)

In a previous chapter, we quoted *posekim* who are puzzled by various sources that clearly indicate that the tribe of Levi did in fact participate in fighting.[7] Two good examples are their participation in the biblical war against the Midianites[8] and the battles against the Greeks led by the Hasmonean family, who were *kohanim*. It seems, we noted there,

---

5. See both the ibn Ezra and the Abarbanel, ad loc.
6. *Mishneh Torah, Hilkhot Shemitta VeYovel* 13:12.
7. See chapter 27.
8. According to the *Sifrei,* ad loc.

that *kohanim* may volunteer to serve in the army. Rabbi Yechiel Michel Tukachinsky (1871–1955), a prominent *posek* who served as *Rosh Yeshivat* Etz Chayim in Jerusalem, also debates this question, concluding that *kohanim* and Levites, although exempt from fighting, may volunteer to serve in the army.

Exemptions Related to Personal Circumstances

The Torah mentions that prior to war the soldiers would gather, and the *kohen* would announce that the following soldiers should go home (Deut. 20:8): anyone who has betrothed a woman but has not married her, anyone who has recently bought a house but has not lived in it, and anyone who has planted a vineyard but has not enjoyed its fruit. The *kohen* would subsequently discharge those who were afraid to fight (Deut. 20:5). However, the Mishna claims that all the above are still required to help with the war efforts (Mishna Sota 8:7). Regarding the newlywed soldier, the Torah elsewhere commands him to stay with his wife at home for the first year of marriage, which implies full exemption for the entire year (Deut. 24:5). This exemption is from all army service and war efforts.

Referring to these exemptions, the mishna remarks: "In what [case] are [all of] these statements [with regard to the various exemptions from war] said? [They are said] with regard to *milḥemet reshut* (elective wars). But in *milḥemet mitzva* (a war whose mandate is a commandment) everyone goes, even a groom from his room and a bride from her wedding canopy." The Rambam accepts this passage at face value and rules accordingly.[9] The ruling of the Rambam seems to obligate both women and Torah scholars. Is this the case?

Drafting Women

Many rabbis have come out against drafting women into the IDF. Their main argument is based on matters of modesty (*tzniut*). In fact, chief rabbi of Jerusalem Rabbi Tzvi Pesach Frank, in his introduction to volume 2 of Rabbi Eliezer Waldenberg's *Hilkhot Medina,* explains that he is not interested in discussing the halakhic matter regarding women's

9. *Mishneh Torah, Hilkhot Melakhim* 7:4.

obligation to participate in war due to his understanding that it is unconscionable for women to fight in battle because of modesty.[10]

Sefer HaḤinukh seems to contradict itself in the discussions of two commandments that involve war. Regarding the commandment to kill the seven nations (245), it rules that women are obligated, yet in the commandment of destroying Amalek (603) as well as other commandments related to war, it exempts them. Why would *Sefer HaḤinukh* obligate women to fight against the seven Canaanite nations but not against Amalek, when both are in the category of *milḥemet mitzva*?

Rabbi Chanoch Henoch Eigis (Lithuania, 1863–1941) was one of the leading rabbis of Vilna for over forty years, until he was killed in the Holocaust. He explains that the default position of *Sefer HaḤinukh* is that women are exempt from all wars and battles. However, when it comes to the seven nations, the obligation to kill them applies to women because of the positive commandment of settling the Land of Israel, which is the direct outcome of this commandment.[11] As women are obligated to settle the Land of Israel, they are obligated to rid the country of the seven nations.

The rabbis who have discussed this matter usually focus on the biblical story of Yael, who saved the day by killing the chief of staff of the Canaanite army, Sisera, with a tent peg. The gemara explains: "R. Eliezer b. Yaakov said: From where [is it derived] that a woman may not go out with weapons to war? The verse states, 'A woman shall not wear that which pertains to a man (*kli gever*)' (Deut. 22:5)" (Nazir 59a). Rashi explains that the gemara is bothered by Yael's choice of weapon: "And that is why Yael, the wife of Ḥever the Kenite, did not kill Sisera with a weapon, as it says, 'She picked up the tent peg' (Judges 4:21)." This source, as well as others, give *posekim* like Rabbi Shlomo Yosef Zevin[12] the basis for prohibiting the conscription of women; the fact that Yael

10. See Rabbi Alfred S. Cohen's article about this ("Drafting Women for the Army," *RJJ Journal of Halacha and Contemporary Society* 16 [Fall 1988]: 26–42), especially in the beginning, where he quotes the rabbis who vehemently oppose the draft.
11. Rabbi Chanoch Henoch Eigis, *Marḥeshet* (Jerusalem), vol. 1, *siman* 22.
12. *LeOr HaHalakha,* 25–27.

did not use a traditional weapon, in their opinion, means that women today should not carry traditional weapons.

Rabbi Yehuda Shaviv discusses whether the gemara's prohibition regarding Yael is about going to war or about carrying weapons. He points out that the Rambam, when referring to this passage, does not relate to the question of women going to war, instead focusing on the *kli gever*. Furthermore, the Rambam cites this law in *Hilkhot Avoda Zara* (12:10), which deals with pagan practices, not in *Hilkhot Melakhim*, which deals with war. As mentioned, the Rambam quotes the mishna in Sota and seems to rule that even women are obligated to fight. Rabbi Shaviv explains how this fits in nicely with his interpretation of the Rambam's ruling.[13] In fact, Rabbi Shimon Federbush, chief rabbi of Finland, quoting the Rambam, agrees that this is the Rambam's opinion.[14]

Some *posekim* cannot fathom the possibility that the Rambam permits women to fight and therefore suggest alternatives. In his commentary on *Mishneh Torah*, the Radbaz questions:

> [The mishnaic text] is difficult, for is it really a woman's way to do battle? Does not the verse [praise women and] say: "In all her glory, the princess is inside" (Ps. 45:14)?
>
> But rather it means to say that, since the groom is exiting his chamber, the bride also has to leave her canopy and cannot follow the usual nuptial customs.

In his second answer (which has practical differences from the first answer), he suggests that women are obligated to participate in the war effort but are exempt from combat: "Perhaps in wartime the women used to provide water and food for their husbands."

However, there are other indications that the Rambam believes that women are obligated to fight in war. In his introduction to *Sefer HaMitzvot*, rule 14, he mentions twice that women are exempt from participating in a *milḥemet reshut*, thus implying that they are obligated to fight in a *milḥemet mitzva*.

13. "Nashim BeMilḥemet Mitzva," *Teḥumin* 4 (1982/1983): 79–90.
14. *Mishpat HaMelukha BeYisrael*, 194.

The exemptions from military service in wartime, discussed only theoretically for thousands of years, have become a practical question since the founding of the state. But one final – though crucial and controversial – question about exemptions remains, as we will see in the coming chapter.

30

Operation Cast Lead, 2008

Should Torah Scholars Be Drafted?

A debate has raged in the State of Israel since its birth in 1948 until the present day regarding drafting yeshiva students.

The mishna in Sota, which we quoted in the previous chapter, states that everyone must participate in a *milḥemet mitzva*. The mishna mentions that even a bride and groom must leave their wedding (Sota 8:7). Presumably, the mishna believes that no one is exempt from fighting, including Torah scholars. Below we ask whether this is, in fact, true.

In wartime, when the Jewish people are facing imminent danger, it is very difficult to give an exemption to anyone. Rabbi Yitzchak Minkowski (1788–1851), chief rabbi of the city of Karlin, writes explicitly in his *Keren Ora* that in times of war, even Torah scholars are obligated to participate.[1]

Many twentieth-century rabbis who argue for the exemption agree with the opinion of the *Keren Ora*. However, they take into account an important fact: the lack of Torah knowledge in the aftermath of the

1. *Keren Ora,* Sota 44b.

Holocaust. Their concern is rebuilding the yeshivas that were lost and creating a new generation of Torah scholars. Nonetheless, in the last few years, new arguments have been added to the debate. We will attempt to discuss the main sources and avoid irrelevant political arguments.

MILITARY DEFENSE AND TORAH STUDY

In 1948, as a response to rabbis who opposed the draft, an anonymous leaflet was distributed in shuls and yeshivas, signed by "one of the rabbis." There is a debate as to who wrote the letter. The common opinion is that it was the great *posek* and *talmid ḥakham* Rabbi Shlomo Yosef Zevin. The leaflet argues that, at times of great peril, all must participate in defending and protecting the nation.

Some rabbis quote sources in the Gemara that argue that Torah scholars are exempt from paying taxes for the city's protection because their Torah protects them (Bava Batra 7b). Rabbi Zevin's response to them is the following:

> When actual lives are at stake, may we rely on miracles? In 1929 during the Ḥevron Massacre...did not young students of the yeshiva, whose holiness shone like stars in the sky, fall before the malicious enemy? Please, did these martyrs need protection or not?
>
> If you understand that the scholars need protection in relatively peaceful times and are exempt from building protective walls, what consequence has this when compared to a life-and-death struggle, a war which is a commandment and in which all are obligated? The defense authorities ordered everyone to cover all windows as protection against shattering glass in case of an air raid. Would anyone think that some rabbis would not do so, claiming, "Rabbis do not need protection"? Why did rabbis leave areas under enemy fire along with the rest of the general population? Why did they not rely on this maxim?[2]

2. This article in Hebrew can be found online. See Rabbi Shlomo Yosef Zevin, "LiShe'elat HaGiyus Shel Bnei HaYeshivot," www.ḥerzog.ac.il/vtc/0026394.doc.

The Model of the Tribe of Levi

Those who oppose Rabbi Zevin's view quote the Rambam's opinion:

> And not the tribe of Levi alone but each and every person throughout the world whose spirit has uplifted him and whose intelligence has given him the understanding to stand before God, to serve Him, to worship Him, to know God; and he walks aright as the Lord has made him and he has cast off from his neck the yoke of the many considerations that men have sought – such a one has been sanctified as the holy of holies, and the Lord shall be his portion and his inheritance forever and ever and shall grant him his sufficiency in this world as He has granted to the *kohanim* and the Levites.[3]

The Rambam rules that any Jew who wishes to dedicate his life to God can receive rights that are similar to the rights of the members of the tribe of Levi – including an exemption from serving in the army.

In his famous essay on the ideology of Hesder, Rabbi Aharon Lichtenstein argues that for several reasons, this law does not serve as a proof for exemption. First, he points out, the Rambam brings this halakha in *Hilkhot Shemitta,* and not in *Hilkhot Melakhim*. Moreover, argues Rabbi Lichtenstein:

> Finally, even if we grant that the Rambam's statement does imply a categorical dispensation in purely halakhic terms, it remains of little practical significance. We have yet to examine just to whom it applies. A *levi* is defined genealogically. Those who are equated with him, however, literally or symbolically, are defined by spiritual qualities; and for these the Rambam sets a very high standard, indeed. He presents an idealized portrait of a selfless, atemporal, almost ethereal person – one whose spirit and intelligence have led him to divest himself of all worldly concerns and who has devoted himself…"to stand before God, to serve Him, to worship Him, to know God; and he walks aright as the Lord

3. *Mishneh Torah, Hilkhot Shemitta VeYovel* 13:13.

> has made him and he has cast off from his neck the yoke of the many considerations that men have sought."
>
> To how large a segment of the Torah community, or, *a fortiori,* of any community, does this lofty typology apply? Two percent? Five percent? Can anyone who has negotiated the terms of a salary...look into a mirror and tell himself that he need not go to the army because he is *kodesh kodashim, sanctum sanctorum,* in the Rambam's terms? Can anyone with even a touch of vanity or a concern for *kavod* contend this?[4]

If one understands that the Rambam's opinion regarding the tribe of Levi serves as a precedent for permitting yeshiva students to avoid the draft, then it seems reasonable to argue that the same way *kohanim* are permitted to volunteer, so may the Torah scholars.

Those who oppose the draft often quote Rav Kook,[5] who argues that yeshiva students should remain in the yeshivas rather than go to the army. I find this ruling completely irrelevant. Rav Kook died in 1935, and obviously the circumstances at the time were completely different, as he was referring to drafting Jews into a foreign army.

Rabbi Haim Drukman has an unpublished manuscript written by Rav Kook, which contains the following determination:

> Although the tribe of Levi does not participate in war, it seems this is only the case with small-scale battles, as in the case when a tribe is fighting for its personal territory. However, *when all the people of Israel are faced with war, all must go to battle.* [Furthermore,] fighting the battles of the Jewish people is also service of God; therefore, whoever is more connected to the service of God should be more connected to it. (Emphasis mine.)

4. The article appeared in Hebrew first; it was then translated to English and published in "The Ideology of Hesder," *Tradition* 19, no. 3 (Fall 1981): 199–217; see p. 212.
5. See Rabbi Alfred S. Cohen, "On Yeshiva Men Serving in the Army," *RJJ Journal of Halacha and Contemporary Society* 23 (Spring 1992): 5–31.

I believe that this last paragraph serves as an important argument that the closer one is to God, the more one should be in the armed forces, fighting the enemies of Israel.

The Views of Rabbi Chaim David HaLevi and Rabbi Aharon Lichtenstein

Rabbi Chaim David HaLevi, chief rabbi of Tel Aviv, argues for a full exemption for those who choose to learn Torah.[6] His opinion is a common one even among Religious Zionist rabbis.[7] However, he agrees that when combat begins, all must fight. He adds that as soon as the battle is over, the students must return immediately to the house of study. I find this opinion very difficult to understand. It is obvious that one cannot leave the house of study and go to the front without proper training. How can one exempt yeshiva students from army service and yet expect them to charge the enemy on the day of battle?

I feel it important to mention that Rabbi Aharon Lichtenstein and Rabbi Yehuda Amital were, to my knowledge, the first Religious Zionist leaders to come out publicly with the opinion that all yeshiva students are obligated to serve in the IDF.[8]

As mentioned, the most "lenient" opinions in the Religious Zionist camp at the time, i.e., those views most positively inclined toward military service, merely permitted yeshiva students to serve in the IDF. Most rabbis told their students that the army was just for those who found it too difficult to study Torah all day.[9] Rabbi Lichtenstein's opinion that Hesder is *lekhatḥila* was nothing less than revolutionary at the time.

---

6. "Sherut Tzeva'i BeHalakha," *Torah SheBe'al Peh* 13 (1971): 152.
7. See the opinion of Rabbi Shaul Yisraeli, as quoted by Yechezkel Cohen, *Giyus Ka-Halakha* (Jerusalem: Ne'emanei Torah Va'Avoda, 1993), 78.
8. See Lichtenstein, "Ideology of Hesder," and Rabbi Yehuda Amital, "Raayon Yeshivot HaHesder VeHagshamatan," *Alon Shevut Bogrim* 14 (Nisan 5761): 35–38.
9. See Rabbi Yisraeli and Rabbi Chayim David HaLevi supra. Also see Rabbi Zalman Melamed, "Gedolei Torah – Zehu Tzorekh HaUma," *Teḥumin* 7 (1985/1986): 330–34; Rabbi Eliezer Yehuda Waldenberg, *Sefer Hilkhot Medina*, 2:62.

Military Service as Lovingkindness

Finally, I would like to raise one more issue. In the past few years, many arguments have been made in favor of drafting all Israeli citizens, including yeshiva students. The suggested reasons are based either on ethical arguments or on halakhic sources.

Rabbi Lichtenstein propounds a *ḥiddush,* a novel approach, for why he believes yeshiva students should join the IDF. He mentions the religious principle of *gemilut ḥasadim* (lovingkindness):

> The halakhic rationale for Hesder does not, as some mistakenly assume, rest solely upon the *mitsvah* of waging defensive war. If that were the case, one might conceivably argue that, halakhically, sixteen months of army service was too high a price to pay for the performance of this single commandment. The rationale rather rests upon a) the simple need for physical survival and b) the fact that military service is often the fullest manifestation of a far broader value: *gemilut hasadim,* the empathetic concern for others and action on their behalf. This element, defined by Shimon Hatsaddik as one of the three cardinal foundations of the world, is the basis of Jewish social ethics, and its realization, even at some cost to single-minded development of Torah scholarship, virtually imperative...
>
> When, as in contemporary Israel, the greatest single *hesed* one can perform is helping to defend his fellows' very lives, the implications for yeshivah education should be obvious.[10]

I believe Rabbi Lichtenstein adds a profound element. This source suggests that the question before us has to do with the way we understand the meaning of Torah and the way we implement it in our lives. Based on this idea, I would like to suggest a similar insight – that considerations other than the strictest sense of the halakha must also be taken into account – in our discussion.

10. Lichtenstein, "Ideology of Hesder," 207–8.

The Hands of Esav and the Voice of Yaakov

In the middle of the book of Genesis, Yitzḥak and Rivka debate the question of which of their sons, Yaakov or Esav, should be chosen to continue the Jewish lineage. Rivka supports Yaakov, and this is a reasonable position; but what is Yitzḥak thinking when he chooses Esav to lead the Jewish people?

Rabbi Yoel Bin-Nun[11] suggests that although Yitzḥak is aware of the complexity of Esav's personality, he is more concerned with appointing a strong leader who will deter the potential enemies of our people. Yaakov, at the time, is almost like a yeshiva student who spends his days learning, while Esav is a man of action feared by those around him.

Yaakov dresses up as Esav, entering his father's tent with his hands covered with hairy goatskin to trick his father into thinking that he is his brother. At this point, Yitzḥak is confused; although "the hands are the hands of Esav," "the voice is the voice of Yaakov" (Gen. 27:22). In Rabbi Bin-Nun's reading, a smile spreads across Yitzḥak's face when he realizes that he has been tricked, that before him stands the solution for ideal Jewish leadership.

Nonetheless, it takes years for Yaakov to combine the two: the hands of Esav and the voice of Yaakov. Rabbi Bin-Nun explains it as follows:

> From the exilic Yaakov there emerges Yisrael, who fights with all his strength. Yisrael may be injured, but he will not be vanquished. Then, once again, Yaakov receives the same blessing he received from Yitzchak, this time having demonstrated that he has truly acquired "the hands of Esav." He no longer needs to resort to deception; he is now able to maintain "the voice of Yaakov" while at the same time using his hands in a real struggle...
>
> This suggests that it is neither Yaakov who is blessed by Yitzchak, through Divine inspiration, nor Esav. The figure who actually received the blessings – possessing "the hands of Esav" while his voice was "the voice of Yaakov" (*Bereishit* 27:22) – did

---

11. His main article on this topic is published in *Pirkei HaAvot* (Alon Shevut: Tvunot, 2004), 154–64.

> not yet exist. Only after twenty years of living in Lavan's household, during which Yaakov grew accustomed to placing "the skins of the kids of goats" (27:16) upon his hands, did this figure come into being.[12]

After two thousand years of exile we have returned home. However, in our home we find ourselves constantly surrounded by enemies who wish to destroy us. What type of army do we wish to build to face these challenges? It seems to me that the ideal Israeli soldier should be a combination of the hands of Esav and the voice of Yaakov.

The Unique Ideology of Hesder

My father, Rabbi Binyamin Tabory, who taught in Yeshivat Har Etzion for many years, told me that, years ago, a committee from the French government visited the yeshiva to learn about Hesder. While visiting the yeshiva, they were astonished to meet student-soldiers in the *beit midrash* who were engrossed in talmudic studies. They explained that in their country, the common soldier cannot be found studying. If anything, they argued, the common soldier is better off learning to obey orders rather than studying them.

The Archetype of David

The Gemara (Moed Katan 16b) refers to a name mentioned in II Samuel, stating that it was a nickname given to King David: "These are the names of David's warriors:…he is Adino the Etznite – he wielded his spear against eight hundred victims at once" (II Sam. 23:8). While *adin* means gentle, *etz* means wood. Thus, the appellation "Adino the Etznite" indicates that while engaging in Torah study, David is as gentle as a worm; but while fighting in battle, he is ruthless and tough like wood.

Thus, the gemara tells us, the meaning of the name is that King David is a combination of *safra* (book) and *saifa* (sword), to utilize the

12. Rabbi Yoel Bin-Nun, "War and Morality: Yisrael in the Land," The Israel Koschitzky Torat Har Etzion VBM, December 14, 2016, https://www.etzion.org.il/en/tanakh/torah/sefer-bereishit/parashat-vayishlach/vayishlach-war-and-morality-yisrael-land.

metaphor of the *Sifrei* (*Ekev* 40): "Said R. Eliezer: The book and the sword descended from the heavens, each bound up in the other."

As long as we are forced to live under the constant threat of war, should we not strive to build an army following the ways of King David? Should Torah students and Jewish soldiers be two separate entities, or should they be combined into one personality?

31

Operation Protective Edge, 2014

May Countries Target Citizens During War?

On June 12, 2014, three Israeli teenagers from Yeshivat Makor Chaim in Kfar Etzion were kidnapped near Alon Shevut. Naftali Fraenkel, Gilad Shaer, and Eyal Yifrach were waiting by the bus stop for a ride to take them home when terrorists abducted them. Gilad Shaer called the police and whispered: "They kidnapped me." In the background, the police heard shouting in Arabic and several volleys of automatic gunfire.

At this point, the army assumed the boys had been killed; but as this information was kept secret, hope remained among the families as well as the entire State of Israel that the boys were still alive. The IDF launched an operation named Operation Brother's Keeper (called *Shuvu Aḥim*, return of brothers, in Hebrew) in search of the three boys. In the following days, Israel arrested approximately 350 Palestinians, including nearly all of Hamas's leaders.

The response in Israel society was dramatic. Huge groups gathered to pray all around the country, with the largest gathering at the Western Wall of over 25,000 people.

On June 30, search teams made up of volunteers and IDF soldiers found the bodies of the three missing teenagers in a field near Ḥevron. As had been suspected, they had been shot dead shortly after the abduction. On September 23, the IDF reached the terrorists' hiding place. After they refused to surrender, the soldiers stormed the house, killing the kidnappers.

During this time, Hamas continued to shell Israeli cities with rockets. As the attacks from Gaza increased, Israel responded with a ground invasion. The operation, named Protective Edge (or *Tzuk Eitan*, meaning steadfast cliff, in Hebrew), included two main objectives: destroying the Gaza tunnel system and stopping the rocket attacks. After weeks of fighting, on August 5, the IDF withdrew and a ceasefire was established. During the conflict, 67 Israeli soldiers and 6 civilians were killed, and 469 soldiers and 261 civilians were injured.

On the last day of fighting, an elite force of the Givati Brigade was assigned to search out and destroy a tunnel which, the IDF suspected, reached into Israel. The soldiers were surprised by terrorists who suddenly came out of the tunnel and opened fire on them. When the rest of the force caught up with their comrades, they found their officer and his radioman dead, while a third officer, Lieutenant Hadar Goldin, was missing. Without any hesitation, the soldiers jumped into the dark tunnel to retrieve Hadar. In the tunnel, they found certain articles which proved that Hadar had been killed during the abduction.

As soon as the army realized that Hadar was missing, the code name "Hannibal" was broadcast over the army radio. This code serves as a message to the entire army that a soldier has been abducted and all forces must do everything possible to find him.

In any case, "Hannibal" unleashed a dramatic response on the part of the Israeli forces, who turned around and fought their way back into Gaza. This military maneuver included bombing all possible escape routes from the tunnels. In these bombings, civilians, as well as Hamas terrorists, were killed.

Sadly, Hadar's body still remains in the hand of the Hamas.

During this operation, as well as in the many wars and battles in Israel's history, civilians on the enemy side have been killed unintentionally. Below we learn about this sensitive issue and look at our sources for insights on this topic.

TARGETING CIVILIANS

Before we begin, let us clarify that there are several different wartime scenarios in which armies find themselves facing innocent civilians. The most extreme case is one in which countries target civilians deliberately as part of putting pressure on the other side to surrender. In World War II, for example, the US bombed Japanese cities intentionally, killing thousands of civilians uninvolved in combat. This extreme case is not the type of scenario we are discussing.

Rabbi Shlomo Goren, IDF chief rabbi and later Ashkenazi chief rabbi of Israel, wrote many articles regarding the Jewish attitude toward war. When referring to our issue, he writes:

> Although the Torah commands us explicitly to fight in war, we are also commanded at the same time to show mercy to our enemies. We may not kill the enemy, even during battle, unless it is required for defensive or offensive purposes.
>
> *It is prohibited to harm civilians who are not involved in the fighting, and obviously we may not harm women and children.*[1] (Emphasis mine.)

Rabbi Goren mentions that the Torah commands us to destroy the seven nations of Canaan, as it says: "However, in the towns of the nations that the Lord your God is giving you as an inheritance, let nothing that breathes remain alive" (Deut. 20:16); however, one cannot use this as a template because this was an exceptional case and was limited to the specific seven nations.

Another very different scenario is the case in which terrorists who are launching rockets at civilian targets are hiding behind their own people, using them as human shields. Is it ethically correct to bomb these terrorists, taking into account that civilians might be killed? Must our soldiers endanger their own lives in these situations?

1. *Meshiv Milḥama* (Jerusalem: HaIdra Rabba, 1982–83), 1:14.

The Dispensation to Kill Soldiers in Battle

First, we must establish the halakhic legal dispensation for killing soldiers in battle. In other words, what is the difference between the severe prohibition of "*Lo tirtzaḥ*," "You shall not murder," which is a capital crime, and the commandment of participating in a war, an act which is encouraged?

The obvious answer would be the famous talmudic rule which we quoted earlier: "Rise to kill whoever comes to kill you" (Sanhedrin 74a). However, the Torah permits us to declare war in various situations in which *pikuaḥ nefesh* is not necessarily at issue – e.g., in the case of a *milḥemet reshut* (non-obligatory war). Clearly killing people in battle is not necessarily based on the principle of rising to kill those who come to kill us!

Rabbi Naftali Tzvi Yehuda Berlin, the Netziv, is often quoted in this context, making the following argument: "There is no prohibition of engaging in war (because of the possible issue of *pikuaḥ nefesh*), just as the king is not cautioned against waging a *milḥemet reshut*. The situation of war is different.... In war, one is allowed to endanger himself."[2] This idea appears in his commentary on the book of Genesis as well. The Torah teaches us the prohibition regarding murder immediately after the Flood: "And for your own lifeblood I will demand account; I will demand it from every wild beast. For human life I will demand account, of every man toward his fellow man" (Gen. 9:5).

The Netziv limits the prohibition of murder to apply only

> at a time when it is otherwise appropriate to act with brotherhood. But this is not the case during war, when it is a time to hate. Then it is a time to kill, and there is no punishment whatsoever for so doing; for this is the way of the world. The king of Israel is allowed to conduct even an optional war, although people will be killed.[3]

---

2. *Haamek Davar*, Deut. 20:8.
3. Ibid., Gen. 9:5.

His understanding is based on the argument that war is an accepted phenomenon that legitimizes killing.

Can this principle act as a logical argument for the killing of innocent bystanders (unintentionally of course)? Rabbi Neriya Guttel,[4] in his meticulous article on our topic, concludes that it may.[5] His argument is that the soldiers of Israel who follow the king into battle in a *milḥemet reshut* are no more or less innocent than the bystanders of the enemy; the lives of both are equally precious.

The Story of Shimon and Levi in Shekhem

In Genesis 34, we read about the kidnapping and rape of Dina by Shekhem, the son of the city's king, Ḥamor. The response of Yaakov's sons Shimon and Levi is harsh. They deceive the people and convince them to circumcise all the males among them; then they kill the males of Shekhem and free their sister from captivity.

Rabbi Samson Raphael Hirsch sees fault in the actions of the two sons. In his commentary on the verses (Gen. 34:25–31) he explains:

> Here begins the part deserving of censure, and we do not need to cover it up. Had they killed only Shechem and Chamor, the brothers would certainly have been in the right. But they did not spare the unarmed, defenseless men who were at their mercy. What is more, they looted the city. They made all the inhabitants of the place pay for a crime committed by their master.
>
> *There was no justification for this.*[6] (Emphasis mine.)

The Rambam and the Ramban argue as to whether Shimon and Levi's actions are justified in this instance. The Rambam explains that all the residents of the city are guilty of sins that justify death:

4. A Torah scholar who served until recently as the dean of the women's Orot Israel College.
5. "Leḥima BeShetaḥ Ravui Ukhlusiya Ezraḥit," *Teḥumin* 23 (2002/2003): 35.
6. Daniel Haberman, trans. (Israel: Feldheim and Judaica Press, 2006), on verses 25–31.

> How must the non-Jews fulfill the [Noahide] commandment to establish laws and courts? They are obligated to set up judges and magistrates in every major city to render judgment concerning these six [other Noahide] commandments and to admonish the people regarding their observance.
>
> A non-Jew who transgresses these seven commands shall be executed by decapitation. *For this reason, all the inhabitants of [the city of] Shekhem were obligated to die*: [Prince] Shekhem kidnapped; they observed and were aware of his deeds but did not prosecute him.[7] (Emphasis mine.)

The Ramban, in his commentary, questions the Rambam's view. His understanding is that Shimon and Levi's attack is an act of revenge; as such, it is a negative undertaking.

Rabbi Judah Loew ben Bezalel, the Maharal of Prague (sixteenth century), justifies the killings by explaining that the battle in the city of Shekhem was not a conflict between individual families but rather a war between nations.[8] In such circumstances, a nation is allowed and perhaps even obligated to respond to another nation's provocation. In responding to another nation's provocation, a nation need not distinguish between another nation's guilty and innocent members. Some *posekim* argue that this opinion may serve as a halakhic precedent to permit fighting battles in populated areas in which civilians may be harmed.[9]

Rabbi Yaakov Medan, rosh yeshiva of Yeshivat Har Etzion, suggests a new approach to the story. In his view, Shimon and Levi are not

---

7. *Mishneh Torah, Hilkhot Melakhim* 9:14.
8. *Gur Aryeh*, Gen. 34:13.
9. Rabbi Chaim Jachter of Teaneck lists the authorities who have based their view on the commentary of the Maharal:

   "Rav Ya'akov Ariel (Arachim BeMivchan HaMilchama p. 83), Rabbi Dov Lior (Techumin 4:186), Rabbi Hershel Schachter (BeIkvei HaTzon p. 207), and Rabbi Asher Weiss (Minchat Asher, Devarim pp. 217–222) all rely upon the Maharal's interpretation of the Shechem episode to allow harming anyone who belongs to an enemy nation during wartime when there is no viable alternative to achieve a military victory." His article can be found at: https://www.koltorah.org/halachah/halachic-perspectives-on-civilian-casualties-in-gazapart-two-by-rabbi-chaim-jachter?format=amp.

committing an act of revenge or punishment; rather, it is a rescue mission. As part of their attempt to rescue their sister, they

> kill every adult male; what this appears to mean is that they kill all of the available fighters in Shekhem. Any male who could raise his sword against them is killed. Shimon and Levi could not extricate Dina from the house of Shekhem and return to their father's house without killing Shekhem and Chamor, all of their bodyguards, and the rest of the soldiers who stood in their path. *This is what happens in a rescue operation: innocents are killed as collateral damage.*

Rabbi Medan compares the biblical story to modern days:

> In modern terms, the people of Shekhem should be considered a non-combatant population that cooperates with and protects the enemy. These are people whom the army fighting the enemy does not want to kill but is ready to kill in order to rescue its people from a clear danger. Were they not cooperating with the enemy, the fighting army might refrain from killing them, even if this involves putting themselves at risk.[10]

The Unique Opinion of Rabbi Shaul Yisraeli

On October 12, 1953, terrorists from Jordan murdered a Jewish woman and her two children in the city of Yehud. Israel responded with an attack on the village of Qibya. The soldiers who participated in the attack did not inspect the homes in the village for the presence of residents, and when the army blew up the homes in the village, many civilians were killed.

This attack raised many questions regarding retaliation to terrorists' attacks and the place of revenge in Israel's response. Rabbi Shaul Yisraeli wrote a detailed article on the halakhic angle of this tragic

---

10. See Rabbi Yaakov Medan, "Vayishlach – The Incident in Shekhem," The Israel Koschitzky Torat Har Etzion VBM, November 20, 2018, https://www.etzion.org.il/en/incident-shekhem.

event.[11] In his article, Rabbi Yisraeli expands the Netziv's idea that war is a universally recognized method of resolving conflicts. Rabbi Yisraeli understands that the ethical dispensation for fighting all wars today is also based on the norms which the world we live in accepts. He concludes that, based on this theory, if at any given time the world would agree that there is no justification for any sort of military conflict, then the Jewish people would not be allowed to fight.

Basically, Rabbi Yisraeli argues that ethical and moral questions that arise during war, must **also** be judged by the standards and values of the rest of the world. He mentions the famous rule of *dina demalkhuta dina* (the law of the land is the law), which is usually used in monetary law, and applies it to our case. Combining both principles (that of the Netziv and that of *dina demalkhuta dina),* he argues:

> The outcome of this is that there is room to permit missions of revenge and reprisal against our enemies, and this is considered a *milḥemet mitzva*. Any tragedy that occurs to our enemies, their partners, and their children is their responsibility and they carry the weight of these consequences. There is no reason to refrain from action against the enemy because of the concern that innocents will be harmed, for they are the reason for these results. Obviously, there is no room to permit harming children intentionally, and one should take care not to harm them.[12]

Rabbi Neriya Guttel concludes his article as follows:

> It seems to me that the targeted killings (*sikul memukad*) that occur among the civilian population, the destruction of a house on top of terrorists and other inhabitants, the bombing of civilian territory in which the enemy has deliberately chosen to reside, etc. – as long as such actions are not carried out with the

11. "Peulot Tzva'iyot LeHaganat HaMedina" (*siman* 16), *Amud HaYemini* (Tel Aviv: Moreshet, 1966).
12. Ibid., 199.

> premeditated goal of killing civilians, but rather with operational consideration, these acts are permitted according to Jewish law.[13]

At first glance, the opinions of Rabbi Yisraeli and Rabbi Guttel may seem harsh. Unfortunately, war is a terrible ordeal, involving horror, pain, and tragedy for so many. Although Jewish values and ethics guide us to be sensitive to human life (even during war itself), enemies can take advantage of our compassion. It is primarily such cases that the rabbis are thinking of when they rule that Jewish law permits killing an enemy even if others might be harmed in the process.

13. Guttel, "Leḥima," 42.

32

Moving the Embassy to Jerusalem, 2018

What Is the Religious Significance of an American Embassy in Jerusalem?

The UN Partition Plan of 1947 envisioned a Jerusalem under international control, but the War of Independence left the western half of the city under Israel's authority and the eastern half under Jordanian control. In December 1949, Prime Minister David Ben-Gurion twice made clear – on the fifth and thirteenth of the month – that Jerusalem would be the capital of the newborn State of Israel. In his statement on the latter date, he declared:

> From the establishment of the Provisional Government we made the peace, the security and the economic consolidation of Jerusalem our principal care. In the stress of war, when Jerusalem was under siege, we were compelled to establish the seat

> of Government in Tel Aviv. But for the State of Israel there has always been and always will be one capital only – Jerusalem the Eternal. Thus it was 3,000 years ago – and thus it will be, we believe, until the end of time.[1]

On the twenty-sixth of December, the Knesset formally convened in Jerusalem, and on January 23, 1950, it proclaimed that "Jerusalem was, and had always been, the capital of Israel" and called for the construction of a permanent parliament building there. However, most countries did not accept Israel's position and established their embassies in other Israeli cities.

On October 23, 1995, the Jerusalem Embassy Act was passed by the US Congress, taking effect on November 8. The act recognized Jerusalem as the capital of the State of Israel and called for the relocation of the United States' embassy in Israel from Tel Aviv to Jerusalem by May 31, 1999. However, the law allowed the president to invoke a six-month waiver and to reissue the waiver every six months on grounds of "national security." Presidents Clinton, Bush, and Obama repeatedly renewed the waiver, thus postponing the move.

Finally, on February 23, 2018, President Trump announced that the US embassy would open in Jerusalem. It officially relocated to Jerusalem on May 14, 2018, coinciding with the seventieth anniversary of the Israeli Declaration of Independence.

What is the significance of this move? Some argue (cynically) that it is merely a political decision and has no religious meaning. However, we will see that the recognition of Jerusalem as the capital of the State of Israel has religious and halakhic ramifications.[2]

---

1. See "Statements of the Prime Minister David Ben-Gurion regarding Moving the Capital of Israel to Jerusalem," The Knesset, accessed July 4, 2021, https://www.knesset.gov.il/docs/eng/bengurion-jer.htm.
2. Many of the ideas discussed here are based on my father Rabbi Binyamin Tabory's audio *shiurim*. See "The Kedusha of Yerushalayim and Eretz Yisrael," The Israel Koschitzky Torat Har Etzion VBM, May 30, 2019, https://etzion.org.il/en/holidays/yom-yerushalayim/kedusha-yerushalayim-and-eretz-yisrael.

JERUSALEM'S DUAL NATURE IN THE PAST AND PRESENT

The great poet and kabbalist Rabbi Shlomo HaLevi Alkabetz (Salonica/Safed, ca. 1500–1576) expressed his love and yearning for Jerusalem in his poem *Lekha Dodi*, universally used by Jewish communities worldwide to welcome the holiness of Shabbat. In the fourth stanza, he uses two biblical phrases to describe the two sides of this special city: *Mikdash melekh, ir melukha*, "Temple of the king, city of kingship."

The Gemara teaches us that a coin existed in Jerusalem which mentioned the uniqueness of the city (Bava Kama 97b): on one side, it said *David uShlomo*; and on the other, *Yerushalayim ir hakodesh*, "Jerusalem, city of holiness." The city's dual nature – as a place of sanctity but also a seat of sovereignty – has defined it for generations.

Mikdash Melekh

The Temples were built in Jerusalem, the first by King Shlomo and the second by the returnees from the Babylonian exile. But does the Temple affect the city's status? Or are the Temple and Jerusalem two separate entities?

The Rambam understands that the *kedusha* (holiness) of the Land of Israel, established in the days of Yehoshua, was annulled at the time of the destruction of the First Temple, as we saw in chapter 2. However, the Rambam argues that the original *kedusha* of the Temple remains intact, since its special status was created by God. Thus, even today, when the Temple is in ruins, there are restrictions on who may set foot upon the Temple Mount.

Based on the Talmud Yerushalmi's discussion of whether a lulav is shaken in all of Jerusalem (Sukka 3:11), the Rambam is of the opinion that the *kedusha* of the Temple "overflows" into the city itself; thus he claims that since the days of the First Temple, the *kedusha* of Jerusalem has remained intact.

> Why do I say that the original consecration sanctified the Temple and Jerusalem for eternity, while in regard to the consecration of the remainder of the Land of Israel, in the context of the Sabbatical year, tithes, and other similar laws, it did not sanctify it for eternity?

> Because the sanctity of the Temple and Jerusalem stems from the Divine Presence, and the Divine Presence can never be nullified. Therefore, the verse (Lev. 26:31) states: "I will make your sanctuaries desolate." The Sages declared: "Even though they have been devastated, their sanctity remains."[3]

This opinion of the Rambam has interesting halakhic ramifications, specifically regarding commandments that are connected to the Temple.

Lulav for Seven Days

The Torah commands us to shake the lulav on the first day of Sukkot (Lev. 23:40). However, in the Temple the commandment is to shake the lulav all seven days.[4] The custom of shaking the lulav for the entire week today is based on a rabbinical decree, which mandates that we do so to remember the Temple (*Zekher LeMikdash*). Is there a biblical commandment to shake the lulav in the rest of Jerusalem for all seven days? The Rambam's opinion on this matter is unclear. In *Mishneh Torah*, he mentions the Temple only;[5] however, in his *Commentary on the Mishna*, he argues that the Temple and Jerusalem share the same status (Mishna Sukka 3:10).

The commentators discuss the Rambam's view on this matter. While Rabbi Manoah ben Yaakov (Provence, thirteenth century) understands that the opinion mentioned in the Rambam's *Commentary on the Mishna* is the correct one,[6] Rabbi Soloveitchik endorses the view noted in *Mishneh Torah*.[7]

Posekim debate the relevance of this issue in our days. Rabbi Yaakov Ettlinger questions the status of this commandment in the nineteenth century and concludes that, according to the Rambam, there is a biblical commandment today to shake the lulav in Jerusalem for a full week. He therefore suggests that people living in Jerusalem should

3. *Mishneh Torah, Hilkhot Beit HaBeḥira* 6:16.
4. See Rashi on Mishna Sukka 41a.
5. *Mishneh Torah, Hilkhot Shofar, Sukka VeLulav* 7:13.
6. Ibid., 2:8.
7. See Rabbi Michel Zalman Shurkin, *Harerei Kedem* (Jerualem, 2000), 1:248.

ensure that their Four Species are biblically kosher on all seven days.[8] In fact, there are people who, upon visiting the Old City of Jerusalem during Sukkot, accordingly shake the lulav again, thus fulfilling the biblical commandment.

In his commentary on the Talmud, Rabbi Meir Simcha HaKohen of Dvinsk argues against this opinion.[9] His view is that if a biblical commandment exists at all times (i.e., in the entire city of Jerusalem, and not just the Temple), R. Yoḥanan b. Zakkai would not have needed to create the *Zekher LeMikdash* (remembrance of the Temple) of lulav for all seven days.

Ir Melukha

Since the days of King David, Jerusalem has served as the capital of Israel. When David chose Jerusalem as his capital, it seems that he was unaware that one day it would be the home of the Temple. His reasons, it seems, were pragmatic – to ensure that his capital would "belong" to all the people of Israel. He therefore chose a location that did not belong solely to his tribe, Yehuda, as his former capital, Ḥevron, did.

Rabbi Hershel Schachter discusses the religious importance of Jerusalem as the capital of Davidic kingship.[10] He explains that the king of Israel reflects divine reign in this world. Thus, Jerusalem, the capital of King David, symbolizes the capital of God's kingship in the world. The Rambam's ruling that "only a descendant of David may be appointed as king in Jerusalem"[11] proves this theory, for only a king from the Davidic dynasty reflects divine kingship.

Rabbi Schachter then raises the question of whether the American government's decision not to recognize Jerusalem as the Israeli capital (the book was printed in 2007) is justified or not. On one hand, he argues that the government residing in Jerusalem today is not of the Davidic dynasty, and therefore Jerusalem cannot be recognized as the true capital of Israel. On the other hand, he suggests that the question

8. *Bikkurei Yaakov* 658:1.
9. *Ḥiddushei Rabbeinu Meir Simcha,* 1:242.
10. *BeIkvei HaTzon,* 222.
11. *Mishneh Torah, Hilkhot Melakhim* 1:10.

only arises if the Israeli government is halakhically recognized as sovereign.

The Rebuilding of Jerusalem in the Amida

The idea that Jerusalem's essence is to serve as the capital of Davidic kingship can be proven from our prayers and blessings.

The fourteenth blessing of the *Amida* is *Boneh Yerushalayim* ("Who Rebuilds Jerusalem"), in which we ask God to rebuild Jerusalem and to restore the kingship of David. Note that there are three main parts to the blessing:

1. Return in mercy to Jerusalem, Your city, and dwell therein as You have promised;
2. And rebuild it, soon in our days, as an everlasting edifice;
3. And speedily establish therein the throne of David Your servant. Blessed are You, Lord, who rebuilds Jerusalem.

Several questions arise regarding this blessing.

First, Rabbi Yoel Sirkis questions the order of requests mentioned in the blessing.[12] There is a rule that the concluding "Blessed are You…" must be similar in context to the preceding phrase. Therefore, the request, dealing with the throne of David, should not be recited at the end of the blessing.

He therefore justifies the Sephardi custom which changes the order and ends the blessing differently:

1. Return in mercy to Jerusalem, Your city, and dwell therein as You have promised;
2. Speedily establish therein the throne of David Your servant;
3. And rebuild it, soon in our days, as an everlasting edifice. Blessed are You, Lord, who rebuilds Jerusalem.

However, the mention of the Davidic kingship in this blessing seems odd. Why is the throne of David mentioned here at all? The question becomes

12. *Baḥ, Oraḥ Ḥayim* 118.

especially difficult when we turn to the next blessing of the *Amida,* which is solely dedicated to the restoration of the kingship of David.

The answer to both questions, as put forth by my father, Rabbi Binyamin Tabory, must be that although there is a blessing dedicated to the return of the Davidic dynasty, the mention of it in the blessing for the rebuilding of Jerusalem has to do with Jerusalem itself. We are not merely praying for houses, buildings, and parks to be built in Jerusalem; rather, we pray that the house of King David will return to the city, for that surely is the real essence of the rebuilding of Jerusalem!

The Rebuilding of Jerusalem in Birkat HaMazon

This same idea repeats itself in *Birkat HaMazon,* the Grace after Meals. It is a biblical obligation to recite blessings after eating a meal, although the text we recite was written by the rabbis. The Gemara (Berakhot 48b) quotes an opinion that claims that one must mention Davidic kingship as well. The Gemara seems to indicate that this is a biblical obligation. An obvious question arises: What is the source in the Torah for this ruling?

Let us examine the verse in the Torah that teaches us *Birkat HaMazon*: "And when you eat and are satisfied, you shall bless the Lord your God for the good land that He has given you" (Deut. 8:10).

Each element in the biblical commandment has its parallel in the text of the Grace after Meals.

1. **You shall bless the Lord your God** – first blessing, *HaZan,* the blessing on the food
2. **Land He has given you** – second blessing, *Al HaAretz,* blessing on the Land of Israel
3. **For the good** – third blessing, *Boneh VeRaḥamav Yerushalayim,* as the Gemara explains that the good of the Land of Israel is Jerusalem (Berakhot 48b).

However, the Gemara obligates one to mention the kingship of David; where is that in the Torah? Here, again, the answer is that the rebuilding of Jerusalem **is** the return of Davidic kingship to the city.

Tearing Clothes over the Destruction

Rabbi Yosef Karo, basing his ruling on the Gemara, concludes that one who observes the *ḥurban* – destruction – of Yehuda must tear his or her garments.[13] He mentions three separate locations: the cities of Yehuda, the city of Jerusalem, and the site of the Temple. At each of these locations, a separate tear must be made.

The *posekim* maintain that destruction is not necessarily a physical term describing devastation, but rather the lack of Jewish sovereignty.[14] Based on this logic, Rabbi Schachter explains the custom today not to tear garments while observing the cities of Yehuda, now under Israel's control.[15] The logic of tearing one's garments over the Temple seems to apply nowadays, since the reason is the physical destruction of the Temple. However, what is the reason for tearing garments over the destruction of Jerusalem? There are two possibilities: Jerusalem no longer being *ir melukha* – a seat of sovereignty – or its no longer being *mikdash melekh* – a place of holiness.

If the main reason is the lack of Jewish sovereignty, then after 1967, it is possible that there is no obligation to tear garments. However, if the reason is based on the lack of the Temple, then even today we must tear our clothes over Jerusalem.

Thus, we have seen that the uniqueness of our capital city for three millennia is twofold: it relates both to its role as the home of the Temple and to its status as the home of Davidic kingship. It seems to me that although the US's recognition of Jerusalem as our country's capital is not revolutionary, it is still significant for it has brought us, we hope, one step closer toward Jerusalem being the *ir melukha*.

---

13. *Oraḥ Ḥayim* 561:1–2.
14. See *Baḥ* on *Tur,* ad loc.
15. *BeIkvei HaTzon,* 106–8.

33

The Beresheet Lunar Lander, 2019

What Is the Significance of the Flag in Halakha?

In the seventy-first year of its existence, the State of Israel attempted to become one of the few countries in the world to successfully land a spacecraft on the moon. The lunar lander *Beresheet* was built by Israeli scientists and launched from Cape Canaveral on February 22, 2019. On March 5, the lander sent a selfie back to Israel. In this sensational picture, the Israeli flag could be seen "flying" in space with the Earth in the background.

Unfortunately, Israel's flag did not make it to the moon. On April 11, a malfunction in the spacecraft's systems caused it to crash on the moon's surface.

This attempt was not Israel's first foray into space. On January 16, 2003, Israeli Air Force pilot Colonel Ilan Ramon became the first Israeli astronaut, on the US's space shuttle *Columbia*. Ilan Ramon carried with him a miniature Torah scroll which had survived the Holocaust, and he was advised on halakhic questions regarding keeping commandments in space. Tragically, upon re-entry on February 1, 2003, *Columbia* exploded as it entered Earth's atmosphere. Ramon and the ship's entire crew were killed.

In the mid-twentieth century, the Space Race raised many halakhic questions. As the US successfully landed men on the moon in 1969, Rabbi Menachem Mendel Kasher (Poland/Israel, 1895–1983) dedicated an entire book to the subject, *HaAdam Al HaYare'aḥ LeOr HaTorah VeHaEmuna* (Man on the Moon in Light of the Torah and Faith), which dealt with philosophical and religious questions raised by the landing. Other rabbinic authorities have also confronted the numerous implications of a human race no longer confined to the planet Earth, including how *Kiddush Levana*, the monthly blessing over the moon, should be recited and how to keep Shabbat in space.[1]

We will discuss a topic in the background of Israel's attempt to reach the moon; I am referring to the Israeli flag which was proudly attached to *Beresheet*.

ISRAEL'S FLAG: DESIGN, ORIGINS, AND HALAKHIC QUESTIONS

A nation takes great pride in its symbols. Thus, Israel's blue and white flag with a Star of David at its center, flying tall and high, touches the hearts of Jews worldwide. But does the Israeli flag have any religious value or importance?

The Israeli flag is a field of white with two horizontal sky-blue stripes which are intended to symbolize the stripes of a tallit. The *Magen* ("Star of," or, more literally, "Shield of") *David* at its center is a widely acknowledged symbol of the Jewish people and of Judaism.

David Wolffsohn (1856–1914), second president of the World Zionist Organization, writes in his memoirs what brought him to suggest the design of the Zionist flag:

> At the behest of our leader Herzl, I came to Basel to make preparations for the Zionist Congress. Among many other problems

1. See Rabbi J. David Bleich, *Contemporary Halakhic Problems* (Southfield, MI: Targum Press, 2005), vol. 5, chap. 3.

> that occupied me then was one that contained something of the essence of the Jewish problem: What flag would we hang in the Congress Hall? Then an idea struck me. We have a flag – and it is blue and white. The tallit with which we wrap ourselves when we pray: that is our symbol. Let us take this tallit from its bag and unroll it before the eyes of Israel and the eyes of all nations. So I ordered a blue and white flag with the Shield of David painted upon it. That is how the national flag, that flew over Congress Hall, came into being.[2]

Does the fact that the design of the flag is taken from a religious article have any effect on our attitude toward it?

Flying the Flag on Yom HaAtzma'ut

Many Israeli homes display an Israeli flag around Yom HaAtzma'ut, Independence Day,[3] and there are many stories of rabbis who support flying the Israeli flag on Yom HaAtzma'ut.

The Sadigura Rebbe, Rabbi Avraham Ya'akov Friedman (Vienna/Israel, 1884–1961), lived in Vienna during the *Anschluss* (annexation). He was forced by the Nazis to sweep the streets of Vienna and to raise a Nazi flag. At the time, he made a *neder* (vow) that if he escaped the Nazis and made it to the Land of Israel, he would clean the streets of the Holy Land and fly the Zionist flag over his house. Indeed, there are testimonies that on Yom HaAtzma'ut, the rebbe could be seen sweeping the streets of Tel Aviv, an Israeli flag flying over his home.[4]

The Ponevezh Rebbe, Rabbi Yosef Shlomo Kahaneman (Russian Empire/Israel, 1886–1969), insisted that an Israeli flag be hoisted on the roof of Yeshivat Ponevezh in Bnei Brak.

---

2. Yom-Tov Levinsky, *Sefer HaMoadim*, vol. 8, *Yemei Moed VeZikaron* (Tel Aviv: Agudat Oneg Shabbat and Dvir, 1957), 432. Translation based on Alec Mishory, "Israel National Symbols: The Israeli Flag," Jewish Virtual Library, accessed December 29, 2021, https://www.jewishvirtuallibrary.org/the-israeli-flag.
3. See Aaron Arend, *Pirkei Meḥkar LeYom HaAtzma'ut* (Ramat Gan: Bar-Ilan University, 1998), 103–17.
4. My friend Victor Ofstein referred me to the book *Alei Tamar, Shevi'it* 4:7, where the story is mentioned.

There are also testimonies that the head of the London Beth Din, Rabbi Yehezkel Abramsky (Russian Empire/London/Israel, 1886–1976), who made aliya in 1951, displayed the flag on Yom HaAtzma'ut as well.

Objections to the Flag

In the sixties, the rabbis at an Agudath Israel conference in Jerusalem protested the flag flying over their hotel. The rabbis were uncomfortable with the Israeli flag and were only willing to accept its presence if international flags were flown with it. Doing this, they argued, proved that flying the Israeli flag was merely complying with accepted worldwide practice.

Later that year, at the annual Mizrachi conference, Rabbi Joseph B. Soloveitchik took issue with this approach. He claimed that no one needed the Union Jack to provide a *heter* (dispensation) for the Israeli flag. In his speech, he explained:

> If you ask me how I, as a Talmudic Jew, view the flag of the State of Israel, and whether it has any halakhic value, I will answer you simply. I do not give any weight to the reverence of a flag, or similar ceremonial symbols. Judaism negates the worship of material objects. However, we cannot overlook the law in the *Shulḥan Arukh* (*Yoreh De'ah* 364:4) that one who is murdered by non-Jews is buried in his clothes, so that his blood should be seen and avenged, as it says, "I will not excuse their blood" (Joel 4:21). In other words, the clothes of a Jew achieve a certain holiness when they are stained with his holy blood. This most certainly applies to a blue and white flag which is soaked with the blood of thousands of Jewish youth (religious and irreligious, as the enemy did not differentiate) who fell while protecting the land and the Jewish settlement. It has a spark of holiness which stems from dedication and self-sacrifice. We are all obligated to honor the flag and to relate to it with respect![5]

5. *The Rav Speaks,* 139; see also *Nefesh HaRav,* 139.

Placing Flags in Synagogues

One of the antecedents of the modern Israeli flag is the Jewish flag of the oldest active synagogue in Europe, Prague's Altneuschul. The story of this flag goes back to the fourteenth century, when Holy Roman Emperor Charles IV granted the Jews the right to wave their very own flag. The flag's color was purple and at its center there was a Star of David. The current flag on display at the synagogue dates back to 1716.

In 1957, Rabbi Moshe Feinstein was asked if one is permitted to pray in a synagogue that has Israeli and American flags on display. At the beginning of his responsum, Rabbi Feinstein discusses the *kedusha* of a synagogue. He states that the *kedusha* of a synagogue cannot be annulled by negative or even sinful actions. Regarding the flags, Rabbi Feinstein understands that a flag is merely a symbolic object and that the people who place the flag in the synagogue have no intention of considering it an object of *kedusha*. He refers to the flag as a *davar ḥol* (secular object). Thus, claims Rabbi Feinstein, there is no concern that the flag is an object of idol worship.

However, Rabbi Feinstein also holds that all flags are nonsense (*hevel ushetut*), and therefore he argues that it is not appropriate to bring them into a synagogue; they most certainly should not be placed beside the ark. He concludes that although he believes it is wrong to place flags in a synagogue, no *maḥloket* should be created regarding their removal.[6]

Rabbi Avraham Chaim Naeh (Ḥevron/Jerusalem, 1890–1954) was a prominent *posek* and a Lubavitcher Hasid. In his written responsum on this topic, he objects strongly to the custom of placing a flag in a synagogue. His reasoning is that a synagogue is a place where we worship God, and thus is a symbol of His kingship over the world. The flag, however, symbolizes *malkhut basar vadam* (human sovereignty). Quoting a gemara in Berakhot, Rabbi Naeh argues that it is not appropriate to mix the two.[7]

6. *Iggerot Moshe, Oraḥ Ḥayim* 1:46.
7. The letter was published in Rabbi Meir Amsel, *Shut HaMaor VeZikhron BaSefer* (New York: self-pub., 1967), 1:544, also available online at https://hebrewbooks.org/pdfpager.aspx?req=36014&st=&pgnum=544&hilite=.

Rav Kook's Speech

In 1915, during World War I, the British Army's Jewish Legion was formed. These Jewish soldiers participated in the Great War, and they had their own flag, a Menora against a blue-and-white background. In the years following the war, the flag was displayed in synagogues across England.[8]

On December 17, 1925, the flag was carried to Israel and brought to the Ḥurva Synagogue in Jerusalem. A ceremony was arranged to officially greet the flag. Among those who attended was the Ashkenazi chief rabbi, Rabbi Avraham Yitzchak Kook.

In his speech,[9] he cited the verse in Psalms (20:6): "We will shout for joy at Your salvation and raise a banner in our God's name. May the Lord grant all your requests." Rav Kook noted that the Torah commands the Israelites to form a camp with banners representing the different tribes: "The Israelites shall camp, each by his banner, the ensign of his ancestral house, positioned around the Tent of Meeting at a distance" (Num. 2:2).

He then cited a midrash that explains that 22,000 chariots of angels, each one decked out with flags, attended the Giving of the Torah. The Israelites immediately desired to have flags just like the angels, and God agreed. This request for flags, the midrash teaches, is described in Song of Songs (2:4): "He has brought me to the wine house, and His banner flying over me is love.":

> "He has brought me to the wine-house" – this is Sinai; "and His banner over me is love"...the Holy One, blessed be He, said to them: "What did you desire? To make banners. By your lives, I will fulfill your petitions!" – "May the Lord fulfill all your petitions." Immediately, the Holy One, blessed be He, told Israel and said to Moshe: "Make them banners, as they desired."[10]

---

8. Rabbi Ari Shvat, *LeHarim Et HaDegel* (Jerusalem: Orot Israel College, 2004).
9. The entire speech can be found at "Derashat HaRav Kook Zatzal Al Ḥashivut HaDegel HaYisraeli," Machon Shlomo Aumann, accessed July 4, 2021, https://www.machonso.org/mishol/item.asp?id=698.
10. Numbers Rabba 2:3.

Rav Kook thus expressed that the original flag of Israel began at Mount Sinai, at the Giving of the Torah. He further argued that the flag represents our march toward redemption and signifies (as it does in this case) the international unity behind the Zionist enterprise. The flag also symbolizes those young Jewish men and women who sacrificed their lives in battle for the redemption of the Land of Israel.

Obviously, Rav Kook found it appropriate to place the Jewish flag in proximity to the Ḥurva Synagogue. Although Rav Kook died thirteen years before the establishment of the State of Israel, I believe his speech can help us recognize that the modern Israeli flag has spiritual value for us and has a place in our yeshivas and synagogues. Whether it will have a place in a yeshiva built on the moon remains to be seen.

34

The Return of Zechariah Baumel's Body, 2019

Should Graves Be Relocated from the Diaspora to Israel?

On April 5, 2019, the body of Sergeant First Class Zechariah Baumel, who had been killed in the First Lebanon War some thirty-seven years earlier, was laid to rest in the Mount Herzl Military Cemetery. Zechariah, a student at Yeshivat Har Etzion, was in his fourth year of studies when the war broke out. Together with other Hesder students, he was sent to the north and participated in Operation Peace for the Galilee. Their mission was to protect the northern towns of Israel, which were targeted by terrorist and rocket attacks.

The operation quickly turned into a full-fledged war. On June 6, 1982, hours before the ceasefire was to commence, Zechariah's tank battalion was sent on a mission which turned into one of the most disastrous battles in Israel's history. Near the Lebanese village of Sultan Yacoub, the Syrian army set a deadly ambush for the Israeli tanks. Over twenty Israeli soldiers were killed, many were injured, two were taken captive, and three were declared missing in action: Zechariah Baumel, Yehuda Katz, and Tzvi Feldman.

For the next thirty-seven years, the families of all three MIAs and the IDF did everything possible to discover what had happened to the soldiers. In early April 2019, the IDF proudly announced that Zechariah's body had been discovered in Syria. In a joint military operation, Israeli and Russian forces had exhumed the body, examined it, identified it, and flown it to Israel. Near the body, other articles had been discovered, among them his tzitzit.

The emotions at the funeral were mixed: sadness and grief on one hand, relief and even pride on the other. Zechariah's sister compared her feelings upon hearing the news to those of the Sages when they added *HaTov VeHameitiv* to *Birkat HaMazon*. This blessing was established after the Romans permitted burial for the victims of the terrible massacre of the city of Beitar. The massacre took place in the year 135 CE; according to our tradition, it occurred on Tisha BeAv (Mishna Taanit 4:6). The Gemara mentions that the bodies of the people killed in the massacre were miraculously preserved and did not decay until the burial was permitted; to commemorate this miracle, they composed *HaTov VeHaMeitiv* (Taanit 31a).

This idea is similar to the halakhic situation in which a relative dies and leaves an inheritance. The proper conduct is to recite two blessings: the somber *Dayan HaEmet* for the death of the relative and the joyous *Sheheḥeyanu,* which conveys gratitude to God for receiving the inheritance.

Both these cases prove that in complex emotional situations in which there are conflicting feelings, halakha recognizes that there is room for expressing contradictory emotions at the same time.

THE IMPORTANCE OF *KEVER YISRAEL*

Over the past chapters, we have discussed many questions that come up during wars and conflicts regarding the commandment of burial and how much effort must be invested to perform this commandment. We proved that the *posekim* permit violating Shabbat and Yom Tov during the process, and even endangering the lives of other soldiers (see chapter 11). The *heter* is based on the assumption that the morale of the soldiers, knowing that their country will do all it can to bring them home, is a crucial factor in wartime.

There is no doubt that, in our case, a very important message has been sent to all IDF personnel in the past, present, and future. It is difficult to weigh the tremendous value of this dramatic, courageous message of *kiddush Hashem* for the outcome of future conflicts.

Rabbi Yaakov Medan mentioned in his *hesped* (eulogy) for Zechariah that in the Bible, we find a similar case in which the people of Israel are dedicated to the cause of bringing the bodies of those killed in battle to *kever Yisrael,* a Jewish grave. In the battle on Mount Gilboa, King Shaul and his three sons are killed. The Philistines desecrate their bodies and leave them out in the open. The people of Yavesh Gilad (at the north of the east bank of the Jordan River), who in the past were saved by Shaul's troops, lead a military mission deep into Philistine territory to retrieve the bodies of Shaul and his sons and give them a proper burial (I Sam. 31:11–13).

In chapter 9, in our discussion about the sixty-nine sailors of the *Dakar* submarine found in the depths of the sea, we argued that according to Jewish law they are considered buried in *kever Yisrael,* and thus removing them from their burial site might be problematic. According to Jewish law, it is forbidden to remove bodies from a grave, even if they are to be buried elsewhere.[1] The commentaries quote from the Bible to indicate that this is considered harmful for the dead.[2]

However, Rabbi Yosef Karo mentions numerous scenarios in which one is permitted to relocate graves. One such case is for the purpose of being buried in the Land of Israel.[3]

Burial in the Land of Israel

There are sources in the Gemara that speak highly of the value of being buried in the Land of Israel. In the eyes of our Sages, burial in the Land of Israel has the power to atone for past sins (Ketubbot 111a). The Gemara quotes a disagreement regarding the question of whether one

1. *Shulḥan Arukh, Yoreh De'ah* 363:1.
2. See *Shakh,* ad loc. 1.
3. *Shulḥan Arukh, Yoreh De'ah* 363:1.

is permitted to bring a body to Israel for burial (Y. Kilayim 9:3); the *posekim* agree with the opinion that states that it is allowed.

The Rambam quotes the Gemara:

> One who is buried there receives atonement as if the place in which he is buried is an altar of atonement, as it is stated (Deut. 32:43): "His land will atone for His people." For retribution, it is stated (Amos 7:17): "You will die in an impure land."

However, the Rambam points out:

> There is no comparison between the merit of a person who lives in the Land of Israel and ultimately is buried there and one whose body is brought there after his death. Nevertheless, great sages would bring their dead there. Take, for an example, our Patriarch Yaakov and Yosef the Righteous.[4]

The great philosopher and poet Rabbi Yehuda HaLevi (Toledo/Jerusalem, ca. 1075–1141), who loved the Land of Israel dearly, condemns the practice of those who choose to live outside of Israel and return only once they are deceased.[5] He supports his claim by quoting the above gemara and the verse "I brought you to a fertile land, to eat its fruits and bounty, but you came and defiled My land, and made My heritage an abomination" (Jer. 2:7).

Well-known leaders of the Zionist movement like Theodor Herzl and Ze'ev Jabotinsky, who passed away in the Diaspora, were laid to rest in Israel. In 1960, Sephardi Chief Rabbi Yitzchak Nissim arranged to bring the body of one the greatest Sephardi *posekim* of all time, Rabbi Chaim Yosef David Azulai (the Ḥida; Land of Israel/Europe, 1724–1806), to be buried in Israel.

Sir Moses Montefiore (1784–1885), the great Jewish philanthropist, was buried at his estate in Ramsgate, England. Since Sir Moses was a great lover of Israel and very active in Zionist causes, the question of

4. *Mishneh Torah, Hilkhot Melakhim* 5:11.
5. *Sefer HaKuzari* II:23.

moving his body to Israel arose. Rabbi Moshe Feinstein disapproved. His main reason, he writes, is the precedent that would be set by performing such an act.[6] Rabbi Feinstein argues: "Why only him? There are many *gedolim,* saints and righteous people who deserve to be brought to Israel." On the other hand, two Sephardi chief rabbis, Rabbi Ovadia Yosef and Rabbi Mordekhai Eliyahu, approved the suggestion.[7]

Rabbi Tzvi Pesach Frank, chief rabbi of Jerusalem, was asked for his opinion regarding bringing the body of the Karliner Rebbe, Rabbi Yochanan Perlow (1900–1956), who passed away in the US, to Israel. Rabbi Frank disregarded the opinions that object to the idea and ruled that it is clear to him that the body should be brought to Israel.[8]

Military Funerals

Zechariah Baumel was laid to rest in a military cemetery. Families of fallen soldiers have the option of having a full or partial military funeral. The custom of many armies is to bury soldiers in a military funeral which involves several military features including honor guards, the firing of volley shots as a salute, and the draping of a national flag over the coffin.

Rabbi Betzalel Zolty (Poland/Israel, 1920–1982), chief rabbi of Jerusalem, came out against military funerals.[9] His central argument is that these customs are prohibited due to the Torah's prohibition of following *ḥukkot hagoyim* (non-Jewish practices; Lev. 18:3). In the ancient world, there was a practice among both Jews and non-Jews to burn the king's belongings after his death. The Talmud refers in two separate places to this custom, but why does it not fall under the prohibition of *ḥukkot hagoyim*? While both references agree that the custom is permitted, they give different reasons. One explains that this act serves as a symbol of importance (*ḥashivuta*; Avoda Zara 11a); the other argues that it is only permitted because there is a biblical source for this custom,

6. *Iggerot Moshe, Yoreh De'ah* 153.
7. See *Yeḥaveh Daat,* 4:57. Rabbi Eliyahu's responsum is quoted by Rabbi Pinchas Toledano of London in his article "Pinui Atzmotav Shel Montefiore LaAretz," *Teḥumin* 8 (1987): 387.
8. *Har Tzvi, Yoreh De'ah* 274.
9. "Issur Halikha BeḤukkot HaGoyim," in *Noam* (Jerusalem: Mekhon Torah Shelema, 1958–59), 2:161.

thus proving it was a Jewish custom before it became a non-Jewish one (Sanhedrin 52b). The *Tosafot* question what seems to be a contradiction between these sources.[10] In their answer, they reach the conclusion that the prohibition includes two separate types of customs: one constitutes idol worship; the other does not. In the latter case, if the custom is mentioned in Jewish sources, proving that there is a Jewish precedent for the act, then it is permitted.

Other *Rishonim,* such as Rabbi Yosef Colon of Italy (Maharik; ca. 1420–1480), explain that practices that are initiated by non-Jews for logical reasons and are not acts of *peritzut* (immodesty) are not considered *ḥukkot hagoyim,* and they are therefore permitted. Many *posekim* agree with the Maharik's conclusion,[11] but the Gra (Rabbi Eliyahu ben Shlomo Zalman, also known as the Vilna Gaon; 1720–1797) rules more strictly: even customs that serve a reason and purpose are prohibited unless they are mentioned in the Torah.[12]

Rabbi Zolty explains that according to the common ruling, military funerals should be permitted, as there is no element of idol worship involved. Furthermore, they serve a purpose, as they give honor and respect to the fallen soldiers. However, due to the Gra's ruling, he finds it difficult to be lenient; therefore, he forbids the practice.

Rabbi Yechiel Yaakov Weinberg disagrees with Rabbi Zolty.[13] In his responsum, which discusses the modern practice of celebrating a girl becoming a bat mitzva, he defines the halakhic parameters of *ḥukkot hagoyim*. He argues that even the Gra only prohibits it in a case in which the reason for the custom is to follow the ways of the non-Jews; however, in a case in which there is good reason for the custom (as in the case of a military funeral), one is permitted to follow the ways of the non-Jews.

It is my hope that this act of *kiddush Hashem,* the burial of Zechariah Baumel, brings his family and the Jewish people comfort. We close with the prophecy of Yeḥezkel, which Rabbi Medan read at his funeral:

10. In both Avoda Zara and Sanhedrin.
11. See Rema (*Yoreh De'ah* 178:1), as well as Rabbi Ovadia Yosef (*Yabia Omer, Yoreh De'ah* 3:24).
12. In his commentary to *Yoreh De'ah* 178:7.
13. *Seridei Esh* (Jerusalem: HaVaad LeHotzaat Kitvei HaGaon HaRav Yechiel Yaakov Weinberg, 1999), vol. 2, *siman* 39.

O dry bones, hear the word of the Lord. So says the Lord God to these bones; Behold, I will cause spirit to enter into you, and you shall live. And I will lay sinews upon you, and I will make flesh grow over you and cover you with skin and put breath into you, and you will live, and you will then know that I am the Lord. (Ezek. 37:4–6)

Afterword

This work has covered seventy years of halakhic developments, beginning with the founding of the modern State of Israel. These years comprise a mere fraction of the thousands of years of the Jewish people's history. However, the events of the past century are far from usual or mundane. They mark a shift in the two-millennia-long journey of a perennially oppressed and scattered nation. In a sentence: The Jewish people have returned home.

These epic chapters in Jewish history have been challenging on many fronts. The road to independence and freedom has been paved with many sacrifices. The reader will notice that, unfortunately, many of the historical events discussed in the book revolve around war and death. However, I urge the reader to observe that even with all the pain and difficulties, Israel has managed to prosper economically, technologically, militarily, and, of course, demographically.

But this book has not focused on these events from a purely historical perspective; rather, the aim has been to demonstrate their religious impact. This has been done on two planes.

First, I have tried to demonstrate that the halakhic questions raised during these seventy years have created a new genre of halakhic literature. Besides relying on halakhic precedents from the Bible and Talmud, this novel approach must relate to the governing of a state and take the needs of the broader society into account. In many cases I noted the shifting halakhic process that resulted from the national sphere. Receiving monies and reparations from other countries, infiltrating the enemy for the purpose of spying, and engaging with terrorists who have taken captives are just a few examples. It is fair to say that, in such cases, normative halakhic rulings before 1948 would have been different.

On another level, our book has probed the theological meaning of the State of Israel's establishment. These events created much debate within the religious community, and we have encountered the success stories as well as the tragic ones.

Running through this book is the belief that the State of Israel is living proof of the biblical prophecies materializing in our days and that, after the terrible years of the Holocaust, God's presence is felt within the historical return of the Jewish people to their homeland.

Throughout this book, we saw the new world of halakha that has come alive as it faces challenges that could only exist within a dynamic and growing Jewish state. Moreover, the miraculous nature of events that have transpired since 1948 should be clear; it is my hope that we can all say, with conviction, "This was from the Lord; it is wondrous in our eyes" (Ps. 118:23).

Halakhic Decisors and Commentators Cited

Abrabanel, R. Yitzhak. Lisbon/Venice, 1437–1508.
Abramsky, R. Yehezkel. Russian Empire/London/Jerusalem, 1886–1976.
Abudarham, R. David. Seville, fourteenth century.
Adler, R. Shemarya Menashe. Poland/England, 1869–1959.
Alkabetz, R. Shlomo HaLevi. Salonica/Safed, ca. 1500–1576.
Amiel, R. Moshe Avigdor. Vilna/Land of Israel, 1883–1946.
Amital, R. Yehuda. Romania/Israel, 1924–2010.
Asevilli, R. Yom Tov ben Avraham (Ritva). Seville, 1260–1320.
R. Avraham ben David (Raavad). Provence, ca. 1125–1198.
Azulai, R. Chaim Yosef David (Ḥida). Land of Israel/Europe, 1724–1806.
Babad, R. Yosef. Poland/Ukraine, 1801–1874.
R. Baḥya ben Asher. Spain, 1255–1340.
Berlin, R. Naftali Tzvi (Netziv). Russia/Poland, 1816–1893.
Bornsztain, R. Avraham. Sochaczew, 1838–1910.
Colon, R. Yosef (Maharik). Italy, ca. 1420–1480.
de Leon, R. Yitzhak. Spain, fifteenth century.
Duran, R. Shimon ben Tzemach (Rashbatz). Spain, 1361–1444.
Ehrenberg, R. Yehoshua Menachem. Hungary/Israel, 1904–1976.
Eigis, R. Chanoch Henoch. Lithuania, 1863–1941.
R. Eliezer ben Shmuel. Metz, 1115–1175.
R. Eliyahu ben Shlomo Zalman (Gra or Vilna Gaon). Vilna, 1720–1797.
Ettlinger, R. Yaakov. Germany, 1798–1871.
Federbush, R. Shimon. Finland, 1892–1969.

Feinstein, R. Moshe. Minsk/US, 1895–1986.
Fogelman, R. Mordechai. Kiryat Motzkin, 1898–1984.
Frank, R. Tzvi Pesach. Kovno/Jerusalem, 1873–1960.
Friedman, R. Avraham Ya'akov. Vienna/Israel, 1884–1961.
Friedman, R. Natan Tzvi. Bnei Brak, 1914–1993.
Gershuni, R. Yehuda. Grodno/Israel, 1908–2000.
Gombiner, R. Avraham Abele (*Magen Avraham*). Poland, 1635–1682.
Goren, R. Shlomo. Poland/Israel, 1917–1994.
Grodzinski, R. Chaim Ozer. Lithuania, 1863–1940.
Hagiz, R. Yaakov. Morocco, 1620–1674.
HaKohen, R. Meir Simcha. Dvinsk, 1843–1926.
HaLevi, R. Chaim David. Tel Aviv, 1924–1998.
HaLevi, R. Yehuda. Toledo/Jerusalem, ca. 1075–1141.
Hertz, R. Joseph Herman. UK, 1872–1946.
Herzog, R. Yitzhak. Poland/Land of Israel, 1888–1959.
R. Hezekiah ben Manoah (*Ḥizkuni*). France, thirteenth century.
Hirsch, R. Samson Raphael. Germany, 1808–1888.
Hutner, R. Yitzchok. Warsaw/Brooklyn/Jerusalem, 1906–1980.
ibn Zimra, R. David ben Solomon (Radbaz). Spain/Safed, 1479–1573.
Isserlin, R. Yisrael. Germany, 1390–1460.
R. Judah ben Barzillai (Ri). Barcelona, eleventh/twelfth century.
Kagan, R. Yisrael Meir (*Ḥafetz Ḥayim*). Russian Empire, 1839–1933.
Kahaneman, R. Yosef Shlomo. Russian Empire/Israel, 1886–1969.
Kamenetsky, R. Yaakov. Lithuania/US, 1891–1986.
Kaplan, R. Avraham Eliyahu (Elya). Lithuania, 1890–1924.
Karelitz, R. Avraham Yeshaya (*Ḥazon Ish*). Belarus/Israel, 1878–1953.
Karo, R. Yosef. Toledo/Safed, 1488–1575.
Kasher, R. Menachem Mendel. Poland/Israel, 1895–1983.
Kimhi, R. David (Radak). France, 1160–1235.
Kohen, R. Shabbetai (*Shakh*). Lithuania/Moravia, 1622–1663.
Kook, R. Avraham Yitzchak. Russia/Land of Israel, 1865–1935.
Kook, R. Tzvi Yehuda. Jerusalem, 1891–1982.
Krochmal, R. Menachem Mendel. Nikolsburg, 1600–1661.
Lichtenstein, R. Aharon. US/Israel, 1933–2015.
Loew, R. Judah ben Bezalel (Maharal). Prague, sixteenth century.
R. Manoah ben Yaakov. Provence, thirteenth century.

Meir, R. Yaakov. Land of Israel, 1856–1939.
R. Meir of Rothenburg. Worms, Germany, 1215–1293.
R. Menachem of Riesbürg. Germany, early fifteenth century.
Minkowski, R. Yitzchak. Karlin, 1788–1851.
Moelin, R. Yaakov ben Moshe Levi (Maharil). Germany, 1365–1427.
R. Moshe ben Maimon (Rambam, or Maimonides). Spain/Egypt, 1138–1204.
R. Moshe ben Yaakov. Coucy, France, 1200–1260.
Naeh, R. Avraham Chaim. Ḥevron/Jerusalem, 1890–1954.
Neria, R. Moshe-Zvi. Russian Empire/Israel, 1913–1995.
Nissim, R. Yitzchak. Baghdad/Israel, 1895–1981.
R. Nissim ben Reuven (Ran). Spain, 1320–1376.
R. Ovadia of Bertinoro. Italy, 1445–1550.
Palachi, R. Haim. Izmir, Turkey, 1788–1868.
Perlow, R. Yehuda Yerucham Fishel. Poland, 1846–1934.
Perlow, R. Yochanan. Karlin/US, 1900–1956.
Reines, R. Yitzchak Ya'akov. Lithuania, 1839–1915.
Reischer, R. Yaakov ben Yosef. Austria, 1661–1733.
Rozen, R. Yisrael. Israel, 1941–2017.
R. Saadia Gaon. Egypt/Babylonia, ca. 882/892–942.
Segal, R. David HaLevi (*Turei Zahav* or *Taz*). Poland, 1586–1667.
Shapira, R. Avraham. Jerusalem, 1914–2007.
Shaviv, R. Yehuda. Israel, 1941–2018.
R. Shlomo ben Aderet (Rashba). Spain, 1235–1310.
R. Shneur Zalman of Liadi. 1745–1812.
Sirkis, R. Yoel (*Baḥ* or *Bayit Ḥadash*). Poland, 1561–1640.
Sofer, R. Moshe (*Ḥatam Sofer*). Pressburg, 1762–1839.
Sofer, R. Shimon. Hungary, 1850–1944.
Soloveitchik, R. Joseph B. Pruzhany/US, 1903–1993.
Soloveitchik, R. Yitzchok Zev (Brisker Rabbi or Griz). Volozhin/Brisk/Jerusalem, 1886–1959.
Rabbeinu Tam. Troyes, 1100–1171.
Tukachinsky, R. Yechiel Michel. Belarus/Jerusalem, 1871–1955.
R. Tzemah ben Haim. Sura, ninth century.
Uziel, R. Ben-Zion. Israel, 1880–1953.
R. Vidal of Tolosa (*Maggid Mishneh*). Spain, late fourteenth century.

Waldenberg, R. Eliezer. Jerusalem, 1915–2006.
Wasserman, R. Elchanan. Lithuania, 1874–1941.
Weinberg, R. Yechiel Yaakov. Poland/Switzerland, 1884–1966.
Yisraeli, R. Shaul. Belarus/Israel, 1909–1995.
Yosef, R. Ovadia. Jerusalem, 1920–2013.
Zevin, R. Shmuel Yosef. Minsk/Israel, 1888–1978.
Zolty, R. Betzalel. Poland/Israel, 1920–1982.

The fonts used in this book are from the Arno family

Maggid Books
The best of contemporary Jewish thought from
Koren Publishers Jerusalem Ltd.